THE ROSE THE BASTARD AND THE SAINT KING

THE ROSE THE BASTARD AND THE SAINT KING

THE MURDER OF HENRY VI

✣

A.W. BOARDMAN

The History Press

First published 2024

The History Press
97 St George's Place, Cheltenham,
Gloucestershire, GL50 3QB
www.thehistorypress.co.uk

© A.W. Boardman, 2024
Maps © A.W. Boardman

The right of A.W. Boardman to be identified as the Author
of this work has been asserted in accordance with the
Copyright, Designs and Patents Act 1988.

All rights reserved. No part of this book may be reprinted
or reproduced or utilised in any form or by any electronic,
mechanical or other means, now known or hereafter invented,
including photocopying and recording, or in any information
storage or retrieval system, without the permission in writing
from the Publishers.

British Library Cataloguing in Publication Data.
A catalogue record for this book is available from the British Library.

ISBN 978 1 80399 709 4

Typesetting and origination by The History Press
Printed and bound in Great Britain by TJ Books Limited, Padstow, Cornwall.

Then stood the realm in great jeopardy a long while,
and every lord that was mighty of men made him strong,
and many wanted to be king.

Sir Thomas Malory,
*Le Morte D'Arthur, c.*1470

Contents

Foreword by Matthew Lewis   9
Acknowledgements   11
Maps   13
Introduction   17

1   Crown of Thorns   23
      Henry VI and the Wars of the Roses

2   The Rose   41
      Edward IV, the Earl of Warwick and the invasion of England

3   The Bastard   58
      Thomas Fauconberg, his family and his career

4   Bloody Fields   80
      The battles of Barnet and Tewkesbury

5   All the King's Men   103
      Medieval London, the city fathers and the Yorkist lords

6   Evil Willers   119
      The culture of rebellion in Kent and the insurgents

7   Bridges of London   136
      The attack on London Bridge and the march to Kingston

8   Bombardment   161
      The siege of London and the second attack on London Bridge

9 The Greatest Jeopardy   176
     The rebel assault on the city gates and Fauconberg's retreat

10 Crushing the Seed   190
     The arrival of Edward IV in London and the death of Henry VI

11 The King's Right Arm   208
     The Duke of Gloucester and the betrayal of Fauconberg

12 The Saint King   220
     The miracles of Henry VI and the aftermath of the siege

Epilogue   233
Select Bibliography   238
Notes   243
Index   257

Foreword
by Matthew Lewis

Readeption is an odd word for an equally unusual moment in England's medieval history. The term might require a second look, which may do little to illuminate its meaning. The reason for this is that it was made up in 1470 to describe an unprecedented moment. The first Yorkist king, Edward IV, was driven from his kingdom by his first cousin, Richard Neville, Earl of Warwick. Helping Edward to his throne nine years earlier and installing his replacement earned Warwick the epithet of 'the Kingmaker'. Warwick restored King Henry VI, the third Lancastrian king, who had reigned from the age of nine months in 1422 until his deposition in 1461, amid a litany of examples of poor rule and failure to reconcile increasingly bitter factions at his court. Readeption was the word created to describe the return to the throne of a king who had ruled before but been deposed.

Amidst the complications of the Wars of the Roses and the frantic politics and battles of the Readeption, one moment can become overshadowed. Hindsight marks it as of little long-term or dynastic importance, but those living through it did not have the benefit of hindsight. Huge numbers had marched out of Kent and Essex. London was laid under siege. The men of power within were forced to weigh their loyalties in the balance once again. They were required to judge how any action might impact the Crown, but also the effect it could have on them and the connection they hoped to maintain between head and neck. What of those outside, though? What drove them to take a risk that so frequently resulted in death?

Within these pages, the siege of London by the Bastard of Fauconberg, an illegitimate cousin of the Earl of Warwick, is drawn into the spotlight from which it has been frequently displaced. The episode offers fresh insights into the actions of key actors, from King Edward IV to his little brother Richard, Duke of Gloucester, still more than a decade from becoming King Richard III. We can see something of the blinding allure of the Earl of Warwick that allowed his plans and his orders to survive his own death at the battle of Barnet. The position in late medieval society of an illegitimate son of an earl, and his desire to alter it, are revealed. Perhaps more compelling is the view of the motivations of counties in south-east England left disillusioned and perennially primed for a leader to drive them into fresh rebellion.

This book restores the siege of London to the position of importance that it occupied in the minds of those living through it, on both sides, in 1471. The Wars of the Roses is a complex jigsaw in which this story is a vital piece, not least in understanding the controversial fate of a King of England. These were days filled with all of the terror and uncertainty of war, of making decisions that cost lives, of risking all for what is believed to be right. Or at least in one's own best interests. Will you man the walls, or storm them? Perhaps you will decide to stay at home and keep out of it. The story that follows will throw you back into those febrile days of tension and fear and offer a new conclusion to the period of the Readeption.

Matthew Lewis
Chair of the Richard III Society and
co-host of the Gone Medieval *podcast*

Acknowledgements

First and foremost, I would like to dedicate this work to my wife, Sheree, to whom I am indebted for helping me fight battles of a different kind while I was writing this book. I cannot express how much her love and support continues to help me find new perspectives in life.

As always, the writing process also provides a welcome antidote to all the anxieties of the modern world, and occasionally disappearing into the fifteenth century has its cathartic merits. However, apart from this, and the unwavering support from my family, I would like to acknowledge the help of certain authors, librarians, professionals and friends who have all contributed to this book in one way or another. I would have been lost for words and images without their expertise, encouragement and kindness in all things medieval.

Of these contributors, Geoff Wheeler has been an inexhaustible well of Wars of the Roses ephemera over the years, and in this book he kindly supplied a host of images when his health was not up to scratch. Special thanks also go out to medieval author and podcaster Matt Lewis for reading the finished manuscript and writing such an insightful foreword to the book. At the Royal Armouries in Leeds I would like to thank Stuart Ivinson, Phillip Abbot and Keith Dowen for helping me sift through their extensive library or just chat, not to mention sharing their knowledge of arms and armour with such enthusiasm.

Toby Huitson and the staff at Canterbury Cathedral Archives and Sally Bevan at the City of London Metropolitan Archives were indispensable when it came to rooting out various contemporary manuscripts, letters and images relating to Fauconberg's rebellion. Among other friends, valued individuals and societies, I would also like to thank

Simon Stanley for sharing his practical expertise on the warbow, Rebecca for all her support, the veteran BBC World correspondent and journalist John Simpson CBE for reading and endorsing the book so generously, and all at The Battlefields Trust, Military History Now and the Richard III Society for providing such accessible historical archives and media support.

Last but not least, I would like to thank Claire, Jezz and all the staff at The History Press for making this book possible and for being so accommodating with their deadlines in a year that has been challenging to say the least.

Finally, most writing is generally done in isolation, and much more time is spent researching – or just occasionally staring out of the window. As my favourite Leeds writer, Alan Bennett, once suggested, writers are two people. One is the person who does the writing, and the other is the one everyone interacts with daily. In my experience, one personality blends into another. Therefore, I would like to apologise for any mistakes I may have made in the book (which are all my own doing) although I could easily blame my alter ego if I so wished.

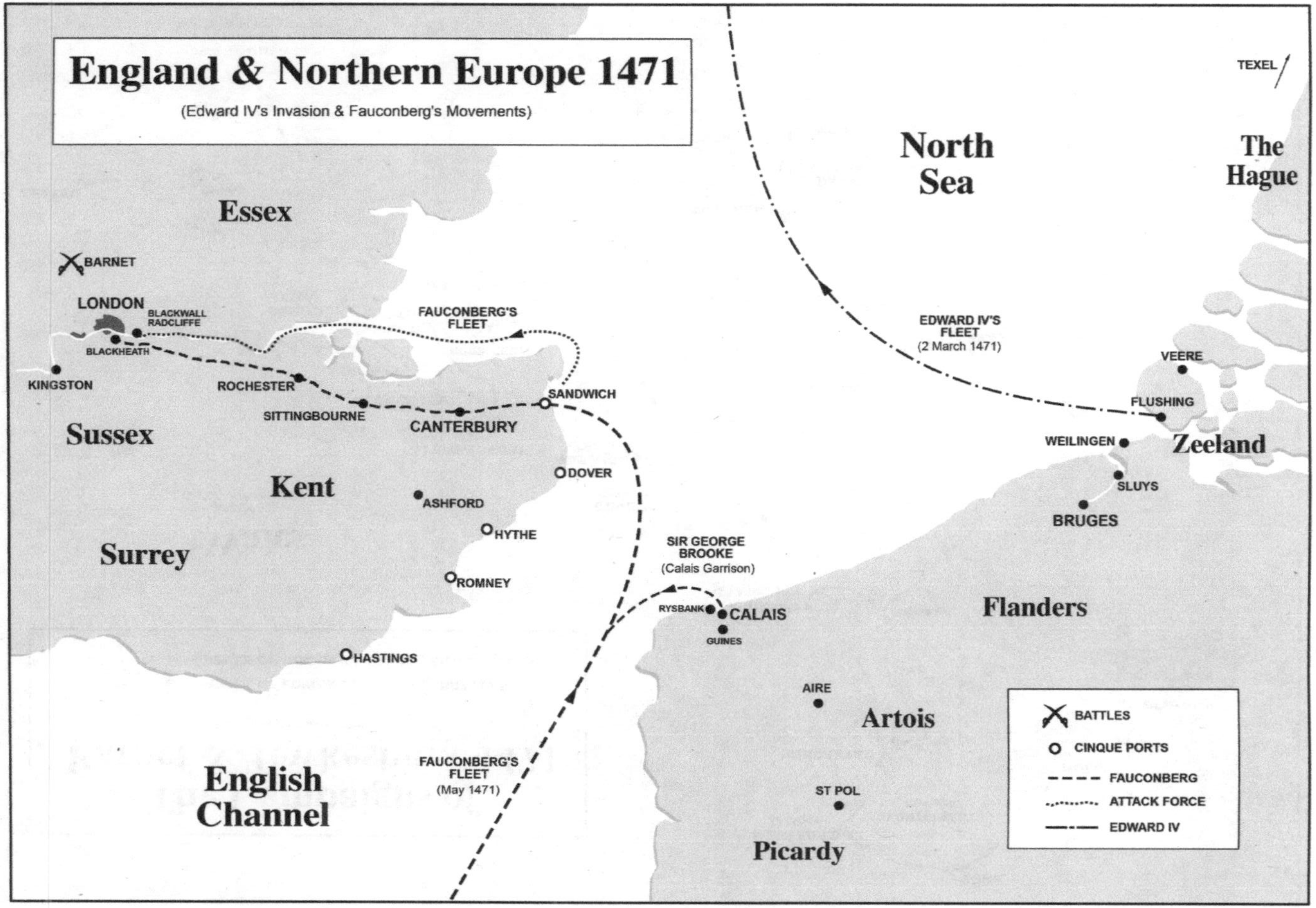
England & Northern Europe 1471
(Edward IV's Invasion & Fauconberg's Movements)
North Sea
The Hague
TEXEL
Essex
BARNET
LONDON
BLACKWALL
RADCLIFFE
BLACKHEATH
KINGSTON
ROCHESTER
SITTINGBOURNE
CANTERBURY
SANDWICH
FAUCONBERG'S FLEET
EDWARD IV'S FLEET
(2 March 1471)
VEERE
FLUSHING
Zeeland
WEILINGEN
SLUYS
BRUGES
Sussex
Kent
DOVER
ASHFORD
HYTHE
Surrey
ROMNEY
SIR GEORGE BROOKE
(Calais Garrison)
RYSBANK
CALAIS
GUINES
Flanders
HASTINGS
AIRE
Artois
ST POL
English Channel
FAUCONBERG'S FLEET
(May 1471)
Picardy
BATTLES
CINQUE PORTS
FAUCONBERG
ATTACK FORCE
EDWARD IV

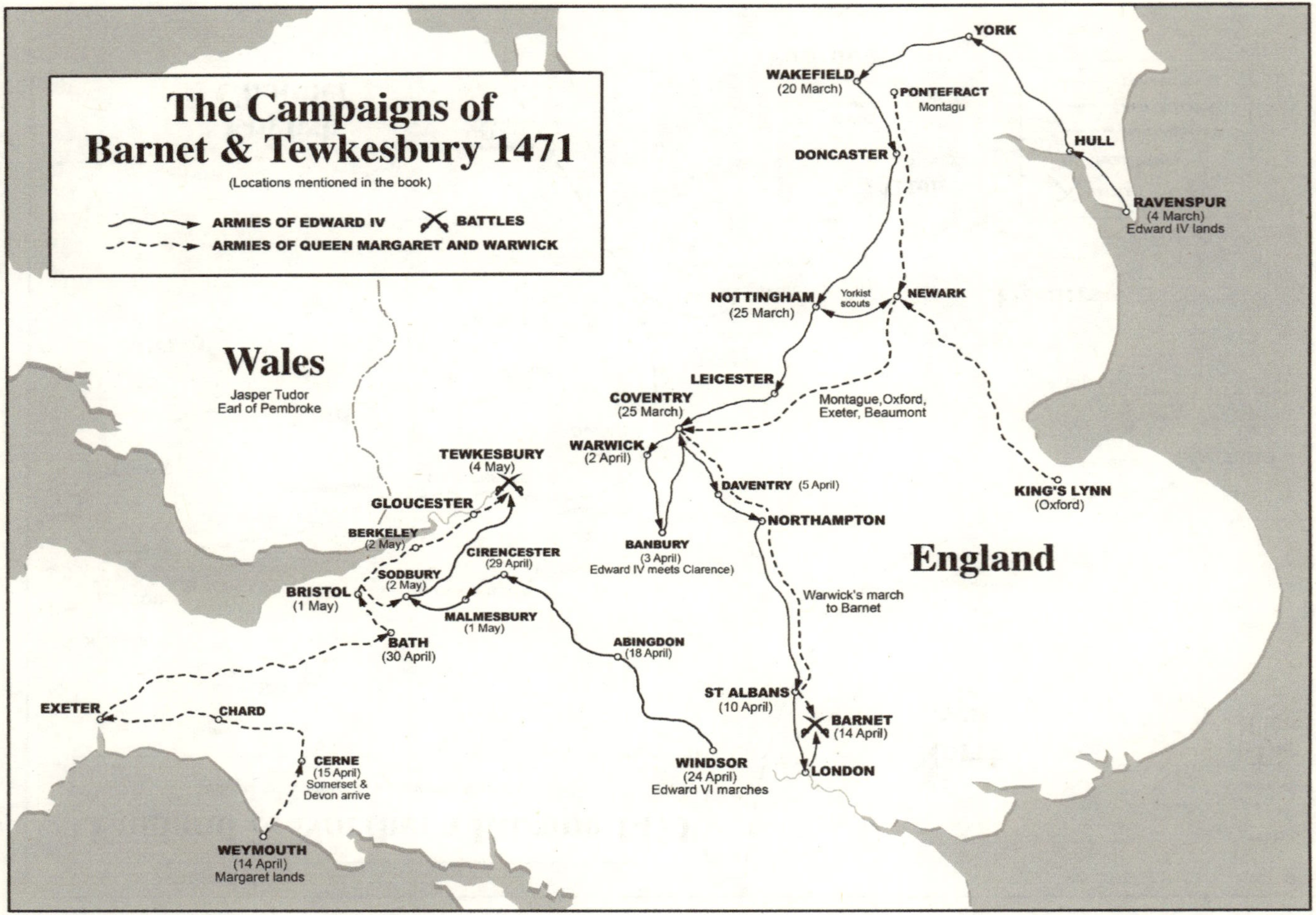
The Campaigns of
Barnet & Tewkesbury 1471
(Locations mentioned in the book)
ARMIES OF EDWARD IV
BATTLES
ARMIES OF QUEEN MARGARET AND WARWICK
Wales
Jasper Tudor
Earl of Pembroke
England
YORK
WAKEFIELD
(20 March)
PONTEFRACT
Montagu
HULL
DONCASTER
RAVENSPUR
(4 March)
Edward IV lands
NOTTINGHAM
(25 March)
Yorkist
scouts
NEWARK
LEICESTER
COVENTRY
(25 March)
Montague, Oxford,
Exeter, Beaumont
WARWICK
(2 April)
TEWKESBURY
(4 May)
DAVENTRY (5 April)
KING'S LYNN
(Oxford)
GLOUCESTER
NORTHAMPTON
BERKELEY
(2 May)
BANBURY
(3 April)
Edward IV meets Clarence)
CIRENCESTER
(29 April)
SODBURY
(2 May)
BRISTOL
(1 May)
MALMESBURY
(1 May)
Warwick's march
to Barnet
BATH
(30 April)
ABINGDON
(18 April)
EXETER
CHARD
ST ALBANS
(10 April)
BARNET
(14 April)
CERNE
(15 April)
Somerset &
Devon arrive
WINDSOR
(24 April)
Edward VI marches
LONDON
WEYMOUTH
(14 April)
Margaret lands

London 1471

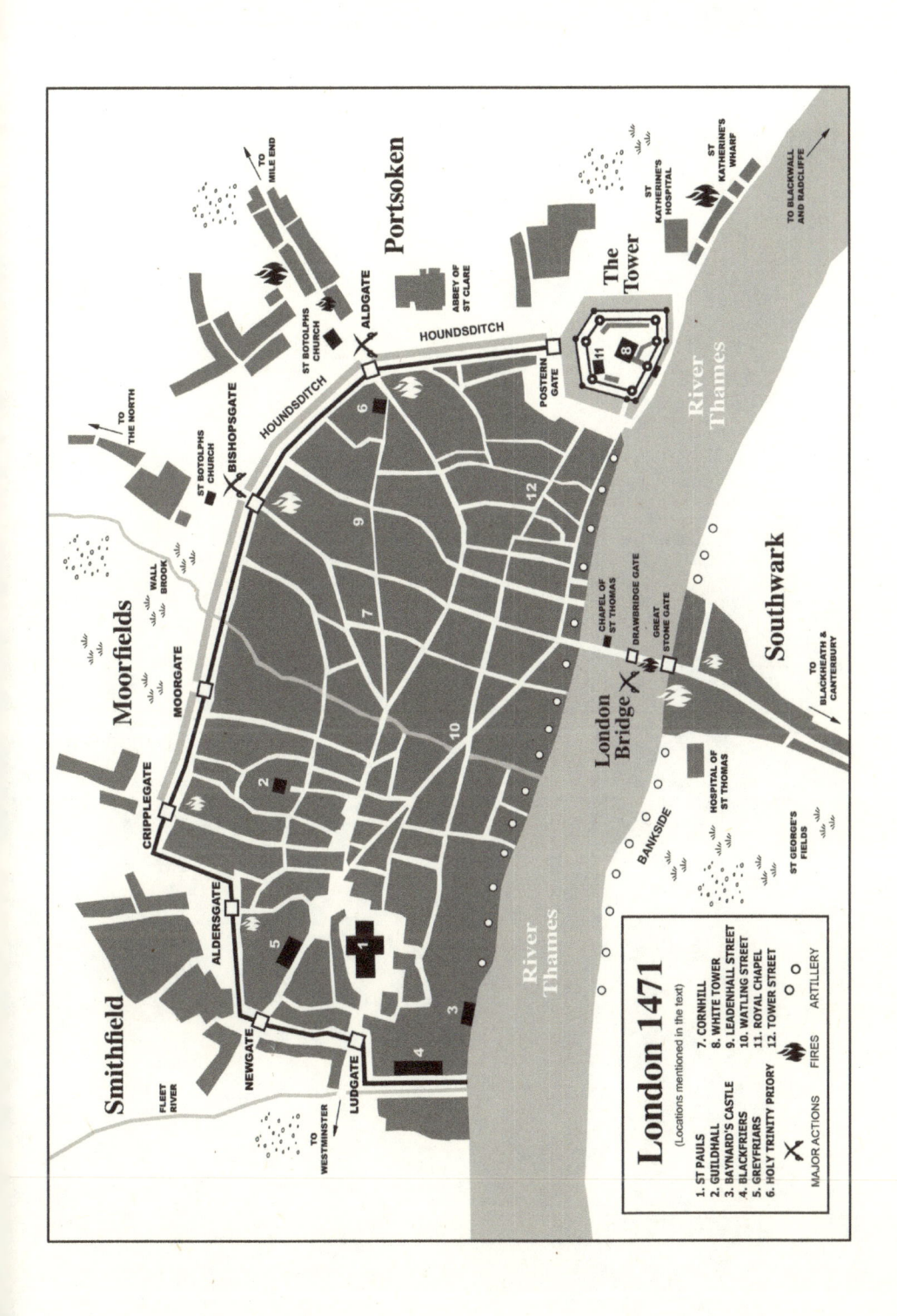

(Locations mentioned in the text)

1. ST PAULS
2. GUILDHALL
3. BAYNARD'S CASTLE
4. BLACKFRIARS
5. GREYFRIARS
6. HOLY TRINITY PRIORY
7. CORNHILL
8. WHITE TOWER
9. LEADENHALL STREET
10. WATLING STREET
11. ROYAL CHAPEL
12. TOWER STREET

✗ MAJOR ACTIONS 🔥 FIRES ○ ARTILLERY

Introduction

Therefore, no more but this: Henry, your sovereign,
Is prisoner to the foe, his state usurped,
His realm a slaughterhouse, his subjects slain,
His statutes cancelled, and his treasure spent,
And yonder is the wolf that makes this spoil.[1]

✧

In Shakespeare's *Henry VI*, Queen Margaret of Anjou encourages her followers to renew the fight against Edward IV (the wolf), who has usurped the English throne. As might be expected, her rousing speech paints a grim portrait of a kingdom divided and in crisis, scarred by civil war, inclined to lawlessness and facing bankruptcy. But how true was Shakespeare's description of England in 1471, a year of battles, rebellion and contending kings? Had the kingdom *really* entered a new dark age reminiscent of Arthur's Britain? And what about ordinary people, who historians say were largely untouched by Shakespeare's carnage? What was their collective response to civil war, local anarchy and a leaderless country?

Doubtless, the spring of 1471 was a defining moment in British history. The conflict, known today as the Wars of the Roses, was still unresolved, and with another serious bout of civil war looming large on the horizon, most contemporaries agreed only more bloodshed would decide the issue. After being forced to flee England by the discontented and politically astute Richard, Earl of Warwick in October 1470, Edward IV returned from exile to recover his throne, fighting two major battles in the process. However, another lesser-known conflict fought in May 1471 proved equally dangerous to King Edward, not to mention his imprisoned rival Henry VI, and this is the central theme of this book.

Although Barnet and Tewkesbury are the most famous battles of 1471, the siege of London has been largely neglected by historians. The conflict is often portrayed as an aftermath (or side issue) of Edward IV's much publicised *Arrivall* in England.[2] Indeed, some modern writers hardly mention the siege in context, which is hardly surprising considering who Edward's enemies were in 1471. Warwick 'the Kingmaker' and Queen Margaret's armies may have tested the king's military competence to the limit, but Edward did not foresee the intervention of Thomas Neville, the Bastard of Fauconberg, who singlehandedly raised a large-scale rebellion in the south-east of England and masterminded the only assault on a walled town or city in the Wars of the Roses.

Fauconberg and his so-called 'lewd company' of commoners, tradesmen and mariners terrorised London suburbs for days before attacking the city defences in a daring attempt to free Henry VI from the Tower.[3] With Henry restored to the throne, backed by thousands of rebels eagerly seeking reform, Edward IV would have been forced into fighting yet again for the Crown. Threatened by Fauconberg's forces in London, his fleet of ships moored in the Thames, his artillery ready for action and the icon of King Henry as a figurehead, contemporaries suggested Edward might have been deposed for a third time in so many years, such was the seriousness of the rebellion.

As for foreign commentators, the Italian writer Polydore Vergil of Urbino was equally certain it was a 'close-run thing' for Edward IV in May 1471. He concluded in his *Anglica Historia* that the Bastard of Fauconberg's 'star, little though it were, yet if it had been raised before, no doubt it would have brought King Edward's affairs great hazard'.[4] That Fauconberg's rebellion was a severe threat to the Yorkist regime is seen by how fiercely both sides fought against each other, knowing that time was running out. Indeed, the struggle for London was much more military-orientated than Jack Cade's popular rebellion of 1450, which preceded the Wars of the Roses – a consideration that has been ignored by writers even though it had far-reaching dynastic consequences.

The reason *why* the Bastard of Fauconberg raised a rebellion in the south-east has never been fully explained by historians and, as a result,

Introduction

Henry VI's tragic death has remained a mystery for centuries. It seems the link between the insurgency and Henry's demise has been forgotten or misinterpreted by writers. Had Fauconberg's rebellion succeeded, it would have been one of the greatest upsets in medieval history. And as for the leading personalities caught up in the rebellion, historians have failed to associate them with another popular rising in 1470 that made the 1471 siege of London possible.

Only vague outlines of Fauconberg's accomplices and adversaries are recorded in most books dealing with the period. The intentions of the key figures are clear but not expanded upon. And there has been no satisfactory answer as to why Fauconberg, a man of insignificant rank and legitimacy, could command an army of thousands. Therefore, this book aims to clarify the rebellion of 1471 by uncovering some of the little-known facts about the participants, using primary and local sources. I will also explain how London was bombarded with artillery and how its defences were attacked by at least two large rebel forces led by determined and well-equipped captains – not by a band of ruffians without a plan. I will trace how popular rebellion had bubbled under the surface in Kent for many centuries and why disgruntled bands of partisans, egged on by obscure leaders, had hurled themselves at London in the past. Fauconberg's call to arms urged ordinary people to march on the capital in their thousands. Therefore, I explore how rebel grievances and impulsiveness were sparked by ancient precedent, how the Lord Mayor of London, his council and relatively few Yorkist lords defended themselves against the insurgency, and what happened to Thomas Fauconberg and his followers once the rebellion ended.

This book also explains the wider events of 1471, their place in British history and the story of two kings of England whose lives were influenced by the bastard son of Edward IV's most valued veteran captain of the 1460s. More than anything, the year 1471 is a story of split-second decisions, devious betrayals and heroic last stands; of determined and brutal campaigning, pitched battles, unrest in the shires and terror on the streets of London. The intentions of the main protagonists could not have been more dissimilar, and the aims of Edward IV, along with his younger brothers, the dukes of Clarence and Gloucester, paint a fascinating picture of family upheaval and political ambition in a dysfunctional royal household.

Primary sources (some never published before) point our way back in time. However, I am also indebted to other historians whose opinions about the Wars of the Roses helped provide a framework to some of the events described here.[5] Since publication, segments of their work have been paraphrased (and often omitted) by others when describing the siege of London, and a single analysis of Fauconberg's rebellion has never been fully fleshed out until now. The resulting study is an exercise in historical cause and effect, and although there are some bolted doors to our knowledge of the period, the main aim of this book is to document the forgotten third battle of 1471 and show how it brought about a sudden and murderous dynastic change in England that may not have been envisaged otherwise.

By reconsidering the contemporary evidence, local topography, and military conventions of the period, several crucial facts about the 1471 campaigns can be redefined. It is possible to enlarge upon how gunpowder weapons and medieval ships played a vital part in Fauconberg's strategy and explain how unforeseen circumstances and chance governed warfare. Using primary sources, we can uncover what kind of logistical problems commanders faced during medieval campaigns, how the chief protagonists adapted to battlefield conditions and siege warfare and what role religious observance played in Wars of the Roses armies. Moreover, we can also revisit the mystery of Henry VI's death in the Tower with a fresh eye, showing how the king's fate was directly linked to circumstance and not affected by personal drama.

My findings will undoubtedly cause further debate about this crucial period in British history, but that is the point of research. Whatever the reader concludes, it is hoped this book bridges a critical gap in the Wars of the Roses that otherwise would have remained unexplored. What Edward intended to do in 1471 was clear enough, but he had many hurdles to cross before securing the throne. Given the simultaneous nature of his campaigns, I also document why rebellions occurred so often in Kent and explain what motivated the Bastard of Fauconberg to commit treason. More than anything, the story of 1471 is an account of ordinary people who saw the Wars of the Roses as a crucial backdrop to their everyday lives. High-level politics and personal military feuding were beyond the scope of commoners. But contrary to the established idea that the civil wars hardly affected the population, I prove that

Fauconberg's rebellion (and others like it) touched thousands of men and women who had simple values. Indeed, we may wonder how their revolutionary zeal was aroused time and time again. Undoubtedly, justice and fair treatment for all were sought-after ideals. However, wholesale pillaging was equally important for some, and we may wonder how Fauconberg could trust an army of malcontents, not to mention a king who had been such a problem to England in the past.

Even today, most writers blame Henry VI's inept leadership for the irreparable divisions in England during the Wars of the Roses, not to mention a north–south divide that made the conflict so merciless among the nobility. Most contemporaries described King Henry as a model of religious virtue. He was over-generous towards some of his nobles, devoid of personal extravagance and tolerant of those who failed him. Other chroniclers claimed Henry VI was the 'true' anointed king, a humble and plain servant of God, yet unsuited to the mantle of medieval kingship in an age of desperate men embroiled in political feuding.[6] As King of England, he ruled intermittently across a period of almost fifty years through bouts of civil war and aristocratic violence not witnessed on such a dramatic scale before in the kingdom. Therefore, if Henry was the cause of the Wars of the Roses, why was he not removed sooner? And why was he later hailed as a miracle worker by those who deposed him and succeeded to the throne?

As will be seen, all these considerations are directly linked to the siege of London in 1471, and the escalation before it explains why so many Englishmen, including Sir Thomas Malory, the famous knight-prisoner and writer of the period, feared for the kingdom's safety. No wonder he concluded in his *Morte D'Arthur* that England 'stood in great jeopardy a long while, and every lord that was mighty of men made him strong, and many wanted to be king'.[7] Shakespeare echoed Malory's concerns in his history plays a century later and concluded that at least three men sought to control the realm in 1471.[8] And as for the Bastard of Fauconberg, he was caught up in one of the most intriguing and complex periods in British history, which confirms how quickly civil disorder can erupt in any age when an embittered population has had enough.

A.W. Boardman
2024

1

Crown of Thorns

Kingdoms are but cares,
State is devoid of stay,
Riches are ready snares,
And hasten to decay.[1]

✢

Historians have always regarded King Henry VI as a much-maligned monarch. When his famous warrior father, Henry V, died at Vincennes in 1422, there is little doubt most of his subjects hoped young Henry would be just as formidable when he reached full age. However, when the king shook off his minority in 1437, aged 16, this perfect dream of sovereignty and warlike ability completely eluded him, and he was later regarded as a man unsuited to his role.[2] Henry VI had been governed from birth by his uncles, and despite being tutored by the best civil and military minds in the land, the king's many failings as a leader proved fatal for England. In adulthood, Henry became uninterested in the real world and later suffered from a debilitating mental illness. In short, Henry V's son was a king in name only, spending most of his reign on his knees at prayer, in the shadows of delirium or watching his dominions in France fall apart one by one.

However, in his early reign, Henry's strange ways and abject holiness were largely tolerated, even in an age of powerful men with feral ambitions. England's belligerent ruling class survived by obtaining key positions at court, and because the king was unable to arbitrate fairly between them, this allowed over-mighty nobles to undermine Henry's authority. More at home in a church rather than in a suit of armour, the king's tragic reign is, therefore, a story of exploitation by others. Those who knew him best realised this and considered him easy prey. Even his advocates regarded Henry as a king who shunned his royal responsibilities, and one later foreign observer measured these failings against his many virtues:

> King Henry was a man of mild and plain-dealing disposition who preferred peace before wars, quietness before troubles, honesty before utility and leisure before business; and to be short, there was not in this world a more pure, more honest and holy creature.[3]

Although the above flattering lines were written after Henry's death, this description of the king, if true, was not one to be admired in the turbulent fifteenth century. Through gross negligence and the unchecked interference of devious ministers, Henry's reign saw the loss of all his father's military conquests abroad except Calais, deep divisions among the English nobility and the makings of a volatile catalyst for intermittent civil war. However, Henry VI was not wholly to blame for these calamities. His many years of personal rule were plagued by crisis after crisis, and powerful nobles who aimed to control, even usurp the throne, thought him poorly served by his councillors and inner circle. Misrule generally translates into rebellion or war in society, and because of this, some people openly described Henry VI as a natural fool. Yet this 'silly weak king'[4] ruled independently from his protectors for almost twenty-five years before being deposed in 1461, and soon after his death, ten years later, thousands of pilgrims visited his shrine at Chertsey Abbey and attested to miracles there. Therefore, we may ask ourselves, who was the *real* Henry VI, and why did his critics tolerate him for so long?

Unlike Edward II and Richard II, who were removed by ambitious courtiers, Henry enjoyed almost saintly status well beyond the reign of his enemies. Even after the death of Richard III, who allegedly stabbed him to death in the Tower of London in 1471, Henry's fame rivalled that of St Thomas Becket in Canterbury. However, while he lived, the king's careless attitude to leadership remains wholly evident, despite successive efforts by Tudor writers to rehabilitate his profile and blame others for mismanaging the kingdom. Indeed, most historians today still conclude that King Henry was no more than a pawn in the hands of others, and the fact that he was allowed to live for so long reveals just how docile and out of touch he was.[5]

In 1459, one contemporary chronicler was particularly scathing about Henry's neglect, and although this viewpoint may seem a personal tirade, there is no smoke without fire:

> [And] at this same time, the realm of England was out of all good governance, as it had been many days before, for the king was simple and led by covetous counsel and owed more than he was worth. His debts increased daily, but payment there was none. All the possessions and lordships that pertained to the crown the king had given away, some to lords and some to other simple persons, so he had almost nought to live on. For these misgovernances, and for many others, the hearts of the people were turned away from them that had the land in governance and their blessing was turned into cursing.[6]

During his reign, there is no doubt Henry VI placed too much trust in unscrupulous nobles, who were driven by power in an age of chivalry and bastard feudalism.[7] According to his chaplain, John Blacman, the king thought governing England was both tiresome and inconvenient compared to his religious pursuits. It is recorded that he admonished government officials when they disturbed him at work, he did not act nor dress in a regal manner as befitting a king, and because of his lack of interest and judgement, factionalism divided English nobles due to indifference or misplaced favouritism.[8] According to one sympathetic writer in 1457, Henry was *simplex et probus* (honest and upright).[9] But this much-quoted and sometimes misunderstood description of the king must be weighed against a host of other royal attributes Henry did not possess. Apart from following a pious and puritanical existence, which prevented him from dealing with state affairs, the king could be wholly self-centred.[10] Even worse, although totally inescapable, in 1453, his mental health became so seriously impaired that others had to govern the realm for him. During the bloody dynastic struggles of the 1460s, Henry was regarded as a political puppet by both Yorkist and Lancastrian factions to the point of absurdity. Indeed, it is the measured opinion of most modern historians that Henry was unfit to rule England and that the foundations of Eton College and King's College, Cambridge, were the only positive endowments of his tragic reign.

So, what are we to make of the king who became the extreme focus of the Bastard of Fauconberg's rebellion in 1471? From Henry's point of view, imprisoned in the Tower of London, he may not have known or cared about the insurgency raging beyond his guarded apartments. On the other hand, knowing this may have contributed to his already fragile disposition. Therefore, tracing Henry's life briefly during the Wars of the Roses is worthwhile to see how each crisis affected his reign and his reasoning. Only then can we understand how a man so ahead of his time (yet so unsuited to medieval kingship) could be such a powerful force for change even though he led a solitary life of religious observance and mental suffering.

See how they disturb me

When his minority officially ended in 1437, Henry VI had been King of England and France since birth. Under his uncles – Cardinal Beaufort, Humphrey, Duke of Gloucester and John, Duke of Bedford – he had enjoyed a largely trouble-free reign and was potentially on the verge of greater things. However, in the 1450s, English military failure in France and localised rebellion at home helped produce a political power vacuum that enabled various factions to emerge that the king was unable or unwilling to control. In short, Henry was unlike his ruthless ancestors, and he set aside problems for others to solve. The popular Kentish rebellion led by Jack Cade in 1450 added to the king's many woes, and it was the first of its kind to present a well-worded manifesto of grievances against Henry's corrupt ministers. The rebels were careful to stay loyal to the king, although this attitude changed when they requested the punishment of those officials who had offended their county. Executions followed when the rebels gained access to London and, as will be explained later, it was not the last rebellion to be put down without a brutal cull of all those responsible.[11]

The idea that rebels had managed to force their way into London was unforgivable, and the blame fell on the king and his ministers, who had lost control of the situation. To add to this crisis at home, the gradual loss of English territories in France added pressure to the king's mounting list of domestic and international problems. Each aristocratic clique sought to influence Henry's decision-making, but a general lack of finance hamstrung the government. The king shifted the blame for the military disasters in France onto other nobles like the Duke of Suffolk, who paid with their lives. Everyone other than Henry was guilty, and this situation aggravated the rivalries of powerful English nobles tasked with winning the war abroad, especially two men who typified the political family feuding of the late fifteenth century.

The most dangerous internal rivalry during the 1450s was the one pursued by Richard, Duke of York and Edmund, Duke of Somerset. York was Henry's heir presumptive while the king remained childless, but even though he was the king's primary beneficiary, his greatest fear was Somerset's royal lineage. If Somerset could validate his own Beaufort claim to the throne, he could also succeed Henry if he died without an heir. Displaced of his command in France, politically humiliated at home on several occasions and owed vast sums of money by the Crown, York's protestations regarding Somerset's incompetence proved wholly ineffective.[12] Even York's armed incursion against his rival at Dartford in 1452 failed to bring about political reform, and this led him into direct conflict with another adversary, whose machinations were wholly backed by King Henry: his French queen, Margaret of Anjou.

Henry had married Margaret in 1445, and she soon proved to be the main driving force behind the throne and later a champion of Lancastrian solidarity. The growing hostility she held for the Duke of York (and later his sons) directly resulted from her experience in France, torn apart by political infighting. But Margaret's main preoccupation in the 1450s was the more critical issue of the succession and how King Henry could be coaxed into fathering a child. Even the Duke of Somerset was earmarked as a willing teacher, according to rumour, which was further amplified in 1459, when biased Yorkist comments about Queen Margaret's 'overmighty' leadership led to questions about the paternity of the Prince of Wales, who had been born six years earlier:

> The queen, with such as were of her affinity, ruled the realm as she liked gathering riches innumerable. She was defamed and slandered that he [who] was called prince was not her son, but a bastard gotten

in adultery. Wherefore she, dreading that he might not succeed his father to the crown of England, allied unto her all the knights and squires of Chestershire for to have their benevolence, and held open household among them.[13]

The result of the queen's determined, and by fifteenth-century standards, *masculine* approach to the succession would later cause deep aristocratic division in England. However, the role and financial acumen of Margaret of Anjou was blown out of all proportion by Yorkist propaganda. The queen was hardly rich, according to royal documents. She had married Henry with a small dowry, and the king owed vast sums of money because of the war with France.[14] Taxes were not forthcoming, and England was heading for a deep recession. In 1459, the various slights aimed at Queen Margaret's methods were bad enough, but disaster had already struck England more shockingly in 1453. The birth of Henry's son, Prince Edward, should have been a joyous occasion for the royal family, but the king's complete mental and physical breakdown at Clarendon Palace in August of that year was a catastrophe of epic proportions that threw England into turmoil.

Henry's condition, in the form of chronic inertia or inherited porphyria,[15] was caused, it is said, by news of the English defeat at the battle of Castillon in France on 17 July 1453. But it is possible that this *and* the birth of the Prince of Wales were related, causing King Henry's total mental paralysis due to the shock. Also, a kingdom fraught with financial problems and division was probably more than the king's frail disposition could stand – a fact that Henry's nobles, ministers and physicians appreciated when they visited him the same year:

> They could get no answer nor sign [from the king], no prayer nor desire, lamentable cheer nor exhortation, nor anything that they or any of them could do or say, to their great sorrow and discomfort. And when [the king] gave no answer, the queen came in and took the Prince [Edward] in her arms and presented him in like form as the duke [of Buckingham] had done, desiring that the king should bless him. But all their labour was in vain, for they departed thence without any answer or countenance, saving only that once the king looked on the prince and cast down his eyes.[16]

King Henry remained unresponsive and in a catatonic state until Christmas 1454, and during his illness, Queen Margaret tried to lay claim to the throne, but failed to gain support among the king's ministers. It was a crisis of epic proportions and soon, almost as a last resort, the Duke of York (Henry's closest adult heir) was voted in as Lord Protector when it became clear the king's disability could not be tolerated any longer and might even be permanent.

However, York's appointment to this high office provided no antidote to England's problems. And to add to the mounting pressure on the government, private family feuding had once again broken out in several parts of England because of local lawlessness. Dangerous alliances threatened to undermine the kingdom. Controlled by a strong monarchy, feudalism was a stable and constructive way to retain law and order, raise armies for foreign war and control land tenure. But during the late fifteenth century, the system changed somewhat, creating a lucrative breeding ground for paid retaining to flourish. Leading gentry became a law unto themselves, and their tenants closed ranks around their lord, not the king. A noble's affinity was essentially a private army, and men received protection and rewards in return for service. They came to rely on their lord's influence in local and national politics, and the agricultural crisis of the Late Middle Ages also influenced the way landed families sought to gain territorial advantage over their neighbours. Thus, local division became commonplace in some parts of the kingdom and family rivalry took hold.[17]

Even the Duke of York, as Lord Protector, found it difficult to control the nobility despite the imprisonment of his rival, the Duke of Somerset. But when King Henry eventually regained his sanity at Christmas 1454 and recognised his newly born son, York's resignation of power heralded a return to abject normality. York wrongly suspected that Queen Margaret was behind his fall from grace, when all the facts suggest that the protectorship was automatically dissolved when the king recovered. However, when Somerset was released from the Tower of London, the Duke of York's position became increasingly isolated. In short, York feared for his life. After acquiring northern military support from his in-laws, the powerful Neville family, whom he had favoured during his protectorate, his next move was to remove Somerset by force.

The non-battle at Dartford in 1452 had been a complete embarrassment to York, and with this in mind, King Henry (no doubt egged on by his ministers) arranged a similar plan at Leicester to deal with the duke's grievances. Henry's new lease of sanity showed how not to treat nobles, who only knew one way to settle an argument. On 22 May 1455, the king and his entourage were intercepted by York and his Neville allies embattled outside St Albans. Henry may have considered reconciling the differences between his leading nobles amicably, but this attitude soon changed when lengthy negotiations failed to prevent violence. Henry's men, under the Duke of Buckingham, barricaded St Albans marketplace, and after a confused and bloody street battle, the Duke of Somerset was brutally assassinated along with other leading members of the nobility:

> [And] at this same time were hurt lords of name: the king our Sovereign Lord in the neck with an arrow; the Duke of Buckingham with an arrow in the visage; the Lord of Stafford in the hand with an arrow; the Lord of Dorset [Somerset's son] sore hurt that he might not [walk] but was carried home in a cart; and Wenlock, knight, likewise [conveyed] in a cart with other divers knights and esquires.[18]

Despite the king's presence, the Yorkist archers seem to have been given leave to shoot at anything that moved in St Albans marketplace, and even the injured king must have been shocked by how easily York had managed to dispose of his rival Somerset in the battle. As a result, Henry had no alternative but to accept York's renewed oaths of loyalty to avoid further bloodshed. Peace at any price was his priority, and later, he willingly assented to a general pardon arranged in parliament for all those Yorkists who had rebelled against him.[19]

Local violence and rivalry had escalated into civil war, and with it, a dangerous family feud had been born out of cold-blooded murder and the failure to curb it by a king who was still far removed from reality. However, four uneasy years of peace followed the (first) battle of St Albans, even though some nobles privately refused to let York's treason go unpunished. To his credit, in 1458, King Henry tried again to bring some accord between the rival factions. In a ceremonial pageant known as 'Love Day', each party walked arm in arm to St Paul's to outwardly show their amity. But the divisions between leading nobles were so apparent that it became a precursor to more violence. The peace-loving king had failed again to manage the situation, and Queen Margaret, no doubt frustrated by his actions, rapidly allied herself with those nobles who had been bereaved at St Albans.

Forsooth ye be to blame

In 1459, using Henry's powers of attainder, Margaret mustered an army in the king's name to crush the Yorkists with charges of high treason. It was a desperate gamble by her, although she knew that York's allies, the Nevilles, were widely scattered in Calais and northern England. However, it was a risk that paid off when the Yorkists attempted to concentrate their forces at Ludlow. Fearful of their recent indictments, the Earl of Warwick and part of the Calais garrison successfully crossed the Channel. They linked up with the Duke of York as planned, but Warwick's father, the Earl of Salisbury, blundered into Lancastrian forces near Blore Heath in Staffordshire as he tried to march south. Henry VI's act of attainder after the battle recorded the rebellious intentions of Salisbury and the Yorkist lords:

> And there [at Blore Heath] in the accomplishment of their false and treacherous purpose [the Yorkists] slew James Lord Audley and many other knights and squires and other of your liege people, and many of their throats [were] cut who were sent thither by your commandment to resist the false and treacherous purpose of the Earl of Salisbury.[20]

The battle of Blore Heath marked the beginning of a new and sustained phase of violence and civil war, although it is evident that no one living in England during the fifteenth century ever saw the Wars of the Roses as a continuous conflict. Some propagandists abroad disagreed for political reasons, but the wars between York and Lancaster must be viewed as intermittent rather than an all-out conflict on the scale of the British civil wars of the seventeenth century. Some compliant Tudor writers vilified the Wars of the Roses, claiming they were unremitting and tore England apart.[21] Even in Shakespearian drama, the wars were used as propaganda to portray a fictional period in English history when armies sporting red and white roses fought bloody battles for no apparent reason. Contemporary chroniclers knew better. Understanding the wars were fought in response to isolated bouts of insurgency, political feuding and dynastic ambition shows that the battles chroniclers described in their histories fail to conform to the accepted model of a country and people divided. Witnesses realised that, aside from the collateral damage incurred in battles and rebellions, ordinary people went about their business as usual. Once conflicts were over, it was extremely difficult to avoid the dispersal of soldiers and, essentially, it was only the tenants of leading nobles who returned to fight another day. Such retainers and 'well-willers' controlled by bastard feudalism formed the nucleus of contingents and large armies that were in no way standing or permanent. In short, England was not equipped to sustain an unremitting civil war, and instead, the military campaigns between 1455 and 1487 are best explained as bouts of cyclic violence, not constant campaigning.[22]

In 1459, the stubborn success of Salisbury's contingents at the battle of Blore Heath reconfirmed that old rivalries were alive and well even after four years of guarded peace. However, the Duke of York was still politically isolated, and when internal treachery by Warwick's Calais garrison forced the Yorkists to capitulate at Ludford Bridge, threats of attainder accompanied their flight into exile. In the eyes of King Henry and the law, York and his Neville allies had rebelled yet again, and their lands were instantly forfeit to the Crown. In retrospect, the Yorkists could expect little else from the embattled king, even though Queen Margaret and her adherents likely influenced him to act forcefully.

Meanwhile, York and his followers had no alternative but to flee the country and plan their next move in exile. The survival of their land and titles was at risk, and in medieval England, a concerted response could only mean boots on the ground. Ireland and Calais were relatively safe havens for the Yorkists to organise a successful return to England, and Calais provided the main springboard from which an invasion was launched in 1460. The Earl of Warwick and York's eldest son, the Earl of March (later Edward IV), along with William Lord Fauconberg and others, successfully raided the south coast of England; and, with Kentish support, their forces soon reached London unopposed. As for King Henry, he and his court were based at Coventry, and when he and his nobles rapidly advanced to Northampton, they were forced into fortifying a camp beside the River

Nene. The Lancastrians were undoubtedly confident of victory, but due to treachery and the notorious English weather, the Yorkists overran their position, capturing Henry VI in the process.[23] It was the last time mediators and churchmen were used before battles commenced, and from then on, the dynastic crisis became wholly personal.

All now eagerly awaited the return of the Duke of York to England. But his rash bid to claim the throne from King Henry was a typical oversight on his part. York was an impetuous man, and his attempted usurpation caused a great deal of consternation among his followers, not to mention ignited a complicated dynastic crisis that forced the compliant Henry VI to disinherit his only son, the Prince of Wales. As a result, the so-called Act of Accord, specifically drawn up by the Yorkists to succeed Henry if he should die, spurred the queen into re-mustering her forces in the north hoping to reclaim her son's lost inheritance. York, 'the rebel' and now 'the usurper', had to be removed in Margaret's eyes, and it was also an opportunity for the new Duke of Somerset and other Lancastrian lords to avenge their fathers' deaths at St Albans in 1455.

Backed by other prominent families in Yorkshire, the Duke of Somerset soon lured his rival into a clever trap, and his combined forces successfully disposed of York and many of his supporters near Wakefield in a brief battle below Sandal Castle in late December 1460.[24] The duke, his son the Earl of Rutland, and other Yorkist lords were slain after rashly attacking what appeared to be a much smaller Lancastrian force than anticipated. It is clear the queen's troops were in no mood for mercy or ransom, and the Wars of the Roses entered a new and bloody phase of violence that saw the final demise of chivalry in a flurry of executions without trial:

> The next day the Bastard of Exeter slew the Earl of Salisbury at Pontefract where, by the council of the lords, they [the Lancastrians] beheaded the dead bodies of the Duke of York, the Earls of Salisbury and Rutland, Thomas Neville, Edward Bourchier, Thomas Harrington, Thomas Parr, James Pickering and John Harrow, mercer, and set their heads upon diverse parts of York.[25]

It was the beginning of a sustained campaign of attrition and regional division when, for a few winter months in 1461, armies seemed to be mustering and marching continually throughout the kingdom. Between

December 1460 and the end of March 1461, the recruiting of nobles' retinues and town militias, not to mention the employment of two commissions of array by rival kings, resulted in an impressive show of manpower that was never again equalled in medieval England.

The killing of the Duke of York, along with some of his chief captains at Wakefield, gave the Lancastrians a clear advantage to consolidate the throne, and if not for York's eldest son, Edward, Earl of March, the civil wars might have ended in the fields below Sandal Castle. However, personal vengeance dictated that the wars would continue, aided and abetted by ambitious nobles and their tenants who wished to capitalise on the carnage. The fight to bring about a dynastic revolution in England escalated the conflict to a new level of adversity, and in 1461, two significant battles were fought at Mortimer's Cross and St Albans, with varying degrees of success and failure.

The queen's bid to free King Henry from Yorkist control at the (second) battle of St Albans ended in a resounding victory against an overstretched Warwick, who had conveyed the pliant Henry to the battlefield. After the fighting ended, the king was found abandoned by his keepers in a state of confusion. Forced out of London and into another stressful situation, he was spotted alone singing psalms under a tree. But due to the fear of northern hoards pillaging London, the victorious Lancastrians and the king were forced by the city fathers to withdraw into Yorkshire to regroup.[26] The queen's campaign was vilified by Yorkist commentators, and as for King Henry, he must have wondered whose side he was on, now he was a refugee in his own country.

Meanwhile, Edward of March was in no mood to let King Henry or his ambitious French queen rule England and capitalise on his father and brother's merciless deaths at Wakefield. After soundly beating the Welsh Lancastrians near Mortimer's Cross in February 1461, he joined forces with the Earl of Warwick, who acclaimed Edward IV king in London amid a widespread propaganda campaign and massive recruiting drive. The outcome of this dynastic challenge against Lancaster was inevitably brutal and bloody, the Yorkists winning decisive victories at Ferrybridge, Dintingdale and Towton, as the *State Papers of Milan* record:

> The number of commoners killed on the [queen's] side was 28,000, while on King Edward's side, only one lord was killed, Lord Fitzwalter,

and 800 men of the commons. The late king, the queen and the prince, with the dukes of Somerset and Exeter, took flight, and King Edward was received into the City of York with honour and great dread. And he sent a great number of men-at-arms in pursuit of the fugitives so that not one might escape when taken.[27]

Despite the 'apparent' death toll recorded by various heralds at Towton on 29 March 1461, the Earl of Warwick was left in command of 20,000 Yorkist soldiers with orders to root out further Lancastrian resistance in the north. It seemed the queen's army had been crushed beyond repair, and Edward was soon crowned king at Westminster in June 1461. His new government attainted all those who had fought against him in the north, and looking back at his reign, Henry VI must have thought the late Duke of York had sired the worst kind of enemy. Edward, it seemed, would stop at nothing to erase the Lancastrian bloodline. However, Henry was wrong about the new king, who would be forced into granting mercy to many Lancastrian nobles still on the run. There is no doubt that Edward IV's orders of 'no quarter' before the battle of Towton prove the point that many refugees had to wait years to be pardoned by the new king. But most Lancastrian soldiers were eventually forgiven, in the hope that Edward could rule England effectively without opposition.[28]

As for the mood of the country, privately many northern nobles and commoners would never forgive Edward for his cull at Towton, and his usurpation of Henry's throne had only put his rival in the shadows, not dug his grave. Lancastrian resistance was forced further north and was weakened in a protracted fight to control the Northumbrian castles. Bamburgh (under Lord Grey) was the only stronghold to withstand a siege by artillery, and most castles fell due to misplaced alliances or trickery. Two more pitched battles at Hedgeley Moor and Hexham in 1464 removed further opposition to Edward's rule, not to mention leading English nobles like the Duke of Somerset, whom Edward had previously pardoned for his crimes. For the time being, the new king directed operations in the north from London, using Warwick and his brother Lord Montagu to effectively neutralise the Lancastrian threat.[29] But when Henry was finally captured wandering the countryside in 1465 and the queen was forced to flee to France with her son, the rebellion lost all credibility. Margaret's only recourse was to live in exile until 1471, from where she would try again to recapture her husband, whom Edward had shut away in the Tower out of sight, but not out of mind.

Ye do foully to smite a king anointed so

By 1465, it may have seemed the civil wars were over in England. But it was not long before those dissatisfied with Edward IV's rule sought to free King Henry from captivity. Edward's main ally, Richard, Earl of Warwick, proved to be central to this insurgency, and over the next few years, he became a persistent thorn in Edward's side. The breakdown in their previous 'loving' relationship stemmed from the king's secret marriage to Elizabeth Woodville in 1464 while Warwick was striving for a more lucrative match abroad. The Woodville family, who had been staunch Lancastrian courtiers, were of 'low birth' according to royal precedent, and therefore, their rapid rise to power threatened Warwick's position and political acumen. However, the earl's embarrassment soon turned to bitterness when the queen's large family came to be preferred above his own at court. Edward's preference for an alliance with Burgundy rather than France and his reluctance to allow Warwick's daughters to marry into the royal family compounded the great earl's dissatisfaction, the result being that 'the Kingmaker' formed a secret alliance with King Edward's ambitious younger brother George, Duke of Clarence, whom he planned to marry to his eldest daughter, Isabel Neville, and then set on the throne.[30]

Fearing Warwick's aptitude for political manipulation, aside from his secret treason, Edward disapproved of the Neville marriage. Still, the determination of his former advisor and comrade in arms knew no bounds, and Warwick's aim to secretly depose Edward with his prospective son-in-law, Clarence, soon became apparent. The means and political climate for this strategy failed to materialise in 1467, even though unrest and unpopularity had begun to threaten Edward's rule. However, the king's victories in northern England and his promises to end Henry VI's mismanagement of the kingdom had not been forgotten by his subjects, and soon large pockets of former Lancastrians and rebels secretly associated themselves with Warwick to topple the Yorkist regime.

Two of these rebel leaders went under the name of Robin, and although the first rising by Robin of Holderness was soon put down by Warwick's brother John, Lord Montagu (the new Earl of Northumberland), the second revolt, captained by Robin of Redesdale, was more aggressive. In fact, it caused Edward IV to eschew his frivolous pursuits, march north in person and call upon Welsh support to put down the rebellion. The Earl of Pembroke and others answered the king's commission, but he and his army were intercepted at Edgecote in July 1469, where he was decisively beaten when some of Warwick's troops, under Sir Geoffrey Gate, appeared on the battlefield.[31] This event exposed Warwick and Clarence as true rebels, and the king uncharacteristically fell into their trap. Caught without sufficient forces to take on Warwick's army, Edward was captured when his contingents deserted him near Olney, and England soon found itself without a king.

Warwick and Clarence now aimed to rule the kingdom in Edward's name, despite the coolness of Lord Montagu, who remained loyal to the king despite his Neville roots. As for Warwick, he soon found out that it was impossible to rule effectively with Edward imprisoned. England needed a monarch in the traditional sense, and in the end, the king's 'release' was driven more by political necessity than desire. As a result, Warwick soon lost control of the government, which caused a resurgence of his former discontentment when he secretly backed yet another northern rebellion in 1470 led by Sir Robert Welles. Domestic unpopularity threatened to engulf England once more, but this time King Edward was not caught off guard. After raising an army and taking Robert's father, Lord Welles, hostage, Edward brought the rebels to battle near Empingham in the Midlands. An anonymous Yorkist chronicler described what happened on 12 March in full view of the rebel army:

> Wherefore his highness [Edward] in the field under his banner displayed commanded the said Lord Welles and Sir Thomas Dymock to be executed. And so forthwith proceeding against the rebels, and by the help of Almighty God, [he] achieved the victory ... where it is to be remembered that at such time as the battles were towards joining, the king with [his] host setting upon [them] they cried out, A Clarence! A Clarence! A Warwick! That time being in the field divers

persons in the Duke of Clarence's livery and especially Sir Robert Welles himself.[32]

The brief battle of Empingham was later called Losecote Field because the rebels, fearing capture, cast off their livery jackets as they fled.[33] It was a rout that settled many personal doubts in Edward's mind, and as for Sir Robert Welles, he later wrote a confession (most likely forced) revealing that Warwick had tried to supplant the king with his brother Clarence. Both men were behind the uprisings that had almost cost the Yorkist king his throne, and Edward was never to trust Warwick again, although his chivalrous nature still offered mercy if the earl and Clarence submitted to his will.

Following precedent, but no doubt fearing another rebellion, Edward sent heralds ordering Warwick and Clarence to give themselves up. But after trying to muster support unsuccessfully in Lancashire from the Stanley brothers, the two dukes fled to France, the insatiable Clarence still believing that one day he would be king. Here in enforced exile, and contrary to what had gone before, Warwick (with the help of Louis XI) arranged an unlikely alliance with his arch-enemy Margaret of Anjou. However, the settlement came at a high price. Understandably suspicious of Warwick's intentions, Margaret insisted that the earl further cement their new relationship by marrying his youngest daughter, Anne, to her son, Edward, Prince of Wales. Moreover, she also declared that Warwick should return to England and free Henry VI from the Tower, and this time, the earl's taciturn brother, Lord Montagu, would play a key role in Warwick's success.

Threatened by Montagu's large forces in the north, Edward could do little until he mustered a sizeable army, and once he knew Warwick and Clarence had landed in England with a fleet of ships and 2,000 French troops, Edward had no choice but to flee the kingdom into exile. He and his brother Gloucester; William, Lord Hastings; and Anthony, Earl Rivers hoped to seek refuge in Burgundy with his brother-in-law Charles the Bold, and it seemed Warwick's gamble had finally paid off. But the earl's role as 'Kingmaker' was not fated to last long. His plan to consolidate an alliance with Louis XI by assisting him with plans to invade Burgundy revealed an uncharacteristic lapse of judgement on Warwick's part. Also, the Duke of Clarence was not pleased with Warwick's new plans to reinstate Henry VI, who was still technically King of England. Clarence had been betrayed, it seemed, and his relationship with Warwick became tarnished despite still being considered a 'spare' if anything happened to Henry VI or his son.[34]

In retrospect, Warwick's discontentment and his part in the various northern uprisings could be directly blamed on Edward IV's inappropriate marriage to Elizabeth Woodville. But other feelings of disillusionment were at work in England in the late 1460s, hence the risings in the north brought on by the king's failure to solve the economic problems in his kingdom. Revolution was in the air, and the need for change was still present in England. Some parts of the country were embroiled in local turmoil, and rival nobles were once again pursuing feuds, which resulted in private battles like that fought at Nibley Green in Gloucestershire in 1470:

> There was a great [rivalry] between the Lord Berkeley and the Lord Lisle for the manor of Wotton-Under-Edge, in so much that they [wished] to fight, and meeting in a meadow at a place called Nibley, Berkeley's archers suddenly shot [their arrows] and the Lord Lisle lifting up the visor of his helmet was by an archer of the forest of Dean shot [through] the mouth and out of the neck, and a few men besides being slain, Lisle's men fled.[35]

Meanwhile, in October 1470, news of Edward's flight abroad and Warwick's arrival in London caused many Yorkist supporters to flee into sanctuary, including Queen Elizabeth, who gave birth to King Edward's son in November the same year. The survival of his family and heir was one reason why the king sought military aid from the Duke of Burgundy. But obviously, the king's main incentive was to regain the Crown and punish those who had betrayed him. Edward IV's policy towards his brother-in-law Charles the Bold would be to appear the injured party. However, the commons in Kent and south-east England directly blamed the absent king for the country's woes. Unlike Henry VI's corrupt ministers, King Edward had broken his promises to heal the divisions in the kingdom and mend the economy, and as a result, Warwick and Clarence's return promised a more acceptable alternative.

As for the newly freed Henry VI, he remained a powerful icon and magnet for Lancastrian resistance, especially in Kent. Queen Margaret was, no doubt, pleased with Warwick's successful invasion, and her return to England was much anticipated so that her son, the Prince of Wales, might reclaim his birthright. But as Sir Thomas Malory would indicate in about 1470, it was a time of personal cravings for the throne, and even young Prince Edward was a contender, according to the *State Papers of Milan*:

> This boy [Edward, son of Henry VI and Margaret of Anjou], although only thirteen years of age [in 1467], already talks of nothing but cutting off heads or making war, as if he had everything in his hands or was the god of battle or the peaceful occupant of the throne.[36]

Prince Edward, aged 16 in 1470, was undoubtedly primed to take the Crown if his father died suddenly or was incapacitated again because of mental illness. And, as will be seen, according to one source, the Earl of Warwick had a tough time protecting King Henry from would-be assassins when he returned to England with Clarence.[37]

To summarise then, Henry VI had reigned intermittently over a period of almost fifty years, although his throne had been effectively usurped by Edward IV in 1461. In those years, Henry had led a traumatic life even though he was no warrior king like his father (Henry V). Put simply, Henry VI had been manipulated, shot at and wounded, suffered several mental breakdowns, been used as a hostage and finally immured in prison for years, never knowing when his life might come to a violent end. We may sympathise with his plight and applaud his piety (for he had nothing else to sustain him), but we cannot say Henry VI was in charge of England when Edward was exiled in 1470. In every sense, he wore a crown of thorns, and Warwick was his master during his brief 'readeption'.[38]

Tragically, Henry of Windsor was barely visible in his later reign, which inadvertently may have saved his life on occasion. He symbolised divine kingship to his subjects, but by this time, most noblemen knew Henry was a weak and sometimes disturbed king who did not matter politically speaking. Shakespeare was correct that England had a vacant throne in many respects. But all this was about to change, and ostensibly the English people, led by a rebel leader called the Bastard of Fauconberg, would inadvertently hasten the king's demise, although the opposite was intended in spring 1471.

2

The Rose

How marvellous to man, how doubtful to dread,
How far past man's reason and mind hath it been,
The coming of King Edward and his good speed,
Out of Dutchland into England over the salt sea.[1]

✣

The new year began in medieval England on 25 March, according to the Julian calendar. Therefore, the date when King Edward returned to win back his throne was 14 March 1470, not 1471, according to modern dating (followed here).

When Edward landed in England almost six months had passed since Charles, Duke of Burgundy had provided safe refuge for the Yorkists in his country. But even considering Charles was married to Edward's sister, Margaret of York, Burgundian help had remained lukewarm until the eleventh hour due to international politics. This coolness was because Louis XI of France closely followed English affairs, and Charles feared that King Edward's presence in Burgundy might provide Louis with the perfect excuse to invade his country. Meanwhile, King Edward could only wait with bated breath and a certain amount of fear that he might never see England again. Indeed, after being exiled by Warwick he was lucky to be still alive.

Before making landfall in Burgundy, Edward's small flotilla of ships had set sail from King's (Bishop's) Lynn on Tuesday 2 October 1470, but storms had separated the Yorkists during their voyage. Edward's ship had been blown off-course to the island of Texel in Holland, and

Gloucester's vessel had floundered near Weilingen in Zeeland. However, despite this separation, the Yorkists were fortunate to weather the storm and a brush with a fleet of Hanse ships intent on piracy.[2] Indeed, it was a wonder the Yorkist lords reached the Burgundian coast alive and had not been forced to put ashore further south in France, where Louis XI might have captured them, a disaster that would have led to a hostage situation with little chance of ransom now Warwick was ruling England through Henry VI.

However, once safely ashore in Burgundy, King Edward sent messengers out for help, and Lord Gruthuse, the Governor of Holland, received Edward courteously. From here, Edward and his crew were accompanied to The Hague, and soon Richard, Duke of Gloucester, Lord Hastings and Earl Rivers were reunited with the king, who set about preparing a plan to invade England at the earliest opportunity. Penniless and, by all accounts, in need of clothing on his arrival in Burgundy, Edward was hardly in a state to bargain with the Flemings, and Duke Charles only sanctioned 500 *écus* per month for his expenses – a paltry sum of money considering the king's family ties. However, like so many other decisions in the Wars of the Roses, international politics were constantly at work behind the scenes. Louis XI had received word of Burgundy's royal guest, which warranted a response from Charles. By all accounts, it was a testing time for the three monarchs, and although Edward IV was allowed to remain with Lord Gruthuse in Bruges for two months, it may have seemed like a lifetime to a king who wished to win back his throne.

As for events in England, Henry VI's 'readeption' depended on the uneasy cooperation of Warwick and former die-hard Lancastrians. On 6 October 1470, Warwick, the Duke of Clarence and their followers, including the Bastard of Fauconberg, had helped Henry VI from the Tower. Despite Warwick's pleas for forgiveness and his offers of loyalty towards the former king, it was a strange situation considering 'the Kingmaker's' track record in the civil wars. But it seemed King Henry, as always, was in a forgiving mood, mainly because, according to one account, he had been badly treated in the Tower by his keepers:

> The Bishop of Winchester, by the assent of the Duke of Clarence and the Earl of Warwick, went to the Tower of London, where King Harry was imprisoned by King Edward's commandment. And there he

was taken from his keepers [who had] not worshipfully arrayed [him] like a prince, and not so cleanly kept [him] as should seem a prince, and they had him out and newly arrayed him and did him great reverence at the Palace of Westminster.[3]

Despite the king's apparent treatment by the Yorkists, moderation was carefully imposed between rival nobles. The king approved pardons, and, soon, Henry was publicly acknowledged in various crown-wearing ceremonies and processions throughout London. In his first parliament as king, very few Yorkists were arrested, although some had already fled into hiding or sanctuary. Commentators said Henry's restoration to the throne was welcomed, although Warwick was undoubtedly in charge, and the king may have been unwell at this time. Despite his imprisonment, an attempt on the king's life by persons unknown may have taken place in the Tower in 1470, although concrete proof of this is lacking considering biased opinion.[4] However, the pretence and process of kingship had to be maintained, or how could Warwick hope to keep his bargain with Louis XI and declare war against the 'accursed Burgundian' Charles the Bold?[5] A truce between England and France had to be signed quickly, and with this in mind, Warwick wrote to the French king, who agreed to denounce the Treaty of Péronne and move his forces into Picardy, threatening war with his neighbour.

Warwick welcomed an alliance with France, but news of the threat to his borders gave Charles the Bold no option but to back Edward IV if he wanted a friendly ally against Louis XI. If Edward could regain the English throne, he would be indebted to Burgundy, and Charles, formerly a Lancastrian sympathiser, likely hoped that England's problems might bring an end to his own. Also, former Lancastrians were still at the Burgundian court, including the dukes of Somerset and Exeter. Therefore, from Charles's point of view, Edward was better supported than spurned. Sandwiched between the fortunes of England and France, Charles could ill afford enmity on both fronts, and this more than anything changed his attitude to his brother-in-law Edward's requests for money and ships. One week after Christmas 1470, Charles granted the king and his companions £20,000 for their expenses and arranged an urgent meeting to discuss the French situation.

Charles finally met King Edward at Aire in Artois on 2 January 1471, and the talks lasted two days. From here, Edward moved to St Pol, where more meetings took place against a backdrop of protest from the exiled dukes of Somerset and Exeter. Privately, Charles tried to persuade the Lancastrians to go against Warwick, but the dukes soon shipped back to England and found favour with Henry VI just before Warwick's peace treaty with France was signed on 16 February. As for Edward, he had finally got what he wanted even though he was now beholden to Burgundy. However, Warwick's letter to Louis XI (dated 13 February) implied he was happy to begin the war with Burgundy at Calais as soon as possible. Therefore, from Charles's point of view, Edward's invasion of England could not come too soon.[6]

Charles the Bold was politically astute and warlike, like most powerful nobles of his age, but he knew if Edward could defeat Warwick in England, a protracted war with France might be avoided. However, the chronicler Philip de Commines, whom the duke employed until his death, wrote a digression about Charles in his memoirs stating he was no coward when it came to warfare. In fact, despite the dire situation now developing on his fragmented borders, he was chivalrous to the core:

> No prince was ever more easy to access by his servants and subjects. He was very splendid and pompous in his dress and in everything else and, indeed, a little too much. He paid great honours to all ambassadors and foreigners and entertained them nobly. His ambitious desire for glory was insatiable, and it was that which, more than any other motive, that induced him to engage eternally in wars.[7]

Charles was to later die in battle at Nancy in 1476, but like Edward, he was a man who desired to imitate the deeds of kings and heroes of antiquity. He was a knight who knew that backing King Edward was one way of defending his honour if he could meet the French on equal terms. Therefore, the duke quickly set in motion military preparations to aid his brother-in-law against Warwick. Three or four Dutch ships were secretly fitted out at Veere on the island of Walcheren while Edward made plans to contact his brother, the Duke of Clarence, through his long-suffering mother, Cecily Neville, the beating heart of Yorkist patrimony. He also wrote to Henry Percy, Earl of Northumberland, who feared being supplanted again by Lord Montagu if Warwick chose to promote him now he was in power. Edward also appealed to Duke Francis of Brittany for help and negotiated with English merchants in Bruges for ships and money. The king even wrote to the Hansards, his erstwhile enemies, to hire sea captains for his fleet now assembling at Flushing.

Great storms, winds and tempests

Eventually, Edward's invasion force consisted of thirty-six ships carrying about 1,200 men and their mounts (2,400, according to another account).[8] Edward's troops were a mix of 900 English and 300 Flemings equipped with handguns, according to one pro-Lancastrian chronicler, and preparations were made to cross the North Sea as soon as possible given favourable winds.[9] Edward aimed to land on the Norfolk coast, but when he eventually set sail on 11 March, he lost one ship, carrying several horses, almost immediately due to yet another storm at sea. He was further hindered when followers of the Earl of Oxford prevented him from landing in England. Warwick's spies were everywhere, and the Bastard of Fauconberg's fleet, financed by Warwick, was patrolling somewhere in the Channel, although not closely enough to stop Edward invading. Spanish, Portuguese and Breton ships were captured by the Bastard when he should have been shadowing the king. However, these actions greatly aided Edward's cause, and he managed to set sail from Norfolk, hoping to make landfall somewhere in Yorkshire where he could at least claim his dukedom.

It was a high-risk strategy by the king with no guarantee of success, and when more fresh storms hit his ships, they became scattered yet again. It seemed all the odds were stacked against Edward's recovery of the throne. But when his vessel, the *Antony*, scraped ashore at Ravenspur at the mouth of the Humber Estuary on 14 March, he must have thanked God for his deliverance, as it was nothing short of a miracle that he and his followers had reached land safely.

But Edward, *The Rose of Rouen*, was made of sterner stuff even though he followed religious portents at every opportunity.[10] Edward was a stubborn and determined man like his father, the Duke of York, but he was brave in the face of adversity. He was also a fortunate man despite knowing little else but the turmoil of the Wars of the Roses for most of his life. Several of his battles were won by taking advantage of weather conditions, leading from the front and using experienced captains – admittedly, the sign of a good commander.[11]

Edward was born at Rouen in France on 28 April 1442 while the Duke of York was campaigning in Normandy, and he was known as the Earl of March when he came of age. He was probably tutored in a typical chivalric environment, first in France and then at Ludlow Castle in the Welsh Marches. His mother, Cecily Neville, was the sister of the Earl of Salisbury, who had been executed at Pontefract after the battle of Wakefield in 1460. But before this, Edward had tasted civil war closer to home. Undoubtedly, while growing up, he was fed stories about Henry's weak and corrupt government and how they had blamed his father, the Duke of York, and not the Duke of Somerset, for losing territories in France. In 1455, Edward may have been an observer at the (first) battle of St Albans, and in 1459, we know he was present at Ludford Bridge, where he witnessed his father confront the king's host and flee for his life. Edward was attainted (as a teenager) along with his father and the Nevilles, and he later fled with the Earl of Warwick to Calais. But it was here Edward came of age, independent of his father, and soon he was carried along by Warwick's audacious plan to invade England.

Edward of York was tall (6ft 3½in, according to his skeleton measured in 1789) and stockily built.[12] According to foreign observers, he was a handsome prince and like Charles the Bold was vain and fashionable in his dress, a fact that was picked up by other writers later in his life:

> He was unusually dressed in a variety of costly clothes, in quite another fashion than we had seen before in our time. The sleeves of his cloak hung in ample folds like those of a monk's frock, lined inside with the richest furs and rolled on the shoulders. Thus, the prince, who was of imposing build, taller than others, presented a novel and remarkable spectacle.[13]

Some chroniclers later commented freely on Edward's liberal sexuality and debauchery, although it is unclear how much of this is true. Several writers speak of his greedy appetite for multiple sexual conquests, and his later adventures with his closest friend and loyal lieutenant, William

Lord Hastings, and his wife's brother, Edward Woodville, point to a man who probably threw caution to the wind in bed and on the battlefield. The author of *Gregory's Chronicle* singles out Edward's 'loving relationship' with his erstwhile enemy, Henry Beaufort, Duke of Somerset, in 1463. But this amorous slight may have been a swipe at the king's character rather than a known fact:

> [Edward IV] made much of [the Duke of Somerset] insomuch that he lodged with the king in his own bed many nights, and sometimes rode hunting behind the king, the king having about him no more than six horsemen at the most, and three were men of the Duke of Somerset. The king loved him well, but the duke thought treason under fair cheer and words, as it appeared.[14]

The author of the above extract may have been writing with hindsight. However, aside from this, we know Edward was a chivalrous man, in the non-romantic sense, amid the utter confusion of the knightly code in the late fifteenth century. He was not wholly opposed to traditional acts of mercy, but on the other hand, he could also be a ruthless killer on an epic scale. When it suited him, he was generous to those who pleased him, and his penchant for religious symbolism and advocating God's judgement was a trait that he exploited to the full on more than one occasion. To summarise, opposites governed Edward IV's life, and three things ruled the Yorkist Achilles in adulthood: his sexual appetite, gluttony and his thirst for battle. And the latter of these traits was rising to the surface in 1460.

When the Yorkist invasion of England was launched from Calais in June 1460, Edward, aged only 18, commanded a division, along with Warwick and Lord Fauconberg. Together they decisively beat the Lancastrians at Northampton shortly after seizing London, and when the Duke of York returned to England, Edward most likely was present when his father's rash attempt at usurpation failed at Westminster. With the help of Warwick, he was named next in line to the throne according to the Act of Accord, which disinherited King Henry's son the Prince of Wales, and Edward took full advantage of this when confronting his enemies in the future. As discussed, in 1460, he had lost his father and brother, along with his uncle, at the battle of Wakefield. Therefore, he was deprived of a major part of his family early on in life, a shock that must have affected him considerably.

Edward likely viewed the killings at Wakefield as cold-blooded murder and planned an act of suitable revenge. When he was posted to the Welsh Marches in December 1460, he managed to recruit a formidable army; here, he also broke free from the guidance of Warwick, who proved to be militarily inferior to him on more than one occasion. By winning the battle of Mortimer's Cross in February 1461, Edward's experience as a commander grew considerably, and after losing the (second) battle of St Albans, Warwick was temporarily cast as Edward's political advisor rather than his chief strategist. According to many pro-Yorkist contemporary accounts, Edward's kingly ambitions were blessed by God and symbolically displayed by nature in the shape of glowing suns (attributed to the Trinity), new vineyards and fragrant herbs. Edward of March had become an accomplished celebrity and soldier in a very short time. Therefore, it would have been against the grain not to expect some sort of violent retaliation when he heard of his family's destruction at Wakefield in 1460. Indeed, Edward was likely set on a course of Lancastrian slaughter because they had been offered no mercy. However, unlike his two younger brothers, Edward was of a certain age to vent his anger personally in battle, and this was fleshed out at Towton in 1461, where he culled the Lancastrian cause in absolute fashion.[15]

The years between 1461 and 1470 were testing and uncertain times for Edward IV. Lancastrian rebellions sprouted everywhere in England, especially in the north, and Warwick became the instrument of his downfall and final exile to Burgundy. But when Edward's ship was blown ashore at Ravenspur on 14 March 1471, there could have been few doubts in Edward's mind about the uphill struggle facing him. His first intention was to strike inland and gather support in Yorkshire, claiming his father's title as Duke of York. His second task was to seek out Warwick, the chief architect of his displacement as king. But when Hull refused to open its gates, Edward quickly marched west to avoid being trapped against the sea. He undoubtedly was in an unforgiving mood and wanted the English throne swept clean of Lancastrian traitors. But little did he know how difficult and dangerous this final harvest of his enemies might be and how unfriendly the City of York and northern England still was towards him ten years after the battle of Towton. *Warkworth's Chronicle* provides the details:

And there rose against him all the country of Holderness, whose captain was a priest and a parson in the same country called Sir John Westerdale. For the same priest met the king and asked the cause of his landing, and he answered that he came thither by the Earl of Northumberland's advice and showed [him] the earl's letter sent to him under his seal to claim the Duchy of York, which was his inheritance and right. And so, [Edward] passed on to the City of York, where Thomas Clifford let him in, and there he was examined again. And he said to the mayor and aldermen, and to all the commons of the city, the same as he had done in Holderness at his landing; that is to say, that he would never claim any title, nor take upon himself to be King of England.[16]

As might be appreciated, some parts of the north still wholly rejected Edward's rule due to the enormous death toll at Towton.[17] Indeed, the prudent Henry Percy, Earl of Northumberland, whose father had been killed at the same battle, failed to come to the king's aid in force. However, the earl's letters of support were good enough to gain Edward time to pass through Yorkshire unmolested. As one pro-Yorkist chronicler recorded, Percy and his northern retainers chose a different tactic rather than promote the king's invasion. The biased Yorkist chronicler of the *Arrivall* agreed that the legacy of 1461 was to blame for Edward's unpopularity:

> Having in their remembrance, how the king [Edward], at his first entry and winning of his right to the realm and crown of England, had won a great battle in those same parts [Towton] where their sons, their brethren, and kinsmen, and many other of their neighbours were killed. Wherefore, and not without cause, it was thought that they could not have borne him very good will and done their best service to the king at this time and his quarrel. And so, it may be reasonably judged that this was a notable good service and politically done by the Earl [of Northumberland]. For his sitting still caused the City of York to do as they did, and no worse, and every man in all those parts to sit still also, and suffer the king to pass as he did, notwithstanding many were right evilly disposed against the king, and especially his quarrel.[18]

As the *Arrivall* suggests, prior contact with the Earl of Northumberland proved crucial to Edward's plans, and he was also lucky that his small force was not ambushed by Lord Montagu, who was based at Pontefract Castle. Still disgruntled by the surreptitious loss of his northern earldom, Montagu was politically unsure of his next move, especially concerning his brother Warwick's campaign against Edward. As for 'the Kingmaker', he was busy raising troops in the Midlands after warnings in East Anglia prompted commissions of array to be issued in King Henry's name. Likely, there was also some panic in other parts of England following Edward's sudden arrival from Burgundy. Many nobles were uncertain who might prevail, and when Edward left Sandal Castle near Wakefield on 20 March, the nervous Montagu was still 'sat still', much like Henry Percy, hedging his bets.

King Edward's fabricated story that he had only returned to England to claim his rightful inheritance was a distant echo of Henry Bolingbroke's perjury in 1399. However, unlike Bolingbroke (later Henry IV), Edward's lie was wearing thin by the time he reached Doncaster, and this was likely the last town where his real intentions remained hidden from public view. By the time he reached Nottingham and Leicester, thousands of men had been drawn to his standard, some commanded by Sir William Stanley. William Lord Hastings supporters also responded to their master's call to arms when Edward's plans were finally unveiled. A well-connected man like Hastings had a large following of retainers and 'well-willers' in the Midlands, where Warwick and Clarence were still frantically trying to drum up support. Therefore, it is logical to assume that long-standing local indentures of service far outweighed Warwick's official royal commissions of array in some parts of England. However, according to the sources, the earl's army was formidable when fully concentrated.[19] Pro-Lancastrians further afield had also been contacted by Warwick's messengers, and the Earl of Oxford had written to his retainers to meet him at King's Lynn on Friday 22 March, to march west to Newark.

But evidently all was not well with Warwick's supporters. Fear caused Oxford's men and those of the Duke of Exeter and Lord Bardolf to beat a hasty retreat when they heard how close the Yorkist army was to their position. When Edward's scourers (scouts) were spotted in Newark, it was presumed the king was also nearby, which was not the case. In fact,

Edward was 3 miles away, and when the king eventually arrived in the town, he found the Lancastrian forces had dispersed, forcing Warwick to take refuge with his army behind the walls of Coventry.

After dispatching Clarence into the west to recruit more men, Warwick closed the town's gates against Edward, who embattled his forces ready for action. It was the king's chance to test his cousin's courage with a formal chivalric challenge. If Edward could entice Warwick out of Coventry and beat him in open battle, he could resume his march on London and rid himself of his most dangerous threat. However, if the earl refused to fight, then Edward would have no choice but to march south, leaving Warwick free to recruit and potentially threaten his rear:

> And when [the king] understood the said earl [was] within the town with a great people to the number of six or seven thousand men, the king desired him [Warwick] to come out, with all his people into the field, which the same earl refused to do at that time, and so he did three days after ensuing.[20]

Edward's invasion and dogged persistence to confront Warwick in battle is a credit to his courage. But the earl's reluctance to fight only postponed the inevitable face-off to another time and place. More than likely, Warwick was still waiting for Oxford and Exeter to arrive from the east, and Clarence to muster troops in the west. As for Edward, he needed to recruit more men to face three armies at once, and London was the only place that could provide such substantial Yorkist support. By delaying his march, the king might suffer desertions in his army. Therefore, he quit Coventry, and after issuing proclamations as King of England, he advanced on Banbury, where yet another army was spotted by his eagle-eyed scourers.

While Warwick was bottled up in the Midlands, Edward's brother, the Duke of Clarence, had recruited a large following in the west. He had been actively testing the mood of certain nobles for weeks after receiving worrying letters from his mother and sister, Margaret of York, Duchess of Burgundy, asking him to make peace with his brother Edward and heal the rift in the family.[21] Edward had also written to Clarence from Burgundy, no doubt putting him in the picture. However, it seems the duke had already decided to betray Warwick in a dramatic about-turn.

Promises had not been kept by 'the Kingmaker', although none of this is recorded by the sources, which only state that Clarence was 'accompanied by more than 4,000 men' who blocked Edward's march.[22]

Edward by the grace of God king

Despite the bad press given to the Duke of Clarence by historians, he was no different from many other nobles in the civil wars who bent with the wind. Therefore, when Edward IV arrived outside Banbury on 3 April and saw Clarence's embattled forces, he decided to give his brother another chance. Cautiously, Edward rode out into no man's land with the Duke of Gloucester, Earl Rivers and Lord Hastings, aiming to use this goodwill to enlarge his army. Clarence followed suit, and when he saw Edward, he immediately dismounted and fell to his knees. According to the biased Yorkist chronicler in the *Arrivall*, Edward spoke to him pleasantly, and there were *no* submissive gestures. The king embraced his brother, as did the Duke of Gloucester, who, it is recorded, had private words with Clarence later that may not have been so forgiving. Given his brother's betrayal and insistence that Warwick should also be pardoned, this was probably a step too far for Gloucester's teenage temperament, and he may have even renounced Clarence for his betrayal and held a grudge. However, Richard of Gloucester was not Edward IV. Clarence had a large, useful army at his back, and instead of arresting his brother on the spot for high treason, Edward ordered that they should all return to Coventry, where Warwick's forces were gathering strength:

> The Duke of Exeter, the Marquess Montagu, the Earl of Oxford, with many others in great number, by whose coming daily grew [had now] increased [Warwick's] fellowship. The king with his brethren this considering, and that in no wise he could provoke him to come out of the town, nor thinking it [wise] to assail, nor to tarry for the sieging thereof, thought it more expedient for them to draw towards London.[23]

It is telling that shortly after this setback, the author of the *Arrivall* depicts Edward in a semi-religious mood, instead of as a man in command of his destiny. We may also wonder at the king's insecurity and isolation when it is recorded that a sign from God, much like that witnessed at Mortimer's Cross in 1461, was needed to give Edward's cause added credibility.[24] Being exiled by Warwick and leaving his army free to manoeuvre cannot have been an enviable position. Facing the prospect of appeasing various truculent nobles in London must have been another concern that needed divine and moral support.[25] Therefore, when King Edward arrived at Daventry on Palm Sunday 1471, it was clear that something special was needed to sanctify his return to the English throne. And we can only wonder at the miracle that biased Yorkist chroniclers conjured up. Coincidence or not, when the king went in procession to the local church followed by a large crowd, it was not about to be an ordinary Palm Sunday service by any stretch of the imagination:

> And in a pillar of the church, directly before the place where the king knelt [there] was a little image of Saint Anne, made of alabaster, standing fixed to the pillar, closed and clasped together with four boards, small, painted, going round about the image, in [the] manner of a compass. And this image was shut, closed, and clasped, according to the rules that in the churches of England, all images [must] be hidden from Ash Wednesday to Easter Day in the morning. And suddenly, during the service, the boards encompassing the image about gave a great crack and a little opened, which the king well perceived and all the people about him. And anon, after, the boards drew and closed together again, without any man's hand touching [them] as though it had been a thing done with greater might, they opened [fully], and so the image stood, open and discovered, in sight of all the people there being.[26]

After suitably thanking God and St Anne for the above sign, Edward marched directly to London via Northampton, leaving behind him 'a good band of spears and archers' to guard against the enemy if they sought to attack him.[27]

As for Warwick, he quit Coventry and sent out messengers with letters to his brother George Neville, then Archbishop of York, and other friendly nobles in London. His orders were to provoke the city against Edward and resist him the best they could. On 9 April, the mayor and aldermen managed to muster a large force, although this may have been an exaggeration. By taking King Henry out of confinement and parading him through the streets between St Paul's and the Bishop's Palace, it was thought that Edward's return to London could be opposed. However, the sight of the humbled King Henry and Yorkist nobles in the city destroyed the pretence. The pro-Lancastrian *Warkworth's Chronicle* explains why:

> And on the Wednesday before Easter Day, King Harry and the Archbishop of York with him rode about London and desired the people to be true to him, and every man said they would. Nevertheless, [Thomas] Urswick, Recorder of London, and divers aldermen, who had the government of the city, commanded all the people who were in arms, protecting the city and King Harry, to go home to dinner. And during [this] time King Edward was let in, and so went to the palace of the Bishop of London and there took King Harry and the Archbishop of York and put them in ward the Thursday next before Easter Day. And the Archbishop of Canterbury, the Earl of Essex, Lord Berners, and such others as bore towards King Edward goodwill, as well in London as in other places, produced as many men as they could [so that] he had 7,000 men, and there they refreshed themselves well all that day and Good Friday.[28]

Now was the time for Edward to strike back at the House of Lancaster for all the trouble it had caused him. But Edward's decision not to dispose of King Henry was dictated more by design than inclination and undoubtedly influenced by other practical considerations. Edward hoped Henry's presence might soften some wavering hearts in Warwick's advancing army when the time came to fight. Edward also needed a hostage to dissuade any would-be Lancastrians from retaking London while the situation remained volatile. As for Henry VI, we can only wonder at his state of mind and how he felt about being manipulated once again, especially by a man who, by rights, should have disposed of him immediately. One contemporary recorded Henry felt *safe* in Edward's care when all about him were regarding him as a puppet in Yorkist hands. By all accounts, six years of confinement in the Tower had reduced Henry to a shambolic, weak and trusting wreck of a man and he embraced

Edward, saying 'my cousin of York, you are very welcome. I know that in your hands my life will not be in danger.'[29] As discussed, when Edward entered London, George Neville, the Archbishop of York, had tried unsuccessfully to drum up support for Warwick in the city, and even the mayor and his councillors were amazed at the dismal spectacle of majesty they witnessed in the streets:

> And so, with a small company of gentlemen going on foot before, and one being on horseback bearing a pole or long shaft with two fox tails fastened upon the shafts end, they held with a small company of serving men following. [But] the progress before showed was more like a play than the showing of a prince to win men's hearts, for by this mean [King Henry] lost many and won none or right few, and ever he was shown in a long blue gown of velvet as though he had nothing more to change into.[30]

Therefore, Edward's victorious entry into the city had been bloodless, with a little help from Thomas Urswick, the Recorder of London. Some of the city fathers had lost faith in the House of Lancaster, apart from those die-hard nobles like the Duke of Somerset, his brother, and the Earl of Devon, who quickly exited London by an unguarded gate to join Queen Margaret's expected invasion. Somerset's objective was to rendezvous with her when she landed in England with forces supplied by Louis XI. Warwick was marching with a large army towards St Albans as planned and all was set for a final confrontation with Edward IV despite Clarence's defection. Undoubtedly, Warwick was still trying to keep his promise to Queen Margaret and the French king despite Edward's landing. He had likely contacted the queen and the Duke of Somerset via messengers long before Lord Montagu and the earls of Oxford and Exeter swelled his ranks. According to sources, Warwick had also sent word to the Bastard of Fauconberg and his fleet in the Channel informing them of the overall plan. But considering his track record, how confident was 'the Kingmaker' of victory against Edward, and crucially, was he a competent field commander on the battlefield?

The simple answer is that the Earl of Warwick was no match for Edward's well-known leaps of faith and courage on the front line. The earl was a politician first and foremost, a schemer and a master of propaganda. Jehan de Waurin, the Burgundian chronicler, and a former soldier at Agincourt, went to see the earl in 1469 and noted only the earl's kindness and affability, not his martial prowess:

> The Earl of Warwick had in great measure the voice of the people because he knew how to persuade them with beautiful soft speeches; he was conversable and talked familiarly with them, subtle, as it were, to gain his ends. He gave them to understand that he would promote the prosperity of the kingdom and defend the interests of the people with all his power, and that as long as he lived, he would never do otherwise.[31]

To some writers, Warwick could never be content with mediocrity. He was constantly planning his next move politically and financially. He was a proud man, 'a trickster and a coward who was a hero in his own thoughts and a child in his actions, a fool and a traitor rushing towards his end', according to one biased writer.[32] The earl was second only to the king, yet there is no faithful likeness of him, and his character is even more challenging to pin down.

Warwick was 42 in 1471 and had been at the top of his political game for decades. However, ten years earlier, Edward IV had grown in stature; indeed, in military matters, he had taken the limelight. Obviously, at the time, the comparisons were always in doubt, but Warwick had never won a battle through feats of arms. He had been on the winning side and had succeeded in mustering Yorkist manpower when it was needed most, but his track record in terms of soldiering speaks for itself. At the (first) battle of St Albans, one of his northern captains had won the battle for him by breaking into the marketplace; at Ludford Bridge, he had escaped to Calais and directed others from there; at Northampton, treachery had won the day; at the (second) battle of St Albans Warwick had lost spectacularly and barely escaped with the shirt on his back; Ferrybridge and Towton were mainly Edward's victories (in fact Warwick may not have fought at Towton due to an arrow wound received at Ferrybridge) and later in the northern war his brother Montagu and others had taken charge of siege operations in his place. During the rebellions of 1469 and 1470 the earl had supported, but not taken an active part in the various battles, and only in the next campaign (Barnet) was Warwick able to take sole command of his destiny and understand the true nature of medieval warfare.[33]

In contrast, Edward IV had finally reached London from exile in Burgundy, and it was one of his greatest triumphs, on a scale not witnessed since his crowning victories in 1461. However, on 12 April 1471 (Good Friday), news arrived that the Earl of Warwick had reached St Albans to the north of the city with his large army, and, informed of this, Edward prepared to move the royal family to the Tower of London for safety. The next day, the king received an oath of allegiance upon the Holy Evangelist from Warwick's brother, George Neville, the current Archbishop of York, before also confining him to the Tower. Edward then dined well, we are told, and rode out to meet his army of English and Flemish soldiers encamped in St John's Field. The Duke of Gloucester, William Lord Hastings and the queen's brother, Anthony Earl Rivers, accompanied him, along with many other confirmed Yorkists. The two sons of Lord Berners also rode out with the king, and Edward kept the Duke of Clarence close at hand, considering his recent acts of betrayal and association with Warwick.

That afternoon (Easter Saturday) the Yorkist army marched north from London along with Henry VI, suitably guarded by the Duke of Gloucester, in the vaward. But Edward could not have anticipated that the English weather and mistaken identity would turn his final battle with Warwick 'the Kingmaker' into a nightmare of uncertainty. He also had no idea that more enemies were gathering strength across the Channel, hoping to deliver the southern thrust of a pincer movement that would aim to destroy his dynasty once and for all.

3

The Bastard

For doubt it not, he would have been,
Lord and master about the round sea,
And keep it sure to stop our enemies hence,
And won us goods and brought them thence.[1]

☩

Meanwhile, as Edward IV and his army marched out of London towards Barnet, the winds of change were gusting in the English Channel. Thomas Neville, the Bastard of Fauconberg, was in command of the Earl of Warwick's navy and had been for some time, according to chroniclers.[2] Thomas was making a name for himself as a pirate and was soon about to steer a course for England to aid his kingmaking cousin against Edward IV – providing Warwick's captains in Calais could determine his whereabouts at sea.

Contemporaries say Thomas had been busy attacking ships off the Breton coast. He commanded a large fleet during March 1471, and one account records that he had managed to capture twelve Portuguese vessels returning from France loaded with booty.[3] Among other goods, these ships carried three expensive religious tabernacles bearing the effigies of saints, belonging to the King of Portugal, and Fauconberg likely saw the vessels as fair game despite them being protected by peace with England. However, in 1473 (long after Fauconberg's death), an investigation was launched into this serious breach of faith that suggested that Thomas had been abusing his captaincy at sea for many years:

Commission to [John] Bishop of Rochester, John Dinham of Dinham, knight, Walter Blount of Mountjoy, knight, John Morton, Keeper of the Rolls of Chancery, and John Russell, secondary in the Office of the Privy Seal, to enquire into the complaint of John de Elbys, knight, licentiate in civil law, orator, ambassador and proctor or advocate fiscal of the king's kinsman Alfonso, King of Portugal, that Thomas the Bastard of Fauconberg and divers other pirates in the ninth year of [Edward IV's] reign plundered divers ships of Portugal, notwithstanding the alliance between the king and his said kinsman, and to cause restitution to be made and to arrest the offenders and bring them before the king and council.[4]

Evidently, Fauconberg had been instructed by his master Warwick to raid everything that moved in the Channel after King Henry's 'readeption', a fact that can be proven by the earl's generous commission to act on his behalf on land and sea. It appears every ship was fair game, and two of the plundered Portuguese vessels mentioned above were still laid up at Sandwich in 1473, awaiting repatriation. All of which establishes the fact that piracy was the Bastard of Fauconberg's main occupation before his rebellion of May 1471.[5]

Piracy around English coasts was a serious problem for many fifteenth-century governments, and it had been a danger to trade since the mid-1430s. In fact, sea robbing had been rife since the advent of shipbuilding. Henry VI's advisors showed concern for English vessels, but there had been no firm policy to stop piracy over the years. The government responded to raids on ships and ports as they occurred rather than implement some form of permanent strategy. Combating piracy was the biggest preoccupation of what was left of Henry V's navy, and English ships were as corrupt as other foreign vessels when it came to amassing personal wealth or financing their military interests such as maintaining the Calais garrison or pursuing war abroad.[6]

However, Thomas Fauconberg was no conventional hit-and-run pirate. Indeed, as discussed, the Earl of Warwick had instructed him to prevent King Edward from crossing to England from Burgundy in March 1471. Fauconberg's fleet was tasked with patrolling the Channel, although what it could have done to stop Edward's invasion is open to question. We know from several sources, including the *Arrivall*, that storms hampered Edward's voyage from Flushing and his landing on the east coast of Yorkshire on 14 March. This may be why Fauconberg failed to locate Edward's ships, given the problems of medieval seafaring in the fifteenth century. Another reason Thomas was at sea and engaged in piracy in March 1471 is revealed by his close family connections, especially those that involved his diminutive father, Lord Fauconberg, who was also a part-time privateer during the Wars of the Roses.

William Neville, later Lord Fauconberg and Earl of Kent, was the younger brother of the Earl of Salisbury, who had been beheaded at Pontefract Castle after the battle of Wakefield in 1460. But before his brother's death, William had been a soldier of some repute, and his loyalty towards Henry VI had been impeccable. Sources tell us he was small in stature, and according to the traditional ballad *The Rose of Rouen*, he was a renowned knight and a notable veteran of the Hundred Years War. No doubt William made an impression on his bastard son, Thomas, while he was alive, and due to his later links with the sea, William may even have promoted his son's maritime career to some extent to provide him with a lucrative income. The simple fact is that the Neville family were all seafarers at some point during the Wars of the Roses, and it is certain that Salisbury's eldest son, the Earl of Warwick, was a master privateer with a substantial fleet long before Thomas Fauconberg transferred into his service.

Born in about 1405, Thomas's father, William Neville, was the second son of Ralph Neville, the first Earl of Westmorland and his second wife, Joan Beaufort. Joan was the legitimised daughter of John of Gaunt and Katherine Swynford. Therefore, William was a great-grandson of Edward III, making his son Thomas related, at least in modern terms, to medieval royalty. However, Thomas Fauconberg was an illegitimate child. He was an outsider in every sense of the word, and when it came to inheriting property, this was generally forbidden to bastard children by English law. Property could be bequeathed, but Thomas was quite literally *filius nullis*, or in English, the son of no one.[7] However, his father was one of Ralph Neville's many sons, a leading member of the nobility and a candidate for military fame in the wars with France. Therefore, it is inconceivable that Thomas did not benefit in some way from Neville pre-eminence in the north when he came of age.

The Bastard

In 1425, when Ralph Neville died, his son William was bequeathed the barony of Bywell and Styford in Northumberland. But before this, he was married into a family who could potentially further Neville firepower in the north. William's marriage to Joan Fauconberg of Skelton occurred in about 1422, and she was variously described as 'an idiot from birth'.[8] Joan was about the same age as William, and her father, Thomas Fauconberg, who had died in 1407 after spending most of Richard II's reign in prison for treason, was also certified mentally ill, according to his peers. Thomas may have suffered from birth, although this fact cannot be proven. Therefore, if records can be believed, Joan may have had the same hereditary illness as her father, although this, too, is not certain. Thomas Fauconberg was 'not of sound mind' although he had lucid intervals, stated his gaolers. Marrying William and giving birth to four daughters (most of whom married well) goes some way to prove Joan's malady, if present, may not have been debilitating when it came to bearing children, unless, of course, William forced himself on her.[9]

However, aside from this picture of aristocratic madness and lucrative landed interests in the north, William Lord Fauconberg sired at least two bastard children during his lifetime (which was not unusual among the nobility). One was Thomas Neville, born about 1429, and the other was called William; both figure in our story. It was common for married women to accept their husband's bastard children during the medieval period, although we may have some sympathy for Joan's plight if she did. She may have recognised that the Fauconberg line might become extinct with no male heir to succeed to the title. Therefore, all may not have been well in the Fauconberg household. For the most part, William led a military life, and his place in northern politics likely kept him busy for most of the time. Essentially, the harsh truth was Joan Fauconberg's influence fitted in well with Neville plans of aggrandisement against the Percys, earls of Northumberland, who were still trying to rehabilitate themselves after their failed rebellions of 1403 and 1408. Primogeniture was precarious in the fifteenth century, and this is likely why Ralph Neville forged so many strong alliances for his children before he died.

As for Lord Fauconberg's career, he had been knighted by the 4-year-old Henry VI in 1426. William had followed a traditional military upbringing in France, and he may even have fought against Joan of Arc's army at the siege of Orleans in 1428. As a professional soldier, William soon rose through the ranks of the gentry to serve on the Scottish Borders in 1435, and in the following year he accompanied Richard, Duke of York back to France, where he fought alongside lords Talbot and Scales at Crotoy in 1437 and Meaux in 1439. As a reward for his services to the Crown at Harfleur, he was made a Knight of the Garter in 1440, and later William achieved the custody of Roxburgh Castle for sixteen years, drawing £1,000 per annum during peacetime and twice this amount when waging war with the Scots. However, in 1449, Fauconberg's fortunes changed when he returned to France as part of a diplomatic mission for Henry VI. Quite by chance, he was captured by an enterprising French raiding party at Pont L'Arche and was held to ransom.[10] According to one source, Lord Fauconberg was almost killed by an archer when the French tricked their way through the gates of the castle, and while William was lucky to be captured alive and offered mercy, he soon fell into debt at home.[11]

Before leaving for France, Fauconberg had instructed his officials to spend his income on supporting the upkeep of Roxburgh, and due to parliament's neglect, by 1451, he was owed £4,109 – a considerable amount of money considering his annual income. William's debt only increased when he was ransomed in 1453 for 8,000 *écus*, and although he still retained the custody of Roxburgh Castle, he became perilously short of money.[12] What with his previous outlay of cash for garrisons in France, he was still owed by the Crown. William tried to settle this debt by accepting a grant of 1,000 marks from the customs at Newcastle, although this was nowhere near the amount he was due. In short, William was being side-lined by the king's council, and it is no wonder he threatened to step down from commanding Roxburgh on several occasions. As the historian R.A. Griffiths rightly pointed out: 'What is so remarkable about this tale is that the Lancastrian crown could command [Fauconberg's] loyalty.'[13]

However, at some point during the next two years, William's allegiance *did* change, probably due to his mounting debt and the Crown's unwillingness to settle it in full. William joined his nephew, the Earl of Warwick and Richard, Duke of York, in their quarrels with Henry VI's government. Fauconberg soon became a member of York's council, and during the king's madness in 1453 he was among the delegates who went to visit him at Windsor Castle. He too reported that Henry showed no signs of recognition or understanding. The crisis hit all government offices, and when York became Protector, William and the Nevilles were shown favouritism in the north against the Percys. However, that said, due to William's unswerving loyalty to Henry VI, he found himself on the wrong side of the fence when the king recovered his sanity and York faced the Duke of Somerset at the (first) battle of St Albans in 1455.

It is implausible that William took part in the street fighting against his family, who were accessories to cold-blooded murder. Indeed, some sources say William was in France on an embassy to Charles VII.[14] Either way, and due to his connections with Warwick and the Nevilles, Fauconberg emerged still in favour with the Yorkists, and his appointment by the Duke of York to be joint Constable of Windsor Castle after St Albans proves William was now a firm supporter of York. He also served his nephew Warwick at Calais in 1459 when England marched blindly into another bout of intermittent civil war — a war where William would make his mark as a notable Yorkist commander and veteran strategist in the battles to come.

As for William's bastard son, Thomas Neville, he was already an accomplished mariner, or, more correctly, a pirate of some note. It is reported that he had received the freedom of the City of London for his 'work' in the Channel and the North Sea against foreign shipping in 1454.[15] His uncle, Richard, Earl of Salisbury, was a commissioner for keeping the seas from 1453 to 1455, and soon the Nevilles became notorious in their own right for attacking all kinds of ships for private gain. For instance, in 1457, it is recorded that Thomas aided Warwick with several acts of piracy in the Channel. Lord Fauconberg was briefly imprisoned for the same crimes. Therefore, we may conclude that Thomas was also directly involved in the Nevilles' rapid rise to power in England, be it only financially.

As discussed, privateering was a lucrative business in the fifteenth century whereby the Crown licensed seafarers to attack the ships of hostile nations. But the trouble with piracy was that it was an uncontrollable enterprise. Money was needed to support the military infrastructure of England, but consequently legitimate trade, safe conduct and general transportation to and from the continent suffered terribly. Sea robbery was one way to raise large sums of money, and most nobles who could buy ships used piracy to line their pockets and enlarge their fleet. However, for some privateers, the Statute of Truces, passed in 1414, made piracy a crime.[16] Attacks on friendly vessels could be construed as treason. Therefore, Lord Fauconberg was lucky to be bailed by his nephew Warwick in 1458 rather than face a long-term prison sentence, or worse, as the *Patent Rolls* record:

> Commission to Humphrey, Duke of Buckingham, and Richard, Earl of Warwick, reciting the complaint of Martin Ochoa, master of a ship called Le James of Spain, that the said ship laden with divers goods and merchandise, in coming to England under confidence of letters of safe-conduct, was taken by pirates in the company of William Neville of Fauconberg knight, and spoiled of its goods contrary to the Statute of Henry V.[17]

It was claimed that Lord Fauconberg was responsible for seizing the above ship to provide for Warwick's impoverished Calais garrison during declining customs revenue. The garrison had to be paid, or it would mutiny; therefore, the Captain of Calais (in this case Warwick) acquiesced despite the complaint from the Spanish authorities. William was again accused of piracy the following month, and it seems Henry VI's council was rapidly losing patience with the Neville family and their Yorkist in-laws despite the need for military finance. Salisbury, Warwick, Fauconberg and his bastard son Thomas were all at work in the Channel during this period despite Warwick's involvement in commissions, and something had to be done. Each family member commanded several private sailing ships, much like their armies of retainers. And similar to the effects of livery and maintenance, piracy was readily forgiven despite its detrimental effects on English commerce.[18] However, this may have been another reason why Lord Fauconberg and Warwick were attainted along with York and Salisbury for their rebellious actions against the king in 1459, as collectively they were becoming too over-mighty on land *and* sea to be controlled.

A knight of great reverence

When civil war broke out again in 1459, Lord Fauconberg was likely still based at Calais. There is no mention that he took part in the battle of Blore Heath or was present at Ludford Bridge when Warwick arrived with the Calais garrison to aid the Duke of York against the king. However, when the Yorkists were forced to flee into exile, Lord Fauconberg was once again thrust into the limelight. Like many other nobles in England, he had to choose sides, and when York was forced to flee with Warwick and the Earl of March, the two earls took ship to Calais to prepare for an invasion. Here Fauconberg played a crucial role in the events that followed in 1460. He was also involved in preventing the various attempts by the Duke of Somerset and other Lancastrians to capture Calais from their nearby camp at Guisnes. William also won the battle of Newham Bridge against Somerset in April of that year.[19] But against all the odds, the Yorkists held onto the only English foothold in France; thereafter, cross-Channel raiding and widespread propaganda played a significant role in securing a vital bridgehead in Kent.

Thomas Fauconberg likely helped his father and uncle with this raiding, especially the taking of Sandwich – one of the five Cinque Ports on the south coast of England.[20] However, when the Yorkists eventually landed in Kent, Thomas did not return permanently to England with his father, Warwick and the Earl of March. No doubt he was still at sea or based at Calais, and this is where the Yorkists saw Thomas's strength. The confidence placed in him was rewarded by an uncharacteristic expression of loyalty from Warwick in 1470, and this would be one of the reasons he would be trusted a year later when given the command of the Kentish rebels.

Similar to later successes in Kent, a highly charged propaganda campaign preceded the Yorkist invasion of England in June 1460. Warwick's recruitment drive in the south-east included ballads nailed to public buildings and town gates, including Canterbury, which inflated the returning Yorkist objectives. A contemporary profile of each of their commanders and their attributes, including Lord Fauconberg, is revealed in a popular ballad of the time which was distributed in England to encourage risings in Kent and other neighbouring counties:

Send home thy true blood unto its proper vein,
Richard Duke of York, Job thy servant insigne,
Edward Earl of March, whose fame the Earth shall spread,
Richard Earl of Salisbury named prudence,

> With that noble knight and flower of manhood,
> Richard Earl of Warwick shield of our defence,
> Also, little Fauconberg, a knight of great reverence.[21]

After London was secured for the Yorkists, and they gained an all-important victory over Henry VI's forces at Northampton on 10 July 1460, the king was captured amid much confusion. Henry was found surrounded by the dead bodies of leading nobles, and according to sources, Lord Fauconberg had commanded the Yorkist vaward who first broke into his fortified camp.[22] It had been a whirlwind invasion of England, and when the Yorkists returned to London, all awaited the return of the Duke of York from Ireland, who had ill-advised usurpation on his mind. The infamous Act of Accord was the result, and the coming winter was where the now ageing Lord Fauconberg showed his true colours as a Yorkist when Queen Margaret went on the offensive. William was 55 when York's claims were rebuffed in 1460, but despite his age he was soon to command significant forces in the field for the Yorkists, including thousands of archers equipped with devastating warbows, in a final bid to bring about dynastic change in England.

In contrast, records are silent about his son Thomas during the blood-letting that removed the Duke of York and secured Edward IV the English throne. But this is probably due in part to a change in the monarchy and government offices, which always causes lapses in historical evidence. However, we can be sure Thomas Neville was not in England at this time, but likely based in Calais with Warwick's fleet. Whereas his father is mentioned (by his heraldic device) in a famous ballad of the period that predates the battle of Towton:

> The Fish Hook [Lord Fauconberg] came to the field in full eager mood,
> So did The Cornish Chough and brought forth all her brood,
> There was The Black Ragged Staff that is both true and good,
> The Bridled Horse, The Water Bouget, by The Horse stood.
> Blessed be the time that ever God spread that flower![23]

During the winter of 1460–61, the Earl of Warwick and Lord Fauconberg took charge of Henry VI in London. The Earl of March was sent to Hereford to recruit against the threat of Lancastrian troops assembling in

Wales, and York with the Earl of Salisbury marched north to stamp out Lancastrian disturbances in Yorkshire. After the Duke of York was killed at Wakefield in December 1460, Lord Fauconberg and the Earl of Warwick tried to stop Queen Margaret's advance on London at the (second) battle of St Albans. However, the result was an utter disaster for the Yorkists, and only the Lord Mayor of London stood between the queen's northern army and a pillaging spree in the capital. Warwick and Fauconberg's army had been routed but miraculously they managed to join forces with Edward, Earl of March, whose victory at Mortimer's Cross assured the queen's retreat. It had been a trying time for the Yorkist commanders, but when Edward was acclaimed King of England on 4 March there was only one way to solve the dynastic problem, and Lord Fauconberg was instrumental in the campaign that followed.

On 11 March, Fauconberg was put in command of Edward IV's Yorkist vaward of 10,000 men when it left the city to face Queen Margaret's army in Yorkshire. At Ferrybridge, Fauconberg led a flanking mounted pursuit of Lord Clifford's force, managing to destroy it and its leader near Dintingdale before nightfall. The next day at the battle of Towton on 29 March, Fauconberg's studious command of the Yorkist vaward (comprised mainly of archers) forced the Lancastrians under Somerset to make an uncoordinated attack, causing horrendous casualties, and after their defeat, the war in the north centred on the vital garrisons and strongholds of Northumberland.[24]

After Towton, Henry VI, his queen and other Lancastrians were still at liberty. However, this did not stop the ageing Lord Fauconberg from pursuing them, supported by Warwick's brother Lord Montagu, who hemmed in royalist support behind thick castle walls. Fauconberg was rewarded by Edward IV for his services in the field soon after and became Earl of Kent in 1461. He also acquired the title of Admiral of England, and in this capacity, he captured Le Conquet, near Brest, in September 1462. Thomas Neville (then aged 33 and *called* Thomas Fauconberg)[25] may have been with his father during the raid. But when William was called back to supervise the siege war still raging in northern England, his glowing military career ended abruptly. He died suddenly aged 58 in January 1463 and was buried at Guisborough Priory in Cleveland, where his landed interest had been established on behalf of his wife, Joan.

With Lord Fauconberg's death, the earldom of Kent became extinct, the barony of Fauconberg fell into abeyance and Thomas Neville looked more to his cousin, the Earl of Warwick, as his master. There is no doubting his loyalty towards the earl, and our next reference to him traces his alliance with Warwick during his attempt to displace his former protégé Edward IV by instigating northern rebellions.

On 4 March 1470, Thomas was still retained by Edward IV. He was paid £50 by the Exchequer to serve at sea with Sir John Howard against the Hanseatic fleet, which was attacking English shipping, and 'other outward enemies, rebels and traitors' in the Channel.[26] In February, Thomas was with Warwick's great ship, the *Trinity*, at Southampton, which formed part of Howard's fleet under its master, John Porter. But when the wheel of fortune turned full circle in 1470, Warwick found himself at the mercy of Edward IV. After the failed Lincolnshire rebellion of that year, Warwick and the Duke of Clarence were declared traitors and forced to flee England. Howard's fleet, including some of Warwick's ships, were prevented from sailing from Southampton, and Thomas Fauconberg's loyalty was doubtless questioned regarding Warwick's treason. Thomas was still at Southampton on 18 March when Howard's fleet was scheduled to sail against the Hanse. He may have received covert messages from Warwick at this time, but by mid-April, just before Warwick attempted to secure his ships from Howard by force, Fauconberg disappears from the record.

It is not known for sure what occurred at sea in April 1470, other than Warwick's main attack was cleverly beaten off by Anthony Woodville, Earl Rivers, and that some of Warwick's captured ships were prevented from leaving port. Their captains, including Sir Geoffrey Gate (of whom more later), were taken prisoner before they had a chance to join Warwick. However, the whereabouts of the *Trinity* is not recorded, and it may have already put to sea. Indeed, Fauconberg may have covertly slipped its moorings with other ships intended for Warwick's use. Thomas likely escaped Howard's blockade before Warwick engaged Earl Rivers, considering he was with Warwick when he tried in vain to gain entry to Calais. He was also present when his master attacked forty Burgundian and Breton ships in the Channel on 20 April. Therefore, by this date, Thomas had returned to his Neville roots and Warwick's guidance, becoming a wanted man. Their combined fleets must have been significant, led by the *Trinity*, which is next mentioned as Warwick's 'great ship' moored in the Thames soon after Henry VI's 'readeption' in November 1470.[27] But in April the earl and Fauconberg were still at sea in every sense. They had been fired on when they tried to re-enter Calais harbour and Warwick's thoughts immediately turned to France and a plan to topple Edward and put Clarence on the throne.

Warwick was forced to seek a safe haven in the Seine estuary where, now with a fleet of some eighty ships, he planned to restore his former glory. Thomas Fauconberg was likely Warwick's second in command by April 1470 and remained so in his coming campaign of 1471. There is every reason to believe that Thomas commanded great respect from his master and those who sailed with him, or he would never have been given command of Warwick's fleet to land in Kent. From his base at Honfleur, Fauconberg remained active for at least a month, seizing fifteen or sixteen Dutch ships, and he even raided the Burgundian base at Sluys on 23 May to further aid Warwick's bid to invade England.[28] Thomas also fought a rear-guard action at sea when Earl Rivers attempted to dislodge him when he tried to blockade the Seine.

English squadrons raided Harfleur on 2 July, and other ports came under attack in August while Warwick was trying to negotiate terms with Louis XI. However, Warwick's surprise reconciliation with Margaret of Anjou at Angers in late July 1470, the earl's landing in Devon on 13 September and the capture of London in October of that year shocked everyone, including Edward IV. As discussed, as part of Queen Margaret's terms, she wanted Henry VI reinstated as king and, to seal the bargain, Warwick's daughter Anne Neville would be married to the Prince of Wales, a settlement that benefited everyone politically apart from the Duke of Clarence, as he was now left out in the cold without a crown.

As for King Edward, he was caught unawares, and when Lord Montagu in the north and others declared for Lancaster, his situation became critical. Thomas Fauconberg was mentioned along with Warwick, Clarence and others when they landed in England in September 1470. Their aim was to march inland and recruit on the way, and in *The Great Chronicle of London*, the author singles out Fauconberg's name when describing the main Lancastrian commanders involved in Warwick's surprise invasion:

In the said month of September, landed at Plymouth and Dartmouth in Devonshire the Duke of Clarence, the Earl of Warwick, the Earl of Pembroke, the Earl of Oxford and the Bastard of Fauconberg with many other to the number of 2,000 people of whom the Earl of Pembroke went into Wales and the other lords to Exeter and did proclaim in the name of King Henry that all men from the age of sixteen to sixty should be ready to defend the said lords with King Henry against King Edward. And the Sunday after the feast of Saint Michael [there] was given a sermon at Pauls Cross by Doctor Goddard declaring by certain bills that King Henry was the true king and not Edward, whereupon King Edward fled and Queen [Elizabeth] went out of the Tower by water in the night to Westminster the first of October, on which day the sheriffs of London took their oaths in the Exchequer, and the same day watch [was] kept in London, for the soldiers were so plenteous in the city, who robbed and spoiled in Southwark and at Blind Chapelton making the Flemings fly out of the city.[29]

The Kentish rebellion of September–October 1470 features significantly in our story. The pillaging of London 'by soldiers' mentioned above was an anathema to the city fathers, and their fears were to be repeated during Fauconberg's rebellion the following year. Many unrelated tensions were present in the city during the insurgency, and foreigners became targets for rebel attacks, which affected relations and trade abroad for obvious reasons. According to the antiquarian John Stow, basket makers, wire drawers, and other foreign traders were permitted to have premises in Southwark, Blanche Appleton and St Katherine's Wharf. During the 1470 rising, thousands of rebels were let loose in these areas at the behest of Warwick, who had paved his way well with propaganda guaranteed to inflame Kentish hearts and topple the Yorkist regime in London.[30]

Warwick's coup was achieved with lightning speed. However, the pillaging in London continued unabated despite his presence in England. The Kent rebels overran the suburbs, namely St Katherine's, Southwark, Radcliffe and other places where Dutchmen lived and managed their beer houses. They robbed and burnt their homes without mercy, and Warwick's retainer, Sir Geoffrey Gate (who had been captured by Lord Howard in March 1470), escaped with others from prison to pillage the suburbs anew, sparing no one. Therefore, the grandly titled 'readeption' of Henry VI had its ugly side, and many onlookers likely wondered how the king might be allowed to live with the city in such turmoil. The Earl of Warwick may have secured himself a foothold in England and was keeping his bargain with Louis XI and Margaret of Anjou, but fears of further rebellion and rioting in London reached fever pitch, and the memory of it would dictate the course of Fauconberg's rebellion in 1471.

With Edward and his followers galloping towards King's Lynn, hoping to flee to Burgundy and Warwick's forces nearing London, the Yorkist government went underground. It was clear only one man could stop the mayhem in the city, and 'the Kingmaker', along with Clarence and Fauconberg, set about doing so soon after they arrived in the city, although Clarence had every reason to be disgruntled:

> On the Wednesday following, the Tower was yielded to the Mayor of London, and he, with his aldermen, brought King Henry out of prison, discharged his keepers and on the Friday following came to London the Archbishop of York, brother to the Earl of Warwick, the Prior of Saint John's and others to the number of 2,000 men at arms rode to the Tower of London. On the morrow, being Saturday, came the Duke of Clarence, the Earl of Warwick and the Bastard of Fauconberg, with many others to the number of 4,000 men at arms ready for war, [and they] brought King Henry out of the Tower to the bishop's palace.[31]

It is not widely known that Henry VI survived an assassination attempt immediately after (or during) the 1470 rebellion, although by whom is unknown. John Blacman, the king's chaplain, was a keen advocate of Henry's saintly nature, and he records this 'crime' fervently in his *Memoirs*. The attack appears to have taken place just before King Henry was released from the Tower, when he forgave both the leaders and the men under them for what they had maliciously designed against him:

> Like compassion he showed to many others, and especially to two who were encompassing his death; one of whom gave him a severe wound in the neck and would have brained him or cut off his head, but the king took it most patiently, saying: 'Forsooth and forsooth, ye do foully to smite a king anointed so'. The other smote him in the

side with a dagger when he was held prisoner in the Tower, and after the deed, believing that he had killed the king with his wicked blow and fearing [capture], fled with all speed. However, [he] was caught and brought before [the king] when he had recovered and was set free from prison once more by the favour and act of God.[32]

As indicated above, Blacman does not name the assassins responsible for the attacks. But it may not be wide of the mark to believe that one 'great lord' in particular had the motive, ambition, guile and stupidity to kill Henry without a thought. It will be remembered that the Duke of Clarence had been promised the throne by Warwick in 1469, and clearly, the way had been blocked by Warwick's alliance with Queen Margaret, who wished Henry freed from captivity. Miraculously, we are told, the king survived the above attempts on his life, maybe due to Warwick's intervention, and this led to renewed oaths of loyalty and pardons for the man who 'thought he had killed the king'.[33] By all accounts, Clarence had been assured he would succeed Henry and his son, the Prince of Wales, after they died, but after Warwick's meeting with the queen in Angers, Clarence may have tried to clear a way to the throne once he entered London in 1470. With Henry out of the way, and the Prince of Wales still exiled in France, no doubt he would have been acclaimed king despite his regicide.

Captain of the navy of England

With the government firmly in his grasp, Warwick fulfilled his next promise to Louis XI and Henry's queen. More ships were impressed into service in December 1470 and January 1471, money was raised for a fleet to escort Margaret back to England and preparations were made to attack Burgundy. King Edward's whereabouts were doubtless on Warwick's mind when Henry VI had been urged to sign a truce with France. And as for the Bastard of Fauconberg, he was given command of Warwick's fleet that would carry out the earl's wishes. But when Thomas set sail in March 1470, he was also given orders by Warwick to prevent Edward from landing in England. Fauconberg had been officially appointed 'by the advice of the Earl of Warwick, captain of the navy of England and men of war both by the sea and by land' although the actual commission has not survived.[34] However, Fauconberg's later correspondence with the Lord Mayor of London in May 1471, when he styles himself as the leader of Henry VI's people in Kent, is likely a reworded extension of this indenture (if it existed). Therefore, Fauconberg was Warwick's rising star at this time, and he was a man who the earl thought could be trusted with his large fleet that would attack Burgundian shipping in concert with the French invasion. And here, our story comes full circle.

In March 1471, the Bastard of Fauconberg was resorting to familiar tactics, namely the privateering mentioned at the beginning of this chapter. As explained earlier, by the end of the month, Thomas had already captured twelve Portuguese merchantmen off the Breton coast – although for what purpose, other than profit, remains a mystery. How long he had been in the Channel is difficult to ascertain as he is such an elusive character. But it is doubtful he would have put to sea in December or January when ships were being gathered into winter quarters. However, when he did weigh anchor, Thomas failed to prevent Edward IV and his followers from landing in Yorkshire on 14 March. Therefore, attacking the Portuguese ships may have been Fauconberg's way of enlarging Warwick's fleet, financing the Calais garrison and purchasing supplies for an all-out attack on Burgundy or England. Also, Brittany is a long way from Flushing, where Edward's force set sail, and the Humber estuary, where the king eventually landed, is even more remote, especially in stormy weather. Consequently, Fauconberg was quite clearly in the dark when it came to supporting Warwick's concerted plan, and he needed to be reined in due to the serious political crisis that was now developing in England.

Even though Warwick had been repelled from Calais the previous year, two of his retainers, Sir Walter Wrottesley and Sir Geoffrey Gate, were dispatched to the garrison town with money and a message from Warwick to supply the Bastard of Fauconberg with troops. As former port governors, both Gate and Wrottesley were well placed to persuade the fickle garrison to provide a contingent of professional soldiers that might help raise a rebellion in Kent while Warwick and Clarence rode out of London to face Edward in the field. However, the pro-Lancastrian *Warkworth's Chronicle* gives the details of how small this Calais contingent was, compared with the enormous task at hand:

Sir Walter Wrottesley and Geoffrey Gate, knights of the Earl of Warwick, were governors of the town of Calais, [and] did send Sir George Brooke, knight, out of Calais, with 300 soldiers unto Thomas the Bastard Fauconberg, [who] was on the sea with the Earl of Warwick's navy, that he should the navy save, and go into Kent, and raise all Kent, to the intent of taking King Henry out of the Tower and destroying King Edward if he might.[35]

No doubt Warwick's written orders to Sir George Brooke for soldiers also included news of Edward's surprise landing in England on 14 March. Fauconberg's fleet was needed for a general commission of array issued to all loyal Lancastrians in England on Henry VI's behalf. And he was to act immediately despite failing to stop Edward's crossing and landing in England.

With Edward in Yorkshire and Warwick marching through the Midlands hoping to gather support, the scene was set for a remarkable battle of wills. The Bastard of Fauconberg's accumulation of ships (legitimately acquired and captured as prizes by him over the months) was the southern support of Warwick's overall strategy to topple Edward IV in decisive fashion. Fauconberg's ships could move men to almost any part of the kingdom, and his fleet must have been a true 'navy' in every sense of the word when it sailed into Sandwich on or about 2 May 1471. Indeed, this fleet had become a law unto itself and a powerful military asset to 'the Kingmaker' in his bid to topple Edward IV. But what exactly did Fauconberg's navy comprise in early May? What kind of ships did he command, and how many mariners and soldiers could Thomas supply to Warwick's campaign?

During the fifteenth century, European shipbuilding underwent a significant transformation as maritime technology advanced and global trade expanded. The Wars of the Roses saw the use of ships in various capacities, from transportation and trade to military action.[36] One example of a recently excavated fifteenth-century vessel is the Newport ship, which offers a rare glimpse into the world of medieval seafaring before 1469. The Newport ship was clinker or lapstrake built, using oak planks that overlapped and were joined together with wooden pegs and iron nails. The ship was designed with a flat bottom and a keel, which helped it to sail in shallow waters and maintain stability in rough seas. Shipbuilders during the period were skilled artisans and craftsmen with years of trade experience, and many of them worked in specially built shipyards, typically located near waterways and ports. The Newport ship, although likely built in Spain, is thought to have undergone refurbishment in a medieval shipyard beside the River Usk in Wales, where it was found in 2002. The vessel would have been used both commercially and militarily, and its main purpose was probably transporting goods such as timber, wool and wine abroad. However, the ship's hull shows signs of damage, suggesting that at some time, it may have been involved in warfare or piracy.[37]

During the fifteenth century, ships were constructed using traditional woodworking techniques and innovative technologies. The construction process typically involved selecting and shaping timber, joining planks and frames together and finishing the ship with a protective coating of pitch or tar. Vessels owned by the nobility, such as the Earl of Warwick and Lord Howard, were built to the highest standards, using the best materials and the most advanced technologies of the period. Oak was the preferred wood for shipbuilding as it was strong, durable and resistant to rotting. Once the timber was selected, it was seasoned for several years to remove excess moisture and strengthen the wood. The next step was to shape the timber into planks and frames, and this was done using hand tools, such as axes, adzes and chisels, and larger machines like saws and planes. The planks were then secured using various techniques, including mortise and tenon, dovetail and scarf joints. These joints allowed the planks to fit tightly and form a strong, cohesive structure. Once the basic framework of the ship was complete, the shipbuilders would add additional features such as decks, masts and rigging. Forecastles were added to some ships, giving height and advantage to archers who could shoot down on smaller vessels. Sails were made of canvas suitably adorned with heraldry, and long flowing standards were used for recognition purposes at sea. Rigging was made from natural fibres such as hemp or flax, and some ships were fitted out with deck artillery, which usually comprised small bore *serpentine* or swivel guns.[38]

The Earl of Warwick's navy was known for its powerful and impressive vessels, each with its own unique name. As well as the famous

Trinity, rebuilt in 1469 by John Stone, many of these names are mentioned in official documents, and they include the *Nicholas of the Tower*, the *Gabriel* and the *Mary Fortune*. The vessels commissioned soon after Warwick captured London in 1470 were similar to the types of ships mentioned in the *Patent Rolls* for November and December, including:

> [A] commission to John Porter, master of the ship called the Trinity, at present in the river Thames, to take mariners for the said ship to serve the king [Henry VI] at sea in the company of the king's kinsman Richard, Earl of Warwick and Salisbury. The like to the following: John Rawlin, master of the ship called the Margaret; Richard Hubbard, master of the ship called the Christopher; and Robert Grave, master of the ship called the Ellen.[39]

Other captured ships were also equipped with men and armaments, and they were made ready to put to sea at a moment's notice. Commanders, including Walter Aldrich, master of the ship called the *Michael*, and Thomas Roger, commanding the *Katherine Warwick* were undoubtedly hired to form a fleet that would go against Burgundy when the truce was signed with Louis XI. In terms of prestige, their presence was intended to evoke a sense of power and grandeur, reflecting the importance of the owner's political position, family and affiliation. The contemporary line illustrations on the famous Beauchamp Pageants of around 1475 indicate the flamboyance of the medieval ship in its heyday, and some of the vessels depicted in the roll graphically portray how precarious seafaring could be when storms blew up without warning and how attacks were made against foreign shipping.[40]

During the period, various types of medieval ships were in use. These ships ranged from small, nimble vessels to larger, more heavily armoured warships, and it is recorded in numerous inventories these had already been categorised in the fifteenth century for identification and commercial reasons. For instance, a balinger (or barge) was a small ship commonly used for coastal trade and fishing. It was a single-masted vessel with a shallow draft, allowing it to navigate rivers easily. Balingers were also equipped with oars, which made them more manoeuvrable. They were typically smaller than 'great ships' of the period, carrying around 50 to 80 tons, and they were not usually heavily armed for warfare, being used primarily for transportation. Caravels were also small ships used for exploration and trade. They were relatively fast vessels, able to travel up to 12 knots. with a crew of around thirty men and a weight of about 50 to 150 tons. However, the most common ship of the period was the cog (or deep-sea cog), a sturdy, broad-beamed vessel used for transporting goods and armaments. It was a relatively large ship, which could carry around 100 to 200 tons, and although it was not a particularly fast vessel, it was reliable, hence its popularity during the period for transporting a significant amount of equipment and men to destinations all over Europe.

Like the balinger, the medieval galley was a long, low-slung vessel powered by oars. It was typically used for warfare, with the ability to travel at speeds of up to 8 knots. The galley was heavily armed with guns and had a crew of about 200 men. It was not a 'great ship', but with a tonnage of about 150 tons, it was highly manoeuvrable at sea. As for the carrack, this was a large, three-masted vessel popular during the period. Its design was developed in Portugal (called a *Nao*) and was commonly used for long-distance oceanic voyages. Carracks had a high rounded stern, usually a forecastle and a large central hull. They were heavily armed with breech-loading guns and equipped with various sails, allowing them to catch the wind and travel at speeds of up to 8 knots. Carracks had a crew of about 200 men and could carry up to 400 tons of cargo, making them popular for long-distance trade missions and warfare.

The cost of building a medieval ship varied depending on several factors, including the size, complexity, the kind of materials used and the skill of the craftsmen employed. A typical cog might cost around £1,000 to build, while a larger warship or 'great ship' might cost ten times this amount. As can be imagined, only wealthy merchants, nobles or kings could afford to commission them. Therefore, such ships were highly prized by those, like the Nevilles, who used them to advance their positions and power. But, contrary to popular opinion, affordable, pre-built vessels were readily available. Ironically, Nicholas Faunt, the well-known merchant and Mayor of Canterbury during the 1471 rebellion, was among others who sold ships to Edward IV in the summer of 1467. Faunt allied himself to Fauconberg and lost his life in 1471, but before this, Edward paid him £170 for a vessel, as recorded in the *Issues*

Rolls, and Faunt was not the only one to use private ships to enlarge his business.[41] Once vessels were built, they could often be bought for less money, and various inventories and wills of the period indicate that ships were active in the Wars of the Roses, although not permanently organised into a navy to serve the Crown. As discussed previously, the Nevilles were the most active mariners of the period, followed by the Howards, and Thomas Fauconberg seems to have been the most prolific and constant pirate in his family. But which commanders were involved in the Kent rebellion of May 1471? And, considering Warwick's plans, what did Fauconberg hope to achieve with a large fleet of ships and only 300 professional soldiers?

We know that Sir George Brooke was initially sent with this contingent of troops from the Calais garrison to aid Thomas in his enterprise. But it is also likely that Sir Walter Wrottesley and Sir Geoffrey Gate crossed the Channel to England with their men, given their involvement in the rebellion and later pardons given by Edward IV.[42] However, 300 mercenaries from the Calais garrison do not make an army. According to the evidence, Fauconberg also commanded mariners and other soldiers on his ships, but even considering his large fleet, this still does not amount to a force that could attack London successfully. Moreover, Thomas had divided his fleet sometime in early May, sending ships carrying artillery into the Thames Estuary while others were anchored at Sandwich to guard it against attack. Therefore, where was Fauconberg's additional support supposed to come from to march on London?

Undoubtedly, Warwick's widespread propaganda campaign in the south-east was expected to raise the commons, and this was gathering momentum as Warwick's forces marched north to threaten King Edward's landing in Yorkshire. Canterbury was the obvious muster point for the rebels, but Essex was also in arms, and so were parts of Surrey and Sussex. Their ultimate destination was Blackheath, where previous rebellions had launched their attacks on London. However, by the night of 13 April 1471, when Warwick's forces were awaiting Edward's army near Barnet, Fauconberg was still at sea. Therefore, what was Warwick's overall plan of action and where did the rebels fit in?

Essentially, Warwick's plan was grounded on recent historical precedent. By raising the commons in rebellion and striking at London, the earl likely wished to repeat his successful 'readeption' tactics of 1470. He hoped to threaten the city, cause anarchy in the suburbs and undermine Edward's grip on power using discontented rebels to attack from the east and south-east. The Bastard of Fauconberg was well aware of Warwick's intentions, as was Sir George Brooke, who had briefed him personally to lead the commons and free Henry VI from the Tower. However, it is debatable whether Fauconberg knew or appreciated how he, or those knights affiliated to Warwick by indenture, might siege London or what might happen if 'the Kingmaker' were to be defeated by Edward when he finally faced him on equal terms across the no man's land of an English battlefield.

4

Bloody Fields

King Edward and his brother, doubting no fear,
Lords and other gentlemen in the king's right,
Steadfastly and worshipfully their part did there,
Manly and freshly that day did they fight.[1]

✢

On 18 April 1471, Sir John Paston wrote an unsigned letter to his mother informing her that he and his brother had escaped the battle of Barnet four days earlier. Both Pastons had supported the Earl of Warwick, and although they had survived the desperate fighting, John reported his brother had been injured by an arrow that had lodged in his right arm beneath the elbow. Most injuries from soiled arrows did not heal if they became infected, but the surgeon who dressed the wound said it would mend despite this fear 'within a right short time'. In the same letter, Paston thanked God for his safety and listed some of those killed half a mile north of Barnet on Easter Day. However, a few weeks later, Paston's wounded brother was far from recovered. Not only was he still suffering from his injury, but he was in hiding and penniless. He had 'neither meat, drink, clothes or money' and was in 'the greatest need that [he] ever was in'. He begged his mother to send cash quickly to pay his debtors and to get 'leechcraft' to heal his lacerated arm. He said he hoped to be well within seven days, but like many soldiers who fought in the Wars of the Roses, he soon discovered that festering wounds were not the only price to pay for fighting on the wrong side.[2]

The battle of Barnet had been a decisive victory for Edward IV. However, we may never fully know what happened north of the town on that damp and foggy Sunday in 1471, for two reasons, and the first of these is probably the most obvious and readily understandable. The battle of Barnet was fought in a thick early morning mist – a 'great mist' according to one source in London 12 miles away.[3] The second reason for doubting what happened in the battle is that we have no concrete proof of the positions of the two armies (and their camps) due to their deployment on Easter Eve. All of which invites speculation about where the action took place the following day and does nothing to advance military history.

Most chroniclers of Barnet agree on the murky weather conditions during the fighting. A probable eyewitness to the battle, who did his best to record the fighting there from a Yorkist point of view, is the author of the *Arrivall*. Considering the appalling weather conditions, he recalls how and why Warwick was defeated. He also regards King Edward's approach to the battlefield in the dark as contributing to his survival. Therefore, for these reasons and many other finer details, we may consider this evidence a unique and contemporary account from a Yorkist viewpoint.[4] The author of the *Arrivall* also claims there was a misalignment of both armies during the night, which changed their relative positions when they formed up for battle the following day. The three factors of darkness, fog and misalignment are bad enough, but add to this the effects of gunpowder weapons (handguns and artillery) on the battlefield, and it is hard to imagine a more confusing situation for both armies. Indeed, the usual mayhem of a medieval battle, in all its forms, would have increased significantly compared to fighting in clear, fine weather. Therefore, as might be expected, the battle of Barnet is still a hotly debated subject, and historians have never fully agreed about the positioning of both armies. Indeed, where the Duke of Gloucester's men were deployed and where they went during the fighting cannot be fully traced. And this is before we attempt to calculate the size of both forces and the total casualties involved. Even the historical topography blurs in most accounts, as does the strategy in such foul weather.[5]

Like many other battles of the civil wars, there is a shortage of conflict archaeology in the general area, as most of the Barnet battlefield has been built over and therefore destroyed as far as evidence is concerned.

There is also mention in the sources of several named locations that complicate the interpretation of the site. Features such as hedges, greens, plains, marshes and wooded areas are all mentioned in contemporary chronicles. In local history, there is a reference to a hermitage, a moated manor house and a battlefield chapel where some of the dead were buried. But as with other medieval conflicts, the historical landscape has changed drastically over the years, causing doubts about key locations. Buildings, modern housing estates and new roads have cut through the site. Legends, such as a solitary oak tree and an area known as Deadman's Bottom, are reminders that the battlefield and the ensuing rout reverted to folklore in later years, thus fictionalising the event. Therefore, due to the fragmented persistence of recorded memory, only the ghost of a battle drifts across the landscape, which naturally invites conjecture and historical misinformation.

However, contemporary sources are the first step to understanding the battle, and several of these support the view that Barnet was an extremely bloody affair. An appreciation of the soldier's experience, what weapons he used and the strategies employed in medieval warfare come a close second to the sources. Each grain of evidence must be evaluated alongside the chronicles, letters and archaeology (if significant artefacts are ever found in the future). Given the lack of detail about the initial positioning of the armies, the facts concerning period weapons can be used to show how medieval warfare was limited to time and place. Using optimum ranges of artillery, buried cannonballs and arrowheads may indicate where the armies were embattled if they are mapped accurately onto the landscape. The technology and use of field guns rapidly advanced during the Wars of the Roses, and even if these were shot blindly at the battle of Barnet, as the chronicles record, the recovery of cannonballs is likely to pinpoint the battlefield approximately – given that even an estimated position is valuable when contemporary evidence is lacking.[6]

Underlying the use of military hardware, we must also deal with how the battle might have changed alignment and if this was significant to the outcome. The mistaken identity (confirmed by two independent sources) of soldiers returning to the battlefield in fog may explain why Warwick was defeated, but other contributing factors, such as looting the dead and dying instead of fighting, may also account for the Yorkist victory.[7] If true, such evidence confirms how appalling visibility actually was at Barnet if livery jackets and banners could not be recognised. Acts of betrayal had won several battles before 1471 and would do so again, proving that treachery was expected in the Wars of the Roses and not arbitrary. However, while the mistaking of banners and livery jackets were no doubt common occurrences in medieval warfare, even in favourable weather conditions, such confusion was likely increased tenfold by the reported accounts of soldiers routing. In thick fog or mist, inflamed tensions and nervousness would have led to soldiers seeking safety in numbers to avoid mistakes between friend and foe, and in these areas of conflict, desertions would have been commonplace when communication and cohesion ceased to exist.

Therefore, taking all the evidence into account, how widespread and detrimental was this apparent mistaken identity and pillaging at Barnet? Did the breakdown in formations and lack of discipline win Edward IV the battle rather than something else? And can we be sure documented sources are truthful accounts of the event, considering their traditional bias, the far-from-ideal battlefield conditions and the accuracy of memory?

As mentioned, all the principal elements of the battle of Barnet are interconnected. Essentially, this leads us to conclude that the fighting there was confused beyond the level generally experienced by the medieval soldier. The men who fought at Barnet were no doubt disorientated; their movements were imprecise; terrain features were vague, therefore arbitrary; most formations would have become disorganised as the battle progressed; messages and orders were likely misinterpreted, and most of all, the fighting was likely so indiscriminate that it would have been challenging for any writer or eyewitness to distinguish what was happening when and where. In short, Barnet was a soldier's battle, and no grand tactics or even a veteran commander's skill could do anything once the fighting had commenced. At best, the conflict was essentially a large-scale brawl in the fog, choked with acrid smoke and hindered by an avalanche of noise and dreadful uncertainty. Therefore, given the circumstances, we can disregard any attempt to illustrate the battle diagrammatically. Any effort to interpret further must be done with extreme caution. But clearly, some historians have attempted a coherent narrative, and therefore, specific facts in the chronicles *can* be verified, while others can be discarded.

Given the biased nature of the surviving Yorkist and Lancastrian accounts of the battle (such as those included in the *Arrivall*, the *Short Arrivall* and *Warkworth's Chronicle*), additional information can be extracted from *The Paston Letters*, *The Great Chronicle of London* and a report by Gerhard von Wesel, a visiting merchant from Cologne. From all these contemporary accounts, some written soon after the event, we can draw definite conclusions without resorting to later Tudor writers and local legends. As explained, elements of local history add colour to the written evidence but do not shape it, and the mechanics of medieval warfare, timings and even existing terrain play a significant part in understanding what was possible given the period. All have value, but the written word is the most crucial ingredient to reconstruction.[8]

Most modern accounts of the battle are based on the *Arrivall*. However, as explained, various other sources are not wholly pro-Yorkist, and the correspondence of Gerhard von Wesel, in the form of a newsletter dated three days after the fighting ended, is the most revealing. As for preliminaries before the battle commenced, these are straightforward enough, apart from the debatable estimates of the two opposing armies, which we must analyse with an open mind.

The Earl of Warwick and his brother Lord Montagu, along with the Earl of Oxford (leading the vaward), the Duke of Exeter and Lord Beaumont, marched south from St Albans on 13 April, arriving in the evening north of Barnet along with approximately 20,000 men, according to the *Arrivall*. Based in London, Gerhard von Wesel agreed with this unusually high figure in principle, and that Warwick's army contained artillery and arquebusiers (handgunners). However, it is hard to imagine how von Wesel knew this if he was not at the battle himself, and even if he were, could anyone make such a calculation in thick fog? The pro-Yorkist *Short Arrivall* says the Earl of Warwick had mustered 30,000 men, 'determined [by] themselves', but clearly, all these figures are likely distortions of the truth to make Edward's victory seem more politically appealing to the masses, and this must be considered when forming an opinion.

The *Arrivall* goes on to tell us Edward IV led a more conservative army of 7,000 to 9,000 men, accompanied by artillery pieces and handgunners when it marched north from St John's Field at four o'clock on Easter Eve, which seems a more believable estimate given the partiality.

Henry VI was taken along with the Yorkist army in the vaward (according to what was recorded that evening and the following day). The Duke of Gloucester commanded this (mounted) division, with Edward, Clarence and Lord Hastings leading the main body from London at a slower pace. We are also told that Clarence's men had already taken the Yorkist livery and that many of Edward's followers had emerged from sanctuary to swell his army.[9] However, reports of the casualties at Barnet must be considered if we are ever to reach an acceptable approximation of the armies before the battle commenced, and this will be considered later in the chapter.

Meanwhile, north of Barnet, we are told that the Earl of Oxford 'pitched his field' in a plain a mile outside the town and sent out scourers to determine Edward's position. At about seven o'clock in the evening, there was a brief skirmish at Hornsey Park south of Barnet between Oxford and Gloucester's 'aforeriders', and the latter chased Oxford back through the town, where the Yorkists found Warwick's army encamped 'under a hedge side' beside the St Albans road, according to the *Arrivall*. The rest of Warwick's forces were embattled on 'a broad green', we are told, and when King Edward's main body marched through Barnet that night, they pitched a camp close to, and 'somewhat aside-hand' of Warwick's army in the dark.[10]

During the night, Warwick's guns (*serpentines* and handguns) opened fire blindly on the Yorkists. But they overshot Edward's position, which was much nearer than anticipated (and therefore lower) according to Gerhard von Wesel, 'in a hollow and marsh'.[11] With this danger in mind, Edward ordered his men and artillery to remain silent throughout the night and not to return fire, thus concealing his position. However, due to the previous misalignment in the dark, Oxford's men now overlapped Gloucester's vaward on the left, where Henry VI was positioned, resulting in a spell of Yorkist confusion when dawn broke on Easter Day.[12]

The battle itself began at between four or five o'clock in the morning. We are told that the sun rose later that day, but initially, a blanket of fog enveloped the battlefield so neither side could make out the other. However, despite this, field guns opened fire again on both sides, probably fearful of what was in front of them. Archers shot blindly into the mist and smoke, and Oxford's overextended battleline blundered into Gloucester's flank, causing 3,000 men (probably Gloucester's whole division) to flee due to surprise and encircling numbers. According to sources, we are told that the Duke of Gloucester was slightly wounded in the resulting rout, and Henry VI was briefly captured.[13] The Yorkists were chased through Barnet, although Oxford's men failed to follow up the pursuit. More than one source mentions the earl managed to rally 800 men, and some returned to the battlefield, where they pillaged the Yorkist camp, stealing 7,000 horses, indicating how many in Edward's army rode to the battlefield.[14]

Although Gloucester's wing suffered heavy casualties, a few survivors reached London, warning the city fathers of Edward's defeat at Barnet. However, no one on the battlefield saw the Yorkist disaster unfolding due to the weather conditions, and the success of Edward and Hastings against Warwick's left pushed the battle northwards. As might be expected, Edward's courage was noted by the biased *Arrivall*, although the *Short Arrivall* recorded it in a more factual, official way.[15] However, the struggle was still finely poised, we are told, until some of Oxford's men returned to the field hoping to regain their lines. Many of their soldiers, it is said, were mistaken for Yorkists in the fog, and it seems this was due to Oxford's star with streams livery badge being mistaken for the Yorkist 'sun in splendour', which spread cries of treachery after three hours of intense fighting. However, the pillaging of the Yorkist camp must also have had a detrimental effect on Warwick's army.

As for Warwick himself, he was powerless to act against both these reversals, and it was likely a combination of the two that robbed him of much-needed support. In the resulting confusion, Warwick's brother Montagu was killed by one of his own men after he was spotted trying to escape in a Yorkist livery coat. Meanwhile Edward, supported by Lord Hastings, capitalised on the Duke of Exeter's thinning ranks by pushing his men back into a shallow valley and downslope known later as Deadman's Bottom, where (it is said) many men were slaughtered.[16] Warwick and Exeter fled for their lives, and 'the Kingmaker' was cut down and killed while trying to escape through a thick wood 'by the field of Barnet'. The unfortunate Earl of Oxford was wounded in the confusion of the rout and escaped to fight another day. The Duke of Exeter was left for dead on the battlefield from seven in the morning until four o'clock that afternoon, and sources say there were up to 4,000 casualties on both sides (1,000 according to John Paston, who fought with the Lancastrians).[17] These were eventually buried in mass graves on the battlefield – the majority being interred beside a small chapel of ease already in existence.

As explained, the resulting casualty figure should roughly agree with a percentage of an army's total strength to be believable. Therefore, considering that one source has it that 'on Warwick's side there were a good three or four thousand [wounded] men more than on King Edward's side' we can conclude that both armies must have started with at least 12,000 men at the start of the campaign, probably more on Warwick's side considering his previous recruitment drive at Coventry – a figure that accords with similar musters during the civil wars, except those of the 1461 campaign.[18]

A miserable spectacle

Gerhard von Wesel noted in his newsletter that 10,000 broken arrow shafts were left scattered on the battlefield of Barnet (a small amount for such a large engagement), proving archery was not used to any great extent by either side, probably due to bad visibility. The fighting 'which was always in doubt' lasted three hours according to the *Short Arrivall* (six according to *Warkworth's Chronicle*), and news of the battle reached London at ten o'clock the same morning, along with Edward's gauntlet, sent to his wife Elizabeth to prove he was still alive. As for poor Henry VI, he was recaptured again, having been previously caught up in the Yorkist rout through Barnet. He may have been wandering the battlefield, but King Edward returned to London later that day with him as his prisoner and immediately shut him away in the Tower for safekeeping, never to emerge alive again.

Soon after arriving in London, the king's two shot-torn banners were offered at St Paul's as a token of the Yorkist victory. Masses were sung in praise of Edward's triumph, and the naked corpses of the Earl of Warwick and Lord Montagu were brought back to London in a cart, accompanying Edward's wounded soldiers, who von Wesel says were badly mauled:

And the same Easter Day, King Edward came and brought King Henry home with his people. Those who went out with good horses and sound bodies brought home sorry nags and bandaged faces without noses, etc. and wounded bodies. God have mercy on the miserable spectacle, but all men say that there was never in a hundred years a fiercer battle in England than this last Easter Day.[19]

A contemporary ballad of the period recorded similar grim tales of battle-weary troops returning home, proving that the battle of Barnet was a significant blow to Edward in terms of wounded soldiers and how many he could put in the field again:

To London came the king when the battle was done,
Leaving behind him many a dead man.
Some hurt, some slain, some crying 'Alas!'
Greater multitude than I can tell.
Some wallowing in blood, some pale, some wan.
Some seeking their friends in care and in woe.
In everything, Lord, thy will be done.[20]

The bodies of Warwick and Montagu were displayed in open coffins at St Paul's for three or four days to dispel any rumours they were still alive. But clearly, other problems occupied Edward IV in the coming days. Of course, Warwick was dead, but some of his followers had escaped the battlefield, and the king still had dissident Lancastrians to deal with in Wales. Edward may have beaten Warwick decisively, but Barnet was also a blow to the king despite his victory. His army was bloodied and dispersed, and its morale had likely been affected when the Yorkist battleline had disintegrated under Gloucester. Many men were dead or injured, and even though the king might have put his victory down to God's will, as was customary, it was essentially the freak weather conditions that had dictated the course of the battle.

As already stated, the main controversy surrounding Barnet is founded on where the fighting occurred. We know there were at least two routs that day, but little has been found in the way of artefacts north or south of the town due to the presence of modern housing and the lack of an extensive battlefield survey (incorporating Hadley Green). Usually, one would consider all the contemporary, topographical and archaeological evidence together when placing a battle in its historical landscape. The little chapel half a mile from Barnet, the plain a mile from the town, the broad green and the hedge-side position on the St Albans road are proof enough of location if artefacts can corroborate these areas of interest. Local history and early maps can help with this investigation, but we may never know precisely where Edward and Warwick clashed or what the battlefield looked like in 1471. What happened there can only be imagined from the chronicles, and due to a lack of visual evidence (archaeology) and grave pits (forensic anthropology, usually located where the heaviest fighting took place), a firm location of only Warwick's opening position can be approximated.

According to *The Paston Letters* and *The Great Chronicle of London*, this position was half a mile north of Barnet. This is where Sir John Paston places the action, according to the letter to his mother — somewhere between Hadley Green (the 'broad green' mentioned above) and where the battle monument now stands.[21] The monument (erected in 1740) is a mile north of Barnet at the junction of the Great North Road and the road to St Albans running through Kitts End (a village contemporary with the battle). Therefore, according to one contemporary London chronicle and John Paston's letter, this half a mile between the monument and Hadley Green marks the battlefield with some accuracy. This area is where Paston's list of dead were 'killed upon the field', and, even today, this terrain is indicated by gently rising ground with hollows and water features that are visible and marked on early maps. The parish boundary of Middlesex and Hertfordshire provides a good indication of where the 'hedge-side' crossed the St Albans road, and this is where the contemporary evidence says Warwick was found encamped on Easter Eve by Gloucester's aforeriders.[22]

According to a surviving manuscript, the small chapel where the dead were buried existed long before the battle was fought. Abbot John de La Moote of St Albans endowed it sometime between 1396 and 1401, along with John Beauchamp. The antiquarian John Stow says this chapel became a dwelling house in 1598, and the building has long been identified near Pimlico House, half a mile from Barnet.[23] An alternative site for the chapel may also be further north at a place known as The Hermitage near Wrotham Park (the position of Warwick's rout and Deadman's Bottom). However, *The Great Chronicle of London* places the little chapel 'in the said plain well upon half a mile from the town' and says that it was newly endowed by Edward IV 'to remember the souls of them that were slain at that field'.[24]

Chapels marking mass grave sites generally indicate where battlefields are situated due to the physical work needed to bury so many dead and dismembered bodies. But this is not always the case, especially near well-populated areas where the dead can easily be moved to nearby churches, chapels of ease and consecrated ground. Either way, the battle of Barnet was likely fought in about half a square mile (not including the rout), and this location is marked, with varying degrees of accuracy, on early maps across the road to St Albans. For certain, the fighting was not static or ordered in any way on 14 April, and the area known as Deadman's Bottom may be an actual killing field where many of Warwick's men were cut down in the rout, including the earl himself. Philippe de Commines recorded that Warwick had the habit of mounting his horse when he had ordered his men forward to fight. If the battle went badly, this allowed him to flee in good time. However, his brother Lord Montagu encouraged Warwick to dismount at Barnet to inspire his troops. Therefore, he could only escape on foot when the fighting turned into a rout, which may have some grain of truth about it.[25]

However, one thing is certain: Warwick's involvement in the civil wars was over. News of his death travelled quickly, even by medieval standards, but as luck would have it, the strategies that he and Margaret of Anjou had originally formulated in France still retained some credibility. On the same day the battle of Barnet was fought, Queen Margaret, the Prince of Wales and a small army of die-hard Lancastrians and French troops in seventeen ships landed at Weymouth on the south coast. News of Warwick's defeat no doubt caused some unease in Lancastrian ranks. But after consulting with the dukes of Somerset and Devon at Cerne Abbey, Margaret was persuaded to continue inland, no doubt egged on by the Prince of Wales, who was undeniably conscious of his usurped birthright.

It was also known, and was probably reiterated at the time, that the commander of Warwick's fleet in the Channel, Thomas Fauconberg, was also on hand to aid Lancaster's cause in the south, albeit on a more radical scale than might have been first imagined. Unlike Queen Margaret, Thomas was still ignorant on 14 April of his uncle's demise at Barnet, and undoubtedly, his plans ran analogous to Warwick's original orders to engage Burgundian shipping. In fact, unbeknown to everyone else, he was already contemplating with Sir George Brooke a landing in Kent to capitalise on Warwick's propaganda campaign to raise the south-east in rebellion.

Meanwhile, back in London, King Edward had important decisions to make. Yet again, he had to determine what to do with 'Henry of Windsor', who still represented a potential threat to the Yorkist dynasty and a magnet for Lancastrian sympathisers. Edward knew he would have no peace while Henry's shadow continued to eclipse his throne. However, his decision to have the king incarcerated in the Tower rather than executed was dictated by politics rather than a personal desire to show mercy. Crucially, news of Margaret's landing at Weymouth must have radically changed Edward's thinking to protect Henry VI as a hostage.[26] And so, acting against the next immediate threat to his throne, *The Rose of Rouen*, in characteristic style, put all his efforts into raising a new army to defeat Queen Margaret before she could raise further support in England and Wales.

On his way to his arranged muster point at Windsor Castle, Edward must have also viewed his present situation with ever-increasing apprehension. Regardless of his military prowess and aptitude for leadership, nothing was certain. The cost to his family in the Wars of the Roses had been grave, and as discussed, the conflict had dogged Edward's life from an early age. He had known little else but war, blood feuding and foreign exile. Peace in England was wishful thinking while Henry VI and his son lived. After securing the throne in 1461, he knew he had re-established the Yorkist dynasty by the sword, not by politics. In fact, Edward had never lost a battle. He had put down local rebellions and had recently survived being deposed by the most remarkable political brain and schemer of his age. However, in a country where some of the nobility had come to regard King Henry as a malleable ruler, Edward must have been a rare individual if he did not fear the widespread insecurity still surrounding his throne. So far, the recovery of his kingdom had gone well, but what new hazards lay on the horizon?

As for Queen Margaret, she moved her army inland to Exeter where the whole might of Devon and Cornwall swelled her ranks. From here, her army marched via Taunton and Wells to Bath. She reached Bristol the next day on 1 May, where the Lancastrians equipped themselves with money, men and ordnance, which were badly needed to face Edward on equal terms. From then on, the Lancastrians marched north. Their scourers were sent out to inspect the enemy position and fool the Yorkists into believing they were moving steadily east. Under this smokescreen, Queen Margaret intended to rendezvous with contingents commanded by Jasper Tudor, Earl of Pembroke (a half-brother to Henry VI), who had been recruiting in Wales since the beginning of the year. From here, Margaret hoped to march into Cheshire and then enter Lancastrian territory, where she would instigate widespread insurrection in favour of the king and Prince of Wales.[27]

However, her army's two forced marches would prove detrimental to Margaret's campaign. King Edward had also been advancing west from Windsor since 24 April, and on 1 May, his newly recruited army had reached Malmesbury, perilously close to cutting across the queen's line of march. The scourers and harbingers of both armies blundered into each other at Sodbury the next day and, informed of this, Edward embattled his army on the hill of the same name, hoping that the queen might attack him sometime in the afternoon. Equally surprised by Edward's proximity, Margaret and her forces made for Gloucester, the nearest crossing of the River Severn, and by late evening of 2 May, she had successfully put some 14 miles between her and the Yorkist army.[28]

No doubt angered by his lack of intelligence, Edward immediately dispatched riders to Gloucester and Sir Richard Beauchamp, the town governor, warning him to bar the queen's advance across the river. And it was Edward's foresight and quick thinking that saved him. When the Lancastrians encountered a hostile reception the following day, their only option was to force-march yet again, this time towards Tewkesbury and the next crossing point into Wales. However, almost immediately, the Lancastrian army met with unfavourable terrain, and after a few hours, their soldiers were suffering from thirst and the effects of heat exhaustion. Both armies had encountered severe logistical problems on the march and began advancing almost parallel. Edward's army was equally spent on the Cotswold escarpment, and when the Lancastrians arrived at Tewkesbury at about four o'clock, they could not organise a river crossing. The ferry and ford at Lower Lode were both within easy reach, but due to their march of 24 miles in about fifteen hours, their army was utterly worn out and strung out down the Gloucester road.[29]

Likewise, but undeniably more exhausted, were Edward's men, who had reached Cheltenham at about five o'clock and decided to press on despite their fatigue. After covering a gruelling march of some 35 miles in one day, the Yorkist army pitched their camp 'in the open fields' 3 miles from the great abbey at Tewkesbury. Late that evening, Edward's scourers claimed they had sighted the Lancastrian army nearby. Indeed, these Yorkist aforeriders threatened Margaret's army so much that the Duke of Somerset immediately took up a defensive position with 'foul lanes, deep dykes, and many hedges, with hills and valleys' to his front.[30] This trench-like terrain bordering the southern aspect of a field known today as The Gastons (or *Gastum* in 1471) became the battlefield of Tewkesbury, where Lancaster's fate would finally be decided:

[And] Upon the morrow following, Saturday, the 4th May, [Edward IV] apparelled himself, and set all his host in good array, ordained three wards, displayed his banners, did blow up trumpets, submitted his cause and quarrel to Almighty God, to our most blessed lady his mother, Virgin Mary, the glorious martyr, Saint George, and all the saints, and advanced, directly upon his enemies, approaching to their field, which was strongly in a marvellous ground placed, full difficult to be assailed.[31]

The author of the *Arrivall* briefly sets the scene in a notably biased and chivalric fashion. It seems he had an insider's view of the campaign and what the battlefield of Tewkesbury looked like in 1471. He later recorded in some detail that the Lancastrians had chosen an excellent defensive position. Therefore, it is hard to believe they would abandon it in favour of the offensive unless we consider other mitigating details and the capabilities of fifteenth-century missile weapons.

Notoriously prejudiced in favour of the Yorkist regime, the writer of the *Arrivall* identified himself as a servant of Edward IV who saw, for the most part, all the events he described. Those events he did not see personally were related to him by others 'that were present at every time'. However, we may confidently say most of these authorities were Yorkist sympathisers with similar prejudiced views, and for this reason, an earlier version of the *Arrivall*, called the *Short Arrivall*, is a more interesting document. It is written in a tone more 'official' and factual than the embroidered version, and while the more extended *Arrivall* describes certain topographic aspects of the battlefield in detail, the *Short Arrivall* was probably written first and likely by a herald in the pay of Edward IV. Therefore, as with other heraldic narratives of the Wars of the Roses, both accounts must be read together.[32]

Aside from the *Arrivall* (both versions) and a pro-Lancastrian account of the battle in *Warkworth's Chronicle*, there is also a later source that is undeniably important not only regarding battlefield casualties but also in determining the exact location of the Lancastrian army before the fighting took place. The noted antiquary John Leland, who visited Tewkesbury in about 1540, quoted in his *Itinerary* from an earlier contemporary book recording the abbey's history that Edward, Prince of Wales came to Tewkesbury and 'entered the field called *Gastum* (or Gaston)'. The earlier source names some of those killed at the battle of Tewkesbury and the burials in the abbey church. But more importantly, Leland also confirms that 'The Gastons' was unquestionably the place where, to within 40 acres, the Lancastrians made camp and formed their battles on the morning of 4 May. Therefore, in difference to the battle of Barnet, we have a clear and precise location of the battlefield to compare against the information in other chronicles and topographical accounts.[33]

The battle of Gastum

Today, a significant part of the original Gastons field is a modern housing estate bisected by a turnpike road. However, in 1471, the *Gastum* field was a large open space, probably enclosed grazing land, with distinct boundaries. Even with the intrusion of modern development and rerouted roads, the field's rough parameters can still be traced with some accuracy. Therefore, the area is wholly connected to where, 'in a close even at the town's end, the town and abbey at their backs', the queen's army pitched their camp. Here, the Lancastrians chose to stand and fight; 'a right evil place to approach, as could well have been devised', according to the *Arrivall*.

What constituted this 'evil place' was the terrain immediately south of The Gastons, which fell away, so we are told, into a shallow valley of 'foul lanes, hedges and deep dykes'. The author of the *Arrivall* describes a hill as significant in the ensuing battle and a 'fair place, or close' as the scene of heavy fighting. A park 'and therein much wood' is also mentioned, along with a meadow (called the Bloody Furlong in 1497). The author further states that 'certain paths or ways' had been reconnoitred previously by the Lancastrian command to surprise the Yorkists, indicating that the writer of the chronicle was impartial to some extent. Although expressing favour to King Edward after the event, only someone with military experience and immunity could have known ambushes were planned, suggesting that a herald or pursuivant must have compiled the *Arrivall* and *Short Arrivall*, or how would they have known Somerset's strategy?[34]

As for the composition of the Lancastrian army, Edmund Beaufort, Duke of Somerset was in command of the queen's forces. One of his brothers had been executed by the Yorkists after the battle of Hexham in 1464, and he was, no doubt, seeking vengeance against those who had destroyed his family in the past. Somerset was 24 in 1471, the last male heir of his unlucky dynasty, and was undoubtedly aware of what victory could mean to him if Henry VI was restored to the throne. As discussed, he had not been present at the battle of Barnet with Warwick, but there is every reason to believe that Somerset, even though untried in battle, was a determined soldier, eager to prove himself worthy of his title. In the coming fight, he was prepared to instigate a risky stratagem to turn Edward's flank, therefore, he was either an unlucky commander or a rash paladin who threw caution to the wind when it came to engaging the enemy.

Unlike Queen Margaret, who was safely ensconced behind the Lancastrian lines (probably initially in Tewkesbury Abbey), her only son, Edward, Prince of Wales, was the royal representative and mascot of King Henry's army. He may have assumed command of the Lancastrian mainward himself. However, apart from witnessing the (second) battle of St Albans in 1461 at the age of 7, and being party to the executions there, he was untried in warfare. His ability to command thousands of men may even have been questioned by veteran Lancastrian commanders like Lord Wenlock – a man who had already been bloodied six times in the Wars of the Roses (albeit on different sides). Indeed, Wenlock had an idea of King Edward's mindset, and it is more likely he took command of the centre, not the prince.

As a Lancastrian, John Wenlock of Someries had been wounded at St Albans in 1455 fighting for Henry VI. He was at least 60 in 1471, and earlier in his career, he had been present at Ludford with the Duke of York in 1459. In 1461, he fought at Mortimer's Cross and Towton for Edward IV, but after being given command of the Calais garrison, he switched sides yet again to join the queen's invasion force that landed at Weymouth on 14 April. Essentially, Wenlock used politics and guile to survive the daily hazards of the Wars of the Roses, as many nobles did in the late fifteenth century. However, with his banner on full view in The Gastons field, he had no doubt been targeted for extinction, this time by the Yorkists.

The other Lancastrian commander at Tewkesbury was John Courtenay, Earl of Devon, then aged 36. He had previously fought at Wakefield in 1460, the (second) battle of St Albans and Towton in 1461. He was undoubtedly well-tried in combat. However, when Edward IV executed his brother after Towton, Courtenay joined the Duke of Somerset and when he escaped with him from London before the battle of Barnet, he carried commissions (previously signed by Henry VI during his 'readeption') to raise men in the West Country. Devon commanded the left wing of the Lancastrian army, no doubt hoping to avenge his brother's death, and that time was fast approaching, according to the chroniclers who recorded the battle.[35]

As usual, there is no firm record of the size of Edward's army at Tewkesbury, although estimates of around 5,000 to 7,000 men on either side make this a noticeably smaller battle than Barnet. P.W. Hammond quotes an account after the battle that states that payments to 3,436 archers were made out, and if this figure is doubled to account for billmen and men-at-arms who fought in the Wars of the Roses, we are likely to be near the truth.[36] However, what is known about Edward's army is that it copied the formation used at Barnet, contradicting the 'accepted' military thinking that the medieval vaward (under Gloucester in both cases) always formed up on the right when in line abreast. If this were always true, there would have been little room for tactics or strategy on the medieval battlefield when divisions were oddly matched or affected by personal feuding. Also, medieval armies never moved or fought with Napoleonic precision. Some vawards, mainly comprised of archers, fronted the whole army, as at Towton in 1461, and this is where artillery was usually placed, for obvious reasons. Gloucester's involvement at both Barnet and Tewkesbury on the left (or fronting Edward's army) is proof of this arrangement, contrary to his being given special command of the vaward for no apparent reason.[37]

According to the *Arrivall*, Edward secured his left flank with a detachment of cavalry (spears), which he concealed on a wooded hill before the engagement. This tactic was to prove crucial later that morning as the battle wore on, but not necessarily in the way that Edward expected. The 'spears' may have been mounted men-at-arms, but it is more likely they were a mix of aforeriders and scouts who would not be missed by a dismounted army but who may have been placed there due to the fear that the Lancastrians had laid a 'bushment in that wood' threatening the rear of the Yorkist army.[38]

William Lord Hastings commanded the division to Edward's right, and it is recorded that he was the most veteran and trusted commander of the Yorkist army. Hastings was Edward's close friend. He was about 40 at the time of the Tewkesbury campaign and had been a staunch Yorkist supporter all his life. William had fought alongside Edward numerous times and was also a key figure in his government. He had been knighted by Edward at Towton in 1461 but had also served at Mortimer's Cross before this. He was with Edward when he was forced to flee to Burgundy and when he returned to face Warwick in battle. If we believe the chronicled evidence, he had fought well at Barnet while on the other flank Gloucester's men had been the unfortunate victims of circumstance, and Hastings could muster large amounts of retained troops and well-willers in the Midlands, according to some of his indentures that still exist.[39]

As for the battle of Tewkesbury, it began in a traditional manner when the Yorkist army advanced and used their field artillery and archers to harass the Lancastrian ranks. The Yorkists formed up on open ground before the small valley and hazards described by the *Arrivall*, but it soon became apparent that both armies could not sustain this pounding for long and one side would eventually break ranks and advance due to lack of morale. Indeed, at Tewkesbury, this advance dictated the course of the battle.

The Lancastrian guns and archers had replied well, but the Yorkist vaward under Gloucester was more successful, or they may have had more ordnance than the Lancastrians.[40] According to the *Arrivall*, the Yorkists 'gave them right-a-sharp shower' in The Gastons field, which the Duke of Somerset's men failed to withstand. A continuous hail of arrows was difficult to bear at the best of times. However, a sustained barrage of cannonballs *and* mounting casualties from arrows was a morale breaker on the medieval battlefield, and this caused Somerset to lead an advance with some of his men, unseen by the Duke of Gloucester on his exposed flank:

> [Somerset's] fellowship were sore annoyed in the place where they were, as well with gunshot, as with shot of arrows, which they would not nor durst abide, [therefore], of great heart and courage, knightly and manly [Somerset] advanced himself, with his fellowship, somewhat aside-hand the king's vaward [led by Gloucester], and by certain paths and ways therefore before purveyed, and to the king's party unknown, he departed out of the [Gastons] field, passed a lane, and came into a fair place, or close, even afore the king where he was embattled, and from the hill that was in one of the closes he set right fiercely upon the end of the king's battle.[41]

At this point, Edward IV, fearing that his army might be split in two, attacked Somerset, supporting his brother Gloucester. After heavy fighting, the *Arrivall* says the brothers won the dyke and hedge, entered the close and pushed Somerset's men back 'up towards the hill' and their original position in The Gastons. It seems the Lancastrian attack had been misdirected, and now fighting against two of Edward's battles, Somerset must have been calling for support from Lord Wenlock and the Prince of Wales to his left. However, no help came. Somerset's commanders were undoubtedly occupied, as it is unlikely that Lord Hastings would have stood idle while the battle raged to his left. If Somerset was waiting for Lord Wenlock to advance, he was sadly mistaken. All the Lancastrians had been attacked across the hedges and dykes and Somerset had little time to punish the veteran turncoat. Although the Tudor chronicler Edward Hall reveals that Somerset called Wenlock a traitor and then used his battle-axe to 'strike the brains out of his head', which smacks of drama rather than reality.[42]

Meanwhile, the 200 spears that Edward had placed on the wooded hill to his left (Tewkesbury Park) had joined the fighting. According to the

Arrivall, they were placed 'a quarter of a mile from the field', and their orders had been to prevent an ambush by Somerset or to employ themselves otherwise if the need arose.[43] Even today, the battlefield is easily viewed from this same vantage point, and with Edward and Gloucester under attack from Somerset, the Yorkist cavalry saw an opportunity to strike 'aside-hand, unadvised'. Polydore Vergil writing in 1506 had information from various contemporary sources that Somerset was now hard-pressed on all sides:

> And after [a] long and sharp fight, Edmund the duke, perceiving his small number to be overlapped [by] the multitude of his enemies, drew forth his men back to their standards, that, being close together, they might more easily resist. The same also somewhat refreshed the courage of the soldiers, so that they began more fiercely to lay on. But when the queen [failed to send] fresh soldiers to supply the places of the wearied and wounded, she was overmatched of the multitude, and in the end vanquished, her company being killed and taken almost everyone.[44]

Aside from the fact that Queen Margaret was almost certainly not on the battlefield that day, Vergil's description of this pivotal episode is interesting from a military viewpoint. That standards and banners were used to encourage and rally troops is based on both fact and logic. But when the rest of the Lancastrian line commanded by the Prince of Wales and the Earl of Devon finally broke, support on Somerset's left flank was no longer possible. Most soldiers 'took them to flight into the park and into the meadow that was near', the latter locally called 'The Bloody Meadow' today, which was a dead end (on account of the Mill Avon) and likely this area became the scene of a brutal massacre.

Many refugees were trapped in the various angles created by the tributaries of the River Avon, like the Mill Avon, the River Swilgate and the ponds that served the abbey mills. In the general rout, the Prince of Wales, Wenlock and Devon were cut down as they ran for their lives. Other soldiers headed for the town and Tewkesbury Abbey, along with those nobles, hoping to seek sanctuary from the pursuing Yorkists. There were heavy casualties during the fighting and in the rout, but when the Duke of Somerset and others were found in the abbey, according to the pro-Lancastrian *Warkworth's Chronicle*, they were pardoned by Edward in the presence of an unidentified priest.[45] However, on Monday, 6 May, Somerset and seven others were dragged from Tewkesbury Abbey and arraigned before the court of the Duke of Gloucester as Constable of England and the Duke of Norfolk as Marshal. Not surprisingly, they were found guilty of treason and promptly executed in Tewkesbury marketplace 'notwithstanding the king's pardon', showing how ruthless Edward could be to those who opposed his rule.[46] *Warkworth's Chronicle* reported, contrary to other sources, that Edward IV and his brothers Clarence and Gloucester murdered the Prince of Wales after he had been captured. However, the political bias here is too obvious, and other chronicles, including the *Arrivall*, agree that the prince was not singled out in a Shakespearian melodramatic way but that he was butchered in the general rout like many other desperate Lancastrian soldiers, in a state of panic.

On the Yorkist side, sometime after the battle, Richard of Gloucester arranged for prayers to be said for some of his household men 'slain in his service at the battles of Barnet, Tewkesbury [and] other fields' which goes some way to explain how badly his personal bodyguard were mauled on these occasions.[47] Years later, Edward gave grants for good service, along with annuities, to his lesser soldiers, and many of these are recorded in the *Calendar of Patent Rolls*, most gifts coming from the forfeiture of Lancastrian lands, fees and rents:

> 8 November 1474. Grant for life to Thomas Ash, for his good service to the king in his journeys at Barnet and Tewkesbury against the rebels, of the manor of Burnham Sutton and three tenements in South Lynne, county Norfolk, late of Giles Saintlowe, late of Watford, county Hertford, esquire, and in the king's hands by virtue of an act of forfeiture in Parliament at Westminster, 4 November, [first year of Edward IV] against the said Giles by the name of Giles Saintlowe late of London, esquire, to hold by the accustomed services with knights' fees, advowsons, fairs, markets, rents and services.[48]

> 3 October 1477. Grant for life to the king's servant Thomas Garth, for his good service at Barnet and Tewksbury against the rebels, of all messuages and lands in Toneworth and Apsley, county Warwick, late of Thomas Collings, which Rose Mountford lately had of the grant

of Henry IV, to the value of £101 yearly, to hold by the services of as many knights fees and as many other rents and services as they were held by before 4 March, [first year of Edward IV].[49]

The king dubbed many of his men knights on the field of battle, and *The Paston Letters* recorded those Lancastrians who were beheaded and those who had been killed fighting for Henry VI.[50] Where the unnamed dead were buried after Tewkesbury is unknown. The Gastons and Bloody Meadow would have seen the heaviest fighting and slaughter, and these areas may once have been the site of mass graves (although no records exist today). However, a transcription by John Stow included in J. Bennett's *History of Tewkesbury* has it that many bodies were buried 'in the [abbey] church yard' while others of note were transported elsewhere. As for the Lancastrian commanders, they were interred within the abbey precincts, the Prince of Wales being buried in the choir and the Duke of Somerset, his brother John, the Earl of Devon and many other knights being interred 'in diverse places' some before the altar of St James.[51] Therefore, it seems after the battle, someone made conscious efforts to do the right thing, although who sanctioned the burials is not recorded.

However, because of the death of the Prince of Wales, the flight of Queen Margaret and the execution of her commanders, the Lancastrian cause was now in ruins. It had been a decisive battle, and King Edward immediately dispatched a letter to London informing the mayor of his victory. Margaret and those ladies who escaped with her north knew the prince and their husbands were dead and that further resistance was useless. In fact, their flight appears to have been half-hearted. Edward's men quickly captured Margaret, Anne Neville (Princess of Wales), the Countess of Devon and other ladies 'at a poor religious house' and delivered them directly to Worcester. Here, the king no doubt celebrated his second glowing victory against the odds that year. Even the troublesome queen was a broken woman claiming that 'she should be at [Edward's] commandment', realising the Lancastrian cause would never recover from such a bloody cull of nobles and royal notaries.[52]

But before he marched for London, not only did Edward hear about a dangerous rebellion brewing in North Yorkshire, but he also received disturbing news from the city. All was not well with the Lord Mayor and the Yorkist lords the king had left behind. Kent and the south-east had also risen in rebellion following Warwick's previous propaganda campaign, and thousands had answered the Bastard of Fauconberg's call to march on the capital and free Henry VI from the Tower. Edward may have thought Barnet and Tewkesbury were decisive victories, but his worries were far from over and London's troubles were just beginning.

5

All the King's Men

Strong be the walls that about thee stands,
Wise be the people that within them dwells,
Fresh be the river with its lusty strands,
Blithe be the churches, well plaintive be thy bells.[1]

☦

According to a Milanese ambassador, London was the 'wealthiest city in Christendom' in the late fifteenth century, and this was largely because of trade. In 1461, the Duke of Milan was further informed that Edward IV and Warwick would likely triumph over the Lancastrians in the north because they were backed by Londoners, whose support meant everything.[2] A similar observation was also echoed when Edward was crowned King of England, and the feeling that London was the key to the kingdom proved correct when the Bastard of Fauconberg attacked the city in 1471.

Foreign visitors to London would sail up the Thames or ride through Kent from the south coast. Coming from Calais, travellers would first have to cross the Channel (in a few hours with a fair wind), and if their ship managed to avoid pirates like Fauconberg, they would arrive at one of the Cinque Ports. From Dover or Sandwich, travellers would ride to Canterbury to secure lodgings, and pilgrims might visit the tomb of St Thomas Becket in the cathedral. Their second night would likely be spent at Rochester, and by the third day, they would cross Blackheath, where the remains of Jack Cade's camp could still be seen in 1471. From Shooters Hill, a traveller would see London for the first time, hugging the north bank of the River Thames, and when they rode closer, Southwark would become visible, as would the only bridge over the Thames (London Bridge) and the houses and shops built upon it.

If you approached London by land from the east of England in 1471, you would enter the city via Aldgate, or Old Gate, to give it its original name.[3] But before reaching this, you would ride through the suburbs of Portsoken Ward, one of the twenty-six wards of medieval London established in the eleventh century. The village-like feel of Portsoken might take you by surprise, but this was not the *real* London bustling with activity. This outer ward bore little resemblance to the ghetto-like conditions that lurked beyond the city's 18ft-high walls. Closer to Aldgate, you would no doubt marvel at how cosmopolitan and busy London was compared to other towns and cities in England. Indeed, the city was overpopulated considering its size, and it was filled with all forms of human, animal and insect life – an abundance of rats being a common sight both day and night.

The London Wall enclosed the city streets and houses from the Tower in the east to Blackfriars in the west. The defences stretched for 2 miles, and in most places, the original Roman walls were visible and noticeably different from those added in later centuries. Over the years the city defences were in a constant state of repair, and only in the reign of Edward IV (1478) did the mayor, Sir Ralph Jocelyne, cause the defences to be wholly refurbished between Aldgate and Aldersgate. Therefore, in the early 1470s, the eastern wall may have been structurally unsound in parts and in need of rebuilding. Before the siege of London, several payments were entered into the *Issues Rolls* to pay 'workmen for erecting walls and other fortifications at the Tower of London aforesaid' with a list of names of the carpenters, masons, soldiers, engineers and others to do the work, further indicating the defences were not entirely satisfactory in some places and had to be augmented.[4]

However, despite the condition of the walls, directly abutting them in the east was a wide defensive moat called the Houndsditch, leading north from the Tower to Bishopsgate and beyond, where local refuse (and dead dogs) were dumped before the Tudor period. It was filled in and abandoned, according to the keen-eyed Londoner John Stow, in 1598, and the ditch was remembered as a repulsive eyesore.[5] It was not cleaned out regularly, and despite several efforts to stop effluent from entering the Tower moat lower down, you would likely smell the stagnant ditch as you approached the city in 1471. Most Londoners would be used to this stench, especially those born there. But on a more positive note, the Houndsditch provided another line of defence against any would-be attackers or rebellious mob that might try to storm the city walls from the east.

Undoubtedly, one of the most prominent landmarks you would see rising from the city in 1471 would be the Tower of London (or, more precisely, the White Tower). But also, at least a hundred churches (including St Paul's) were prominent, each of which regularly rang their bells to summon the faithful and sound the curfew when everyone in the city was expected to clear the streets or be arrested for night walking. Outside the city walls, the curfew was generally not enforced. Churches there were like those in local parishes, and as you approached Aldgate, you might notice the imposing St Botolph's Church directly across the road from the gatehouse. To your left, behind the houses and cottages flanking the open road into London, was the Franciscan Abbey of St Clare, founded in 1293 by Edmund, Earl of Lancaster, and to the right, as the London Wall turned westward towards Bishopsgate yet another St Botolph's Church might be seen beside the north road which passed over the start of Moorditch.

To the south, the Tower of London was the most formidable defence of the city. With its plentiful stocks of artillery, men and military hardware, it was the focus of power both royally and militarily. In the late fifteenth century, the Tower was one of the most iconic structures of its time and the construction dated back to the eleventh century and William the Conqueror. In 1471, it was a royal residence and prison consisting of several internal buildings, strategically placed towers and impressive curtain walls. The inner ward of the defences housed the royal apartments, the Great Hall and the Chapel of St John, where Henry VI and his family lived, worked and prayed when they were not on royal progress or conducting business elsewhere in England. Henry III and his son, Edward I, had constructed the outer ward of the Tower in the thirteenth century, along with a wide moat that protected the fortress from landward attack. The River Thames fed the moat, making it extremely difficult for attackers to access the Tower which was essentially a fortified island. The narrow Tower Wharf (used for loading and unloading armaments) was equipped with guns, the walls were several metres thick in places, and barbicans and drawbridges were built for added protection. In addition, the walls were also surmounted with artillery strategically placed to sweep the River Thames of enemy shipping should they venture upriver towards London Bridge.[6]

In addition to London's seven main city gates, north of the Tower, across the moat, was the Postern Gate, marking the southern end of the walls. The London antiquary John Stow remarked that this had once 'been a fair and strong arched gate, partly built of hard stone of Kent and partly of stone brought from Caen in Normandy' after the conquest. But Stow goes on to say that the Postern had become ruinous by 1440 and was replaced by a weak wooden structure providing a convenient haunt for 'persons of lewd life' to inhabit.[7] The gate was also used by merchants and tradespeople who brought their goods into the city from the east and by those visiting the Tower on business. But considering its ruinous state, as described by Stow, the gatehouse still had a drawbridge despite its insignificance.

On your way through Portsoken Ward, between the gaps in tenements and cottages, you might just be able to make out the River Thames indicated by the masts of merchant ships docked beside the cranes and warehouses on St Katherine's Wharf. Here, beer houses and inns owned by Flemings were plentiful beside the river, catering for mariners and merchants who stopped for refreshment and lodgings between journeys. The hospital and church of St Katherine's was situated behind the wharf and was founded by Queen Matilda in 1148. It was formed as a religious community for poor and infirm people, and in 1442, privileges were granted by Henry VI, which made it exempt from London's ecclesiastical and civil jurisdiction. But above all, as you explored the city's eastern suburbs, you would, no doubt, be transfixed by the noise rising from behind the city walls. The hubbub might disorientate you when entering Aldgate under its double portcullis. However, as you ventured further into the city, your ignorance might be shocked by the contrasting sights and sounds of thousands of people going about their daily business and subsistence amid the dissolution of countless streets and alleys.[8]

Aldgate Ward, and the street of the same name, was a bustling hive of activity. Like most of London, it was a mix of residential, commercial, ecclesiastical and industrial properties. The narrow, winding streets were lined with shops and stalls selling various goods, including food, clothing and household items. The area was also home to several markets, while behind the tenements on Leadenhall Street, the Holy Trinity Priory, built in 1108, was one of the earliest Augustinian houses to be established in England. The overcrowding in the streets would be accentuated by the continual traffic of horses and wagons arriving and leaving the city via Aldgate, above which the poet Chaucer once lived. The population of London in 1471 was approximately 80,000, although this figure was never static due to thousands of visitors from home and abroad. In fact, the population was constantly in flux and on the increase. Other English cities might have approximately 10,000 people living and working in them (York was about this size). But London, as England's capital, like Paris and Venice, was the centre of business and a magnet for trade, law and government. Therefore, regarding its relatively small size, as a traveller, you might rightly conclude that London was a heaving metropolis, a melting pot of activity and an extreme fire risk, with most of its buildings made essentially of wood and plaster.[9]

Looking south along the Thames, you would see the only bridge that spanned the river into the city. London Bridge in the late fifteenth century was also a bustling thoroughfare that served the south and the suburbs of Southwark. The bridge was another essential artery for trade and travel into the city, the next bridge upriver being at Kingston, 10 miles away. As a seasoned traveller, you might note that the old bridge was grander and longer than the Rialto in Venice, the Ponte Vecchio in Florence and the Pont Neuf in Paris, and you would be correct. The bridge was constructed of stone and had nineteen arches supported by piers and protected by starlings (artificial islands). It was approximately 928ft long and 20ft wide, and the pitted roadway was lined with shops, houses and other buildings, including a chapel dedicated to St Thomas Becket. The bridge was heavily fortified, with several lines of defence designed to protect the city. In the centre, the crossing was equipped with a large drawbridge, built in 1426, that could be raised and lowered to allow (and prevent) masted ships from passing through, and there were several gatehouses along its length, each with towers and embrasures.

The large gate at the bridge's southern end was an impressive fortress that had stood the test of time. The Great Stone Gate (obviously built of stone) had two towers equipped with arrow slits, murder holes and other defensive features. Halfway across the river was the Drawbridge Tower, and at the northern end of the bridge, two chain barriers could be raised to block the passage of enemy ships. Therefore, overall, London Bridge was a formidable salient that played a crucial role in protecting the city from the south.[10] The Italian 'spy' Domenico Mancini, who visited London in 1483, wrote an overview of the bridge and Southwark in his report to Angelo Cato the same year, which serves as a good basic eyewitness account of the medieval city:

> On the right bank [of the Thames], which is on the south side, is a suburb notable for its streets and buildings which, had it been enclosed by walls, could have been called a second city. This is connected to the city of London by a very famous bridge built partly of wood and partly of stone, on which there are houses crowded together with gates having portcullises: the dwellings belong to various kinds of craftsmen and have workplaces below. Just as the suburb [Southwark] lies on smooth and flat land and is laid out almost in a circle when seen from behind, so the city opposite extends lengthways along the riverside and lies partly on the level and partly on sloping ground.[11]

Although Mancini reported that green fields surrounded London in 1483, several areas just outside the walls were well populated. Bishopsgate Ward to the north-east, and the gate of the same name, was approximately 600 yards from Aldgate. Next came Moorgate, then Cripplegate, Aldersgate and so on, each ward and gate having officials responsible to the Lord Mayor, who in May 1471 was John Stockton, a London mercer. Stockton and a select group of Yorkist lords were responsible for the whole city while Edward IV was busy dealing with the Lancastrians in the west, and under the mayor was an intricate hierarchy of officials that saw to the everyday running of London, and if the need arose, its defence.

As discussed, the city had a rapidly growing population and a thriving economy in the late fifteenth century. London's administration was highly organised, with officials responsible for different aspects of governance. At the top of this hierarchy was the Lord Mayor, elected by the Common Council of the City of London. The mayor's duties included presiding over the Court of Aldermen, who were responsible for managing the city's finances, and the Court of the Common Council, which dealt with the laws and regulations of the city. There were twenty-six aldermen in total, each representing one of the city's wards, and they maintained the peace, collected taxes and enforced the law. In addition to the mayor and aldermen, there were also wardens of the city responsible for specific areas. These included the Wardens of the Bridge House, who maintained the city's bridges (including London Bridge) and the Wardens of the City Walls and Gates, who managed the fortifications.

For the surety of the city

London's administration was driven by an elected body of men, with the mayor and the Court of Aldermen having the final say on all matters related to governance. This centralisation was essential for maintaining order and stability in the overflowing city, as it allowed for quick and decisive action in response to any challenges or threats within the walls. Overall, the administration of London in the late fifteenth century had clear lines of responsibility and accountability. Effective city governance was crucial to ensure London's continued growth and prosperity, even during crisis and civil war. Indeed, being an official responsible for this was a great honour and a means of advancement.[12]

In addition to the mayor, aldermen and wardens, several other officers operated in London in the medieval period. There were two sheriffs of London, elected annually by the Court of Aldermen. Their duties included maintaining law and order, overseeing the city's prisons and carrying out legal processes and writs. The Recorder was an official appointed by the Crown. His duties included advising the mayor and aldermen on legal matters, serving as a judge in the Mayor's Court and presiding over the Court of Hustings. The Common Serjeant was another legal official who served as a prosecutor in the Mayor's Court. His duties included advising the mayor and aldermen on the law, prosecuting criminal cases and representing the city in legal disputes. The Chamberlain managed the city's finances, including collecting taxes, paying expenses and maintaining records. The coroner investigated suspicious deaths and determined their cause. He also presided over inquests, which included formal investigations into the circumstances of a death. The aldermen appointed beadles who maintained public order in their respective wards. They also performed ceremonial duties, such as leading processions and making proclamations, whereas the Clerk of the Market was accountable for regulating the buying and selling of goods. His responsibilities included enforcing laws and regulations, setting prices and ensuring the quality (as far as possible) of goods sold.[13]

All these officials played essential roles in the administration of London in the Wars of the Roses, and their duties were crucial to the smooth functioning of the city's government in times of peace and crisis. An investigation into various London documents, livery company records and contemporary chronicles reveals that the city fathers were predominantly made up of officials who were merchants and traders.[14] These men were elected to fulfil the above tasks as leading members of society, and in May 1471, most had not yet been knighted by the king:

Sir John Stockton – mercer – Lord Mayor
Sir Ralph Verney – mercer – Alderman
Sir Richard Leigh – grocer – Alderman
Sir Ralph Jocelyne – draper – Alderman
Sir John Young – grocer – Alderman
Sir William Taylor – grocer – Alderman
Sir George Ireland – grocer – Alderman
Sir John Stoker – draper – Alderman
Sir Matthew Phillip – goldsmith – Alderman
Sir William Hampton – fishmonger – Alderman
Sir Thomas Stalbrook – Alderman
Sir John Crosby – grocer – Sheriff
Sir Bartholomew James – draper – Sheriff
Sir Thomas Urswick – Recorder of London
Sir John Ward – grocer – Sheriff
Sir Robert Basset – salter –Alderman [15]

Many of the above officials were knighted personally by Edward IV 'in the field' soon after Fauconberg's rebellion, accolades that underline how dangerous the situation in London became when the king was absent from the city. However, contrary to the outwardly robust nature of the above structure, the Common Council (The Commonality) was far from stable, and there were many rivalries between Yorkist and Lancastrian officials to complicate the tense political situation that existed in the Wars of the Roses.

For example, John Stockton (1445–95) was a Yorkist sympathiser. He was the son of Richard Stockton of Bratoft, Lincolnshire, and was appointed Lord Mayor of London from 1470 to 1471 after taking over from Richard Leigh. Before this, Stockton had taken to his bed before the battle of Barnet and was deputised by Sir Thomas Cook (a Lancastrian), who tried to maintain order in the city.[16] On 7 April 1471, Cook fled to France with his son after Edward IV returned to the city, and an alderman, Ralph Verney, had to take over his duties. John Stockton was still 'indisposed' when the Recorder of the City, Thomas Urswick (a Yorkist), tricked the guards at Bishopsgate into letting Edward into London. And it was only the eventual cooperation of Stockton and Urswick, both Yorkists, in May 1471 that encouraged the citizens to act against Fauconberg, unlike before this when London was polarised on more than one occasion.[17] Once he recovered from his 'illness', Stockton was instrumental in defending the city gates and walls, and after the siege, he was knighted by Edward IV for his 'good service' against the insurgents.[18] Stockton died in 1495 and was buried at St Pancras Church, Bow Lane, but despite his prominent position in 1471, other officials were also instrumental in organising and manning the city defences.

Richard Leigh, Ralph Verney, John Young, Matthew Phillip and William Taylor had all been mayors previously. John Crosby, whose altar-tomb still exists in St Helen's Church on Bishopsgate Street, was a wealthy merchant who owned Crosby Place in the same area. In 1483, Crosby was still one of the two sheriffs of London and a great benefactor of the grocer's livery company. William Hampton, son of John Hampton of Minchen Hampton, was famous for setting up stocks in every ward of London for the punishment of vagabonds. He became a sheriff in 1462 and was one of the city's four members of parliament. He was instrumental in offering large loans to Edward IV that tripled when he became Lord Mayor in 1472. Hampton died ten years later after being married twice but fathering no children. He left his estate to his niece, Alice Hampton, who saw to his burial in the now-lost church of St Christopher le Stocks on Threadneedle Street.[19]

Many of these officials fought tooth and nail to defend London against the Bastard of Fauconberg's rebels, and some men were not acclaimed immediately for their bravery. Robert Basset, for example, was an alderman of Aldgate Ward for most of his life, and he, among others, fought in the front line when the rebels attacked the city. As in so many other battles of the Wars of the Roses, most fifteenth-century chroniclers gave men with no grand title short shrift, and Basset, who had previously been a member of parliament and Sheriff of London, was a man who, like Thomas Urswick, played an essential part in the siege. Their courage ranks alongside the martial abilities of the gentry during the fighting, and when Basset was knighted for his services and became Lord Mayor in 1475, he could probably look back and consider himself one of those who saved London for Edward IV.[20]

In contrast, Thomas Urswick (1415–79) was a lawyer who became Recorder of London and later Chief Baron of the Exchequer. His memorial brass still survives, depicting him with his family in the Church of Saints Peter and Paul in Dagenham. His family was from Badsworth in Yorkshire, and he studied law before being elected a Sergeant of the City of London in 1453. He was one of the four members of parliament for London in 1461 who took dangerous risks to help admit Edward into the city on at least two occasions. After the (second) battle of St Albans in 1461, Urswick was tasked with delivering a message to Margaret of Anjou (and Henry VI) that supplies to her victorious army would be delayed, thereby refusing her entry to London but later allowing Edward IV to march in and usurp the throne. In May 1471, Urswick vigorously resisted Fauconberg's attacks on the city and was knighted for his services. The following year, he was appointed to the Exchequer and later received an annuity from the king, which allowed him to keep a large household at Marks Manor near Romford, where he lived with his wife, four sons and eight daughters until he died in 1479.[21]

However, apart from these city officials, the defenders of London were also bolstered and encouraged by the lords who had been left in charge by Edward IV. When he marched against Margaret of Anjou on 24 April, the king had given command of London to his brother-in-law, Anthony Woodville, Earl Rivers. But the Earl of Essex, Lord Duras,

Lord Dudley and other prominent Yorkists had also been tasked with keeping the city and the royal family safe during the crisis. And as the *Arrivall* points out, the presence of all these Yorkist lords was crucial when it came to uniting the citizens against Fauconberg's rebels:

> To the citizens and defence of the city came the Earl of Essex and many knights, squires, gentlemen, and yeomen, well arrayed, which had right great diligence in ordering the citizens, and first to prepare and ordain for the defence and surety of the said city and people thereof where it was necessary and prepared how and where they might best issue out upon them and put them from their purpose. By which ordering of gentlemen and lord's servants, with the citizens, in every part, were greatly encouraged to set sharply upon them with one whole intent, where else it had been likely they should not have willed to have done so much thereto as was done.[22]

There were several veteran soldiers among the Yorkist lords, although which noble had overall command of the city defences is open to debate considering the confused and random nature of Fauconberg's attacks. Sources say Earl Rivers had been given authority, but considering the diverse topography of London, it may have been the mayor who organised who would defend the wards. However, the lords were clearly instrumental in 'preparing and ordaining' the defences. They encouraged and made final decisions based on the availability of men and materials in London, and their experience far outweighed that of the city fathers when it came to actual combat.

John Sutton, Lord Dudley (1401–87) was the oldest veteran among the Yorkists. He was the man who brought the body of Henry V home from France in 1422 and was the chief mourner and standard bearer at his funeral. Dudley was a keen supporter of Lancaster earlier in his career and became Lord Lieutenant of Ireland in 1428. He fought in many early battles of the Wars of the Roses, including Blore Heath, where he was wounded, but he later changed his allegiance before the battle of Towton in 1461. After Towton, he was rewarded for his services by Edward IV, but by this time, Dudley was over 60 years of age and probably no longer suited to the physical strain of medieval warfare. However, he was appointed Constable of the Tower of London from

May 1470 to 1471 and was still in this position during Fauconberg's rebellion, to his credit. He had complete jurisdiction over prisoners in the Tower, including Henry VI, whom he had previously served as a diplomat and councillor. In 1477, Dudley was one of the English ambassadors who negotiated a continuance of the peace treaty with France, and he remained in royal service until he died in 1487 at the grand old age of 86.[23]

Galliard de Durfort IV, Lord Duras (d.1481) was a Gascon noble of the Durfort family. When his father died in 1444, he was a minor, and in 1446, he obtained a safe conduct to travel between England and Aquitaine at his pleasure. He spent most of his early life between England and Bordeaux until the English were routed from Gascony in 1453 at the battle of Castillon. Later, in 1461, he was awarded the Order of the Garter by Edward IV, became Governor of Calais and remained faithful to the king during the Wars of the Roses. In 1470, he became Chamberlain to Charles the Bold, Duke of Burgundy, and he probably returned to England with Edward in 1471, after which he was awarded a £100 annuity for his services despite being born in France.[24]

One of the most prominent veteran nobles of the fifteenth century was the Earl of Essex. Henry Bourchier (1404–83) was related by marriage to Edward IV and, on his mother's side, was a great-grandson of Edward III. He served under the Duke of York in France and was summoned to parliament as Viscount Bourchier in 1446. Essex was married to Isabel of York, the sister of Richard, Duke of York, and therefore, he was Edward IV's uncle. He was created Earl of Essex in 1461 by the king and was Lord High Treasurer for most of his life when the Yorkists were in power. Bourchier was greatly admired for his loyalty towards Edward, most of his eleven children married well and some were killed in the Wars of the Roses. One of his sons had been slain at the battle of Wakefield, and more recently, Humphrey Bourchier, Lord Cromwell, had perished at Barnet. Therefore, despite his advancing years, it is highly likely that Essex was in no mood to stand by while others fought against Fauconberg; he had a personal stake in the outcome.[25]

The heavy burden of London's fate in May 1471 fell on the broad shoulders of Anthony Woodville, 2nd Earl Rivers, who was Queen Elizabeth's brother. As discussed, the Woodville family had risen from Northamptonshire minor gentry to great heights in only a few short years thanks to Edward IV and his infatuation with the Woodville's most voluptuous asset, Elizabeth. However, the marriage set Anthony's family on a rocky road of misfortune and social ridicule that some men, like the Earl of Warwick, delighted in and used for their own ends. As for Rivers, he was a nobleman of contrasting interests. On the one hand, he was a renowned tournament jouster and, on the other, he was a man of great creativity with an apparent love of literature.

In May 1471, Anthony was 31, and like his father Richard, the first earl, he was initially a Lancastrian who had fought against Edward IV ten years earlier.[26] However, when Edward met and married Elizabeth Woodville in 1464, everything changed for the family, and the queen's brother was no exception. Anthony was made a Knight of the Garter and later Lieutenant of Calais and Captain of the King's Navy. In fact, Rivers (then Lord Scales *jure uxoris*) was promoted in every way possible, to the extent that others became intensely jealous of his position. At the tourney, Rivers excelled as a jouster, and when he fought a famous two-day duel at Smithfield against Antoine the Bastard of Burgundy, he became a national celebrity. The contest was ended before it began, and it was declared a draw by Edward IV due to his favourable political connections with Burgundy in 1467. However, two years later, when the Woodvilles became targets of Warwick's campaign against Edward, Rivers' celebrity image was overshadowed by family tragedy. After the battle of Edgecote, Anthony's father and brother were beheaded after a mock trial by some of Warwick's supporters, and this bonded Rivers to Edward IV and the royal family from then on. In 1470, he fled with the king to Burgundy, and when he returned to fight with him at the battle of Barnet, he was wounded. He may still have been suffering from the same wound in May 1471 (which is why he did not march with Edward to Tewkesbury), but overall, Rivers did not shirk his responsibilities. It seems he had principles, and in complete contrast to his chivalric experience on and off the battlefield, he was not a typical nobleman by any stretch of the imagination.

Mancini noted, presumably from his contacts in London, that Rivers was different from other members of his family, especially his brothers who, despite their sister the queen, aided Edward VI in his bouts of excessive living and debauchery:

> While there were many panders who aided and abetted [Edward's] lustfulness, the foremost and of special note among these were three of the aforementioned relatives of the queen: her two sons and one of her brothers. On the other hand, Lord Rivers was always held to be an agreeable man, serious and upright, who had been tested by all of life, whatever his condition, he had obliged many and disobliged none. For that reason, he had in his trust the care and guidance of the king's eldest son [Edward V].[27]

Woodville was also devoutly religious, like many nobles of his age. He yearned to go on a pilgrimage to the Holy Land, and later in his career, he became a keen editor and translator of religious and philosophical works. His translation of the *Dicts and Sayings of the Philosophers* was one of the first books printed in England by William Caxton, and Rivers also wrote many ballads against the seven deadly sins, suggesting he was both honourable and ethical.[28] What brought about this fascination with literature and philosophy is hard to pinpoint apart from the fact that most books of the time were extensions of a noble's education and that Rivers, no doubt, wanted to be part of this circle. He presented a copy of his and Caxton's printed book to Edward IV in 1480, and he may have desired, above all things, to be a learned man rather than a rough and ready knight. However, in his final days, Rivers realised this chivalric ideal fell short of perfection. He still wanted to go on a crusade and planned to depart for Portugal, although this conviction to serve God also came to nothing, we are told.

Like other nobles during the Wars of the Roses, Rivers had enemies within Edward's close circle, namely William Lord Hastings, who quarrelled with him over the Captaincy of Calais and questioned his chivalric honour. Without doubt, Rivers' previous affinity with Lancaster and his puritan ways dogged him for most of his life. In his translation of the *Dicts and Sayings*, even Caxton mocked him when he omitted some parts of the original Arabic text concerning the habits of women, which likely went against his chivalric beliefs – unlike Thomas Malory's *Morte D'Arthur*, which was also sponsored by Earl Rivers and printed by Caxton soon after the author died in 1471.

Overall, it seems Rivers was a man of many talents. Indeed, despite his creative love of all things chivalrous, he may have seen himself as a polymath. Some of Anthony's contemporaries openly accused him of cheating at tournaments and avoiding battle. Stories were invented that his duel with the Bastard of Burgundy had been rigged and that ambitious men like Warwick wanted him killed for his deceit (although Edward's marriage undoubtedly coloured the latter). Rivers, it seems, had been born into a family destined to be hated and ridiculed for their easy rise after 1464. However, the queen's family persisted, and the courage of Earl Rivers was never questioned when Fauconberg stormed London in 1471. Therefore, we may conclude that Anthony was not cowardly or deceitful in any way. But he may have been a cautious man. Rivers took chivalry very seriously and may have even tried to mirror Malory's perfect knight of Arthurian legend. He was undoubtedly a man of many contradictions, who was ridiculed and hated by his peers, although the evidence suggests he never avoided a fight or the possibility of death in battle.[29]

To illustrate this, on 3 May 1471, when news arrived in London that some parts of Kent were being stirred up to revolt, Rivers was among the first of those commissioned to go against the rebels before they had a chance to march on the city:

> Commission to the king's kinsman Anthony, Earl Rivers, Edward [of] Westminster, Neville of Bergavenny, knight, Galliard de Duras, knight, John Scott, knight, William Haute, knight, John Culpepper, knight, and the Sheriff of Kent, to array the king's lieges of that county and to arrest and imprison certain persons stirring up insurrection.[30]

According to the *Patent Rolls*, Edward IV had issued the above commission the night before he marched against the Lancastrian army at Tewkesbury. So, clearly, Earl Rivers must have been aware of the situation before 3 May. It is recorded that he and the knights mentioned in the above commission aimed to march with thirty armed horsemen and forty foot soldiers into Kent. According to sources, gunpowder, warbows, arrows and bowstrings were also requested to help put down the rising (although they were never used in Kent):

> To Anthony Earl Rivers, sent by advice of the King's Council to the county of Kent to suppress diverse rebels there assembled against the

king. In money paid to him for wages for 30 armed horsemen at 12d. per day; 15l. and 20 marks for the wages of 40 foot soldiers at 8d. per day; 22l. 6s. for a barrel of gunpowder, and one firkin of serpentine powder and 50 bows at 2s. each; 100 sheaves of arrows at 2s. [a] sheaf, and three gross of bowstrings at 18s. per gross.[31]

Other prominent Yorkists were ordered to deal with rebels in Essex at the same time, including the Earl of Essex, Lord Dinham and one of Edward IV's squires named Robert Radcliffe, who features later in our story.[32] However, by early May, news must have already arrived in London that Fauconberg had reached Canterbury, and that Kent, Essex and other southern counties were up in arms and ready to march on the city. Thousands had turned out, and Rivers may have thought it best to defend London's walls rather than sally out into a raging storm, such was the seriousness of the rebellion.

But what political message could have been so appealing to the Kentish rebels gathering at Canterbury and elsewhere in 1471? Indeed, it is not enough to *believe* in something; surely, you must be ready to *stand* for something to risk breaking the law and committing treason. Fauconberg had received a mandate from the Earl of Warwick via his adherents based in Calais to spark revolution. But the earl's death at Barnet two weeks earlier must have changed everything. Indeed, what did Thomas now hope to achieve with his master dead and only 300 professional soldiers from Calais at his disposal?

6

Evil Willers

O glorious God, what vexation was then,
To the queen and the lords and the other ladies eke,
To the mayor, and the commons, and the aldermen,
They needed no fear nor sorrow to seek.[1]

⁂

The Bastard of Fauconberg's rebellion of 1471 was similar in many ways to other Kentish risings during the fourteenth and fifteenth centuries. And although it was not the last rebellion in south-east England, its social and military dimensions were serious enough to cause widespread panic in London. The commons of Kent, Essex and other southern counties would not have gathered in strength without good cause, and aside from their willingness to question the power and authority of the king, in this case Edward IV, for his various failings and broken promises, there were other incentives to revolt in 1471. The Earl of Warwick exploited these reasons (as he had done before) through cleverly worded propaganda that appealed to those in society who had suffered from injustice. However, in 1470–71, Warwick's focus was also dynastic and aimed at 'his great rebel and enemy Edward, late Earl of March' who had failed to deliver 'perpetual peace, prosperity and common weal' to his subjects. Warwick's message, therefore, recognised the legitimacy of Henry VI, and his campaign of words greatly helped Fauconberg muster sizeable forces in both Kent and Essex exceeding those of Jack Cade twenty years earlier.[2]

Indeed, there was an engrained culture of rebellion in Kent, and like Cornwall, Lincolnshire and Yorkshire, it was one of the most distinctive and 'tribal' regions in England. Kent was 'a county whose inhabitants held themselves to be descended from the Jutes', and in 1471 they still believed (like Cornwall) that 'their county had never been conquered'.[3] Medieval Kent was also a largely neglected county, and therefore, in terms of governance, it was sometimes left to its own devices. Foreign invasion was a real and everyday threat, and Kentish towns and ports suffered badly from intermittent French raiding on numerous occasions. Kent was on the front line when commissioners recruited for the Hundred Years War, and its hotch-potch of 'hundreds' suffered greatly from the resulting casualties. To add insult to injury, after the English were ousted from France in the 1450s, Kentish soldiers returned home to find themselves neglected, out of work and leaderless. Jack Cade's manifesto may not have touched upon these problems directly, but twenty years later, in 1471, these same grievances were no doubt felt by many discontented veterans who saw war as their only trade. After 1461, misgovernance in Kent passed from Henry VI to Edward IV, and claims of extortion, corruption, vote rigging, injustice and ignorance of the ever-present French threat of invasion were problems deeply felt in Kentish culture. In 1471, the population would have been acutely aware of Cade's demands for change in 1450, not to mention those of the Peasants' Revolt in 1381. And although Fauconberg produced no well-worded manifesto that has survived, there had been little change in Kent's unruly stance since the beginning of the Wars of the Roses. It was still a volatile part of the kingdom, therefore, conditioned to rebellion.

Politically speaking, no one had supplied an answer to Kentish insurgency for almost a century, and the Peasants' Revolt and Cade's rebellion were both products of localised frustration and a lack of overlordship. Even after Fauconberg rebelled against the Yorkist regime, revolts continued to surface in the south-east. Buckingham's rebellion of 1483 and other risings in the sixteenth and seventeenth centuries prove that Kent was a continual hotbed of discontent. For instance, Fauconberg's rebellion even had topographic similarities with previous risings – even to the extent that the rebels attacked virtually the same areas of London. Jack Cade's forces ran riot through Southwark and battled over London Bridge. Aldgate and Bishopsgate were assaulted, and pillaging occurred in the suburbs, which is one reason why the Lord Mayor of London, John Stockton, and his council feared a repeat of the same anarchy in 1471. It is estimated that around 5,000 rebels took part in Cade's uprising, and his force was comprised of the same kind of commoners, tradespeople, merchants and landowners who would rebel again in May 1471. One knight, two MPs and eighteen esquires provided the 'leadership' of Cade's host, but no great noble associated himself with the rebellion. However, this is not surprising if Kentish history is studied overall.[4] The absence of nobility ruling over the county is telling, and hence, bad governance was always blamed on London and especially the king's ministers. This transference of responsibility is reflected in the actions of obscure and charismatic figures like Wat Tyler, Jack Cade and the Bastard of Fauconberg, who provided the revolutionary spark needed to fuel rebellion when overall command in the county was lacking.

In the late fifteenth century, various prominent families owned land in Kent, but the county lacked traditional over-mighty subjects. A monarch was, therefore, only able to recruit minor gentry into his service. However, when royal authority was weak and bad governance predominated, the Kentish gentry tended to ally themselves to those men who represented national politics, and this became a recognisable feature of rebellions. Bastard feudalism was a widespread evil, and private forces led by nobles ran riot and regularly abused law and order, while in Kent landowners measured their service against personal survival and landed prosperity. Initially, the county had been supervised by Henry VI's uncle, Humphrey, Duke of Gloucester, but in the 1430s, Kent began to rethink its allegiance, due to the prominence of the Beaufort family in national politics. Beaufort influence continued while Henry VI was king, and because of family connections with the Kentish gentry, some men were drawn into their circle against the Yorkists. The Wars of the Roses also had a direct effect on Kent when it became a centre for military recruitment and a focus for Warwick's propaganda. Consequently, as Beaufort and Lancastrian hegemony declined and Yorkist control increased in 1461, Kent adapted, switched allegiance and supplied men to those nobles who favoured their county.[5]

For instance, men like Sir John Fogge of Ashford, Sir John Scott and Robert Horne, who were well-known captains of Kent, were initially Lancastrians who later supported Edward IV when he usurped the throne.

After the battle of Towton in 1461, Fogge became Treasurer of the King's Household, and Scott was made its Controller. Many local gentry in the county were recruited and granted annuities for life from lands confiscated from the Lancastrians, and because of this, a divided Kent emerged. In short, the county was soon fragmented into pockets of resistance that Warwick sought to combine when he became Constable of Dover Castle and Warden of the Cinque Ports during King Edward's reign. Warwick, to his credit, became well-liked in Kent, and in the guise of first being a Yorkist sympathiser and then a Lancastrian 'Kingmaker', he managed to remain in close contact with a large following of Kentish knights and landowners throughout the 1460s. However, when Thomas Fauconberg was made Warwick's 'Captain of Kent' in May 1471, some local gentry refused to heed his call to arms. In panic, the Mayor of Canterbury, Nicholas Faunt, sent out riders to ascertain how the gentry might respond to Warwick's muster, and, according to the evidence, some men chose to remain neutral despite their previous affiliation with the earl.[6]

Nicholas Faunt, despite his staunch involvement in Fauconberg's rebellion, remains an obscure leader who had a direct influence on the 1471 rebellion. He was elected Mayor of Canterbury in 1470 and was executed on 29 May the following year for his part in the uprising. Faunt welcomed Thomas Fauconberg and his men (made up of mariners and the Calais troops of Sir George Brooke) into the cathedral city on or about 6/7 May. It is also likely that Warwick's propaganda had drawn many thousands of rebels to Canterbury primarily so they could hear, first hand, Fauconberg's intentions. Supplied with all kinds of weapons and armour, most rebels readily agreed with the denouncement of Edward IV's recent usurpation and Henry VI's legitimacy as the rightful King of England. Faunt was no doubt supported by his city council in this, even though by this time, it must have been common knowledge in Canterbury that Warwick had been killed at Barnet on 14 April.[7] Warwick's naked corpse had been displayed for all to see in London, and Canterbury was only 55 miles from the city. Therefore, other reasons why Fauconberg's rebellion was popular must have fuelled the insurgency.

Some of these reasons can be found in the kind of men that Fauconberg led against London, as documentary evidence still exists of the Kentish rebels and those men in Essex and Surrey who also decided to take advantage of Fauconberg's insurrection. For example, *The Great*

Chronicle of London records that the Essex rebels rose in response to pressing economic grievances:

> In the month of May, Sir Geoffrey Gate and a rover named the Bastard of Fauconberg, having a multitude of rovers in his rule, landed in Kent and there raised much idle people, and afterwards marched towards London, and caused divers of his ships with ordinance to be brought into Thames. Whereof the same being blown into Essex, faint husbands cast from them their sharp scythes and armed themselves with their wives smocks, cheese cloths and old shirts, and weaponed themselves with heavy and great clubs and long pitchforks and ashen staves. And so, in all haste [they] sped towards London making their avaunt as they went that they would be revenged upon the mayor for setting of so easy pennyworths of their butter, cheese, eggs, pigs and all other vittals, and so joined them unto the Kentish men.[8]

The tongue-in-cheek remarks of the chronicler when he refers to the Essex men as 'faint husbands' is clearly a slur by those biased Londoners who saw ordinary people as rural 'yokels' and no more than a rabble armed with agricultural tools wearing borrowed rags. In contrast, their grievances were obviously serious concerns, and popular feelings relating to high taxation and injustice fuelled their decision to rebel. This large host was heading due west, we are told, while Fauconberg was mustering more men in Canterbury. Although there is no surviving roll-call recording the kind of men who marched from Essex to London in 1471, there *are* documents that record those who marched from Kent led by the mayor Nicholas Faunt.[9]

The Canterbury Archives Roll is a fascinating document in that it records the names of those commoners, tradesmen and officials who personally assisted the Bastard of Fauconberg, those who marched freely with him and those who were considered long-term offenders. It also names individuals who were compelled to take part in the uprising, and those who supplied material (military equipment and the like) under compulsion.[10] According to the roll, there was a proclivity of press-ganging in the county, and some men were reluctant to join the revolution, probably due to their past allegiances and political history. The roll lists about 200 men who aided Fauconberg's rebellion in some way, those who had resisted Edward IV and supported Warwick during the 'readeption' are also mentioned, as are those men who saw the king's councillors in London as a threat, and those Yorkists who had proved detrimental to their lives and livelihoods. Many men on the roll were merchants and artisans. Most were working men employed in various trades. Two parish clerks are mentioned, as are innkeepers, grocers, merchants, labourers, drapers, yeomen and a town sergeant who should have mustered for Edward IV but marched with Fauconberg instead – a crime that he paid dearly for when the rebellion ended. Various captains are also mentioned in the document, indicating that the men of Kent were ordered into contingents as they had been during the Hundred Years War and the wider Wars of the Roses. If Essex was a rabble, which cannot be proved, Kent was a force to be reckoned with, as were Surrey, Sussex and those men mustered from the Cinque Ports who applied for pardons later in 1471.[11] Most of the men seeking acquittal in the *Patent Rolls* were 'yeomen' or 'gentlemen'. The squires mentioned were likely trained in arms, similar to the 300 men from the Calais garrison who were seasoned professionals, and others were likely archers or men equipped with pole weapons such as the bill or glaive.

Based in London during Henry VI's 'readeption', it is likely that Edmund Beaufort, Duke of Somerset also sought out similar men in the county and some of his former adherents throughout southern England in May 1471. Recruitment for Margaret of Anjou's invasion would have been uppermost in his mind. Therefore, his 'distant' influence in Kent is a further indication why the popularity of Fauconberg's muster was not clear-cut. Earlier in Henry VI's reign, the county may have enjoyed a more level-headed Beaufort–Lancastrian bias, but this had been affected by at least three changes of government. Memories of the Peasants' Revolt and Jack Cade's rebellion also prove there were more complex reasons why some parts of Kent remained openly independent and hostile in 1471. And to make this point clearer, it is worth exploring the important but little-known Kent rebellion of September–October 1470 for comparisons, as it was a precursor to Fauconberg's rising six months later.

The basic chronology of this insurgency has already been traced. However, it is worth detailed examination, parallel to the siege of London, so that rebels who accompanied the Bastard of Fauconberg to the city can be identified. *The Great Chronicle of London* gives the main details of this important uprising and the involvement of Sir Geoffrey Gate as one of Warwick's henchmen:

> In this while, the commons of Kent along with shipmen came into the suburbs of London to St Katherine's, Southwark, Radcliffe and other such places as Dutchmen dwelled and held beer houses, and they robbed and spoiled [them] without mercy. And then Sir Geoffrey Gate, above named, got into his company such 'sanctuary men' for his master [Warwick] and others [who] had kept sanctuary in Westminster and other places, and so being associated with them, they went unto the King's Bench and other prisons where they knew [some] of their fellows were held, and [they had] them delivered, and then some of them being so enlarged, went after to beer houses and robbed and spoiled them anew, and some set fire and burnt them sparing no Flemings that came into their [sight].[12]

The leadership and aims of those who led this assault on Southwark and its neighbourhood provide a noticeable similarity to Fauconberg's rebellion the following year and also explain why Warwick and Gate thought the same strategy might be worth repeating in 1471. Indeed, some rebels involved in the rebellion of 1470 were present at the siege of London six months later, and judging by their associations with Warwick, they were ready to march again with Fauconberg if not for justice, then for plunder. For instance, Henry Aucher of Newenden was linked to the Earl of Warwick indirectly. Aucher was the brother-in-law of John Guildford of Rolvenden, who was Warwick's lieutenant of Dover Castle. His appointment was significant in Kentish politics, and the Nevilles had firmly established connections in the county that proved helpful in 1471. The Earl of Warwick's kinsman, Edward Neville, Lord Bergavenny was another notable administrator in Kent, and his son Richard Neville had served with the Calais garrison in 1466.[13] Both men could call upon others to follow them, including Aucher, but if Warwick's power waned, so would his influence over the local gentry, which is one reason why so many in the county remained fiercely independent after Warwick was killed at Barnet.

However, by the time Warwick and Clarence had made their peace with Margaret of Anjou and landed in the West Country, London had been alerted to various disturbances in Kent. The gates and portcullises of the city were ordered to be strengthened, artillery was deployed at key locations and militias were raised to deal with an attack. On Monday 17 September, all was set in readiness. When the men of Kent rose soon after Warwick and Clarence's landing, *The Great Chronicle of London* records that towards the end of the month, the Kentish rebels made their move, attacking the homes and businesses of Dutch residents in the city. The chronicle goes on to say that Sir Geoffrey Gate, then in prison, broke out and gathered numerous sympathisers from various sanctuaries. Known criminals and felons were freed and they descended on other London prisons, including the notorious Marshalsea in Southwark, releasing their inmates. The Flemings again became targets of Gate and his men, and an indictment surviving among the records of the Court of the King's Bench provides a positive link between the two events and how indiscriminate the attacks became.[14]

In November 1471, a session of the Court of the Verge at Southwark heard that on 11 October 1470, Henry Aucher, esquire, Robert Aucher, gentleman, and William Squery, gentleman, all from Newenden in Kent, Richard Neville of London, gentleman, John Langrigge of Southwark, mercer, and John Browne, yeoman, plundered the Hospital of St Thomas the Martyr in Southwark. It was a lucrative raid for Aucher, by all accounts, as he and his men were able to carry off a great deal of plunder. The undefended hospital, mainly caring for the poor and sick, was easy pickings for the rebels and no doubt the raid was politically motivated. The above indictment proves that Kentish associates of Warwick were closely linked to the Southwark riots and also that Sir Geoffrey Gate was the instigator.[15] However, what the chronicle fails to tell us is if this rebellion was any different from similar racially motivated riots in the past or if it was something else.

Evidently, it appears that Henry Aucher was personally ordered to coordinate the attacks on Southwark in concert with Warwick and Clarence's landing in England. An entry in the *Canterbury Chamberlain's Accounts* shows a Neville captain called Richard Lovelace and his company was paid £1 not to enter the city.[16] Another entry records that a further captain called 'Quentin' (later associated with the Fauconberg rebellion) was paid 13*s* 4*d* to refrain from damage there, and at least one other Neville retainer of note accompanied the Kentish force.[17] Richard

Neville (who died before 1476) was named in the Aucher indictment, and his involvement as a professional soldier in the Calais garrison was no doubt crucial to coordinating the attacks on Southwark and other parts of the city for Warwick. Neville's link to his father, Lord Bergavenny, and various other local Kentish captains was well established by 1470, and Warwick's move to capture Henry VI was a popular call to arms for many discontented with Edward IV's rule. Some local gentry with proven links to the Nevilles were fully on board with this Yorkist animosity. And as for leadership, we can safely conclude that Sir Geoffrey Gate and Henry Aucher were in Warwick's pay and fully aware that the earl intended to recapture Henry VI and rule England through him. Their actions were initially aimed at Dutch homes and businesses, and as a precursor to Warwick and Clarence's invasion, the riots were intended to cause maximum disruption in the city.

Xenophobia against Dutch migrants had been prevalent for years in London and Thomas Fauconberg was party to the overall plan of action judging by his close association with Warwick and Clarence. He knew each Neville connection intimately and was known to those veterans like Gate who prepared the way for Warwick during the rebellions of 1469.[18] There is no reason to doubt that the same successes of 1470 were anticipated in 1471. Therefore, men like Geoffrey Gate, George Brooke, Richard Neville and some of the other Kentish captains named in sources readily accepted the risks of treasonable action to advance themselves along with their masters. It was, after all, Kentish culture to rebel against authority, and along with a paid contingent of mercenaries from Calais to support their cause, such men became the prime movers that helped Fauconberg conduct the siege of London to free Henry VI and place him back on the throne.

My faithful, trusty and well-beloved friends

As mentioned above, some individuals opposed insurgency due to divided loyalties, including nobles like Lord Bergavenny, who died in October 1476. He had supported Edward IV for most of his life, and even though his son Richard Neville favoured Warwick in 1470 (according to the Aucher indictment), we may wonder if this affected the relationship with his son a year later when Fauconberg landed in Kent. Edward Neville, styled Lord Bergavenny, was a veteran of the Hundred Years War and had been knighted in about 1426.[19] In 1471, he may have kept a low profile as he was approaching the age of 70, but on the other hand, he may have also been ill or infirm. Either way, father went against son, and the split in the Neville family became permanent. Richard died not long after Fauconberg's rebellion ended, but for others, there were financial rather than family reasons to take sides in the rebellion.

For example, Sir Richard Lovelace decided to throw his lot in with Fauconberg to acquire land and property. Richard's brother John supported Edward IV, and like so many other families in the Wars of the Roses, the brothers became rivals, but not altogether due to factionalism. Richard Lovelace was associated with the Earl of Warwick. His father (also called Richard) had taken part in Jack Cade's revolt of 1450 and was, therefore, a rebel at heart. He was pardoned for his actions by Henry VI, but it is clear Richard's son also had a rebellious streak. He was born in 1440 and had fought alongside the Duke of York at the watershed battle of Wakefield in 1460. After the battle, it is alleged, he pleaded for his life when taken prisoner by the Lancastrians at Pontefract Castle. Promising never again to take up arms against the king, he was released, but as Warwick's 'Captain of the Men of Kent' who later met with Queen Margaret's army at the (second) battle of St Albans, he soon faced a dilemma. When Lovelace's men became hard-pressed by the Lancastrians on Bernards Heath and the Kentish line broke due to various defensive contraptions and malfunctioning handguns, Richard became a scapegoat.[20] When the Yorkists fled, it is said the Earl of Warwick directly blamed Lovelace for his defeat. However, there is little evidence to back up the earl's claim if we consider Richard's close association with Clarence and Warwick in 1469–70 and his exile with the said lords in Calais.[21]

However, apart from this involvement in the civil wars, the Lovelace family were major landowners in Kent, and part of their story is typical of other significant property disputes in the late fifteenth century. Richard Lovelace's father held the three Kentish manors of Bayford, Goodnestone and Hever, all of which had other estates associated with them. In his will, proved in 1466, Richard senior bequeathed his first two manors to his eldest son John and Hever to his daughter Katherine.

All three estates should have been distributed equally under the rules of inheritance, but this arrangement left no provision for Richard, and he had to fight for his share of the property when his father died. Naturally furious about the contents of his father's will, Richard illegally took possession of Bayford and Goodnestone and was charged with trespass by his brother, instigating a dangerous family feud.

Feeling that he could not stand alone against John, Richard approached the Duke of Clarence for support. Along with his vast inheritance, Clarence held land at nearby Milton, and Richard managed to enfeoff Bayford and Goodnestone to Clarence and seven others of the duke's affinity in return for service. However, Richard was immediately disappointed with the taciturn Clarence, who in 1468 and 1469 had other things on his mind – namely the Crown. Rebellion was in the air, and in the end, Richard fled the country, taking refuge in Calais. Here, he lived off the proceeds of the enfeoffment being administered in his absence. But despite promises of security, the door was left wide open for his brother to reoccupy the disputed manors.

For a few months, Richard's gamble looked likely to pay off, but when Edward IV returned to power, he was left at the mercy of his brother John once more, who petitioned for his arrest. Richard's response was to fortify Bayford and prepare for a siege, although soon after this, he disappears from the record, and his whereabouts are unknown. The Sheriff of Kent was ordered to bring him to justice but in September of the same year, Richard resurfaces by siding with Clarence and Warwick and taking part in the Kentish rebellion under Sir Geoffrey Gate and Henry Aucher. His hope was obviously to recover his manors from his brother, but he may have been aiming higher to serve Warwick as one of his retainers. However, the outcome of Edward IV's return to England changed everything for the Lovelace family.[22]

On 8 May 1471, Thomas Fauconberg and his army of 'evil willers' left Canterbury and were camped at Sittingbourne, midway between Bayford and Goodnestone, and, by chance, Richard Lovelace was again looking for a way out of his property dispute with his brother. If he could help free Henry VI from the Tower and gain favour with the king, then his father's will might be reversed. Lovelace, it seems, was willing to take a gamble on this despite the risks. Indeed, he may have been desperate. He was likely known by men of the Calais garrison who had accompanied Fauconberg to England due to his service there as a mounted man at arms in 1466. Judging by the Aucher indictment, he could also raise men in Kent. His motivations may have been governed by self-interest, and his past may have been chequered, but like many Wars of the Roses gentry, he was a resourceful man who felt he had been wronged. Therefore, he quickly allied himself with Fauconberg and joined the rebels, no doubt not the only man wishing to capitalise on Henry VI's freedom to solve local feuding.

As to the size of the Kentish forces assembled at Canterbury and Sittingbourne, there is no accurate record. Part of Fauconberg's fleet was somewhere moored in the Thames, loaded with troops and artillery. Thomas had, by all accounts, contacted the Essex rebels to coordinate a concerted attack on the capital. Some of his ships had been 'blown into Essex' according to *The Great Chronicle of London*. However, Fauconberg's entire force is difficult to quantify due to its rural composition of peasants and 'idle people' who were looking to plunder the city. Clearly, some leaders, even prominent captains like a man called 'Spysyng' (a captain of Essex) and a butcher simply named 'Quyntyn' (who may have captained men from Rochester), must remain anonymous to a certain extent. We know Quentin – to give him a recognisable name – had taken part in the 1470 rebellion organised by Gate and Aucher, but other than this, nothing more is known of him. Both Spicing (to give him a recognisable name as well) and Quentin may have been prominent rebels in their own right and 'recognised' for their riotous proclivity. However, we can safely assume that anyone who had a genuine grievance in the south-east of England rallied to Fauconberg's banner in 1471, as they had done in previous rebellions aimed at London. Clearly the rebels recognised something in Thomas's message that stirred their hearts or their pockets, and the total force at Fauconberg's disposal must have been at least 10,000 men, although the 'official' record states it exceeded 20,000.[23]

From Sittingbourne, Fauconberg intended to march to Blackheath. But before breaking camp on Wednesday 8 May, he wrote a letter to the Lord Mayor of London, John Stockton, to test the mood of the city.[24] It is also recorded that Fauconberg wrote a similar letter to the Commonality of London that was part of the Court of the Common Council, intending to appeal to those in the city with pro-Lancastrian feelings:

To the worshipful, my faithful trusty and well-beloved friends the Commonality of the City of London. Your faithful true lover, Thomas Fauconberg, captain and leader of our lord King Henry's people in Kent at this time, sends hearty recommendation letting you know that I am informed how the party of the usurper of our said liege lord's crown hath made you to understand that I with the king's people should purpose to rob, rifle, and despoil the City of London if I came therein. Wherefore they [have] exhorted you to make war on us and keep us out of the city. Certainly, friends, God knoweth whom I call to record, it was never mine intent nor purpose, and therefore, I beseech you to give no credence to their false suggestion and surmise. But trusty friends see it is so that I have taken upon me with the help of Almighty God and the king's true commons to revenge his quarrel against the said usurper and his adherents and to seek him in what parts he be willing [in] the realm of England to a right painful labour, and to short the way of the king's people heartily set and disposed against the said usurper's desire, I pray you courteously to pass through the city in our way and we shall neither take vittals nor anything without payment, be you thereof certain, and that I promise you on my honour for if there is any within the king's host in my company that break the king's cry, they shall have execution according to his offences. No more unto you at this time save we have desired of the mayor and aldermen to have an answer hereof by Friday nine of the clock at the Blackheath, and Almighty God have you and the good city in his blessed care, written at Sittingbourne [on] the eighth day of May.

Your own friend and well-willer &c.
Thomas Fauconberg[25]

Apart from the 'apparent' cordiality of Fauconberg's letter, Thomas's words are quite revealing, and seeing as this is the only correspondence that survives from him, it is worth scrutinising his words in detail to ascertain his character and the intentions of the rebels.

In his message, Fauconberg asserts he is the 'captain and leader of our lord King Henry's people in Kent'. He sends a 'hearty recommendation' to the Commonality and calls Edward IV a usurper and his 'party' liars who have misled the city fathers that he intended to pillage and rob the city. He blames the same Yorkist lords, and not the mayor, for their deceit and tries to justify his mission to go against Edward and his adherents wherever they might be in England. He wants to shorten this journey by passing through the city, but here it is quite apparent that Fauconberg is lying. Instead, he *actually* wants to free Henry VI from the Tower of London, as made clear by the chronicles. If his intention was to confront Edward, he could have ferried his men across the Thames into Essex by water and marched west, although he conceals his real intention with a persistent request to enter the city 'to short the way' to Edward. For what reason, you may ask? Clearly, Thomas intends to free King Henry, gather Lancastrian support in London and then go against Edward with an army that outnumbers him. Possession of London is everything, as it had always been in the past, and with Henry VI free, no doubt many others in England would rally to the royal banner.

Next, Fauconberg promises 'on his honour' to execute wrongdoers who might pillage goods without paying for them in the city. Throughout his letter, he keeps referring to the Commonality as 'my faithful trusty and well-beloved friends', and he says that he has requested the mayor to answer his letter by Friday 10 May at 'nine of the clock', when he will be at Blackheath. The tone of his friendliness, as opposed to what could have been a more formal request, continues to the end of his letter. But the underlying covert issue here is that Fauconberg wishes to free Henry and increase his army with those Londoners supportive of the Lancastrian cause (exemplified by him calling Edward a usurper and repeating the claim that he is not leading an unruly army of rebels but the 'king's host').

This host was exceedingly large, according to the pro-Lancastrian *Warkworth's Chronicle*, although the author may have exaggerated the size of Fauconberg's forces for political reasons. The chronicle states that Fauconberg 'had purposed to have destroyed King Edward, or to have driven him out of the land. And if the Bastard had held forth his way, King Edward could not have resisted him, for [he] had more than 20,000 good men well harnessed, and wherever he went the people flocked to him'.[26] However, the author of *The Great Chronicle of London* recorded a more factual account, although quite naturally he upbraids the quality of the rebel force and their pretended mission:

In this passed time, the Bastard of Fauconberg, increasing his lewd company, sent unto the mayor that he might be licenced to pass through the city intending not to tarry therein but to pass through without disturbance of the mayor or any of the citizens.[27]

Likewise, the pro-Yorkist *Arrivall* counters this claim, although the strength of Fauconberg's combined force is maintained by the author, who as discussed, was an official observer with King Edward's army at Tewkesbury and doubtless learned of the siege of London after the event. However, there are some interesting facts in his chronicle that support the claim that the rebel army may have been unusually large, well paid and equipped, aside from those pressed men who joined Fauconberg 'for fear of death':

[Fauconberg] had brought many men with him from [Calais] into Kent, where he began to gather his people in great number, intending, by likelihood, to do some great mischievous deed. After the king was at Coventry, he had daily messages from the lords in London, how the Bastard had assembled great people, and, both by land many thousands, and by water with all his ships full of people, he came before London, thinking to rob, and spoil, and do all manner of mischief. And thereto many of the country of Kent were assenting, and came with their good wills, as people ready to be appliable to such seditious commotions. Other of Kentish people that would right [preferred] to have sat still at home and not to have run into the danger of such rebellion, by force and violence of such riotous people as were of the said Bastard's company, for fear of death, and other great menaces and threatenings, were compelled to go with the Bastard, in their persons if they had array and might not wage to such as would go, they were compelled by like force, to lend them their array, and harness. And such as were unharnessed, aged, and unable and of honour, were compelled to send men waged or to give money wherewith to wage men to go to the said Bastard's company. So that, right in a short time, the said Bastard and his fellowship had assembled to the number of sixteen or seventeen thousand men, as they counted themselves.[28]

Undoubtedly, some commoners may have feared reprisals but went with Fauconberg out of historical duty. Others did not march on London but were involved in other ways, as the *Arrivall* suggests. The majority went willingly, and of course there were mercenaries in Fauconberg's ranks who had been paid for their services, namely the men of the Calais garrison and various mariners who were used to a rough and ready life of violence, hardship and privateering. Therefore, the claims of the *Arrivall* may have been an accurate representation of Fauconberg's army rather than a biased account loaded with political spin against the Yorkists. As discussed, Kent was well supplied with ex-soldiers versed in warfare and rebellion willing to supplement their meagre incomes by looting the capital if the opportunity arose. Those who marched with Fauconberg were well equipped, it seems, and most had an axe to grind against authority in one way or another. Therefore, Fauconberg's host was not a peasant army by any stretch of the imagination. It had all the trappings of a Wars of the Roses force led by captains who had fought before and would do so again.[29]

Meanwhile, in the west, King Edward had left Tewkesbury on Tuesday 7 May, after ordering the executions of the Lancastrian commanders captured after the battle. After receiving news at Worcester of yet another rising against him that was gaining momentum in the north of England, it is generally accepted that Edward readied his army for yet another march towards Coventry. He already knew of the disturbances in Kent, so this new northern problem was an additional worry in an area that had been equally volatile and unruly in the past. Indeed, messengers and heralds carrying letters had been reaching King Edward since at least 3 May, warning him of risings in Yorkshire, not to mention those predicted in Kent, Essex and other southern counties. The king had already given Earl Rivers and other lords commissions to go out against the rebels in the south-east, and naturally, Edward had informed London of his decisive victory over Margaret of Anjou at Tewkesbury to put their minds at rest. However, nothing was certain in England while Henry VI was still a magnet for Lancastrian agitators. Two rebellions were brewing in the kingdom, and Edward's trials were far from over.

As for Queen Margaret, she was a broken woman. After losing her only son in battle, her reign as queen and head of Lancastrian defiance had reached a grim end. At the age of 41 and left with nowhere else to turn, she had no alternative but to put herself at the king's mercy. Edward IV could have removed her permanently, but he acted chivalrously despite her anti-Yorkist track record. It was a turning point in the Wars of the Roses, and we may wonder if Edward now saw Margaret's past actions as circumstantial rather than calculated. H.E. Maurer suggests the queen was a woman acting on behalf of her husband and her son Prince Edward rather than the vengeful and ruthless 'she-wolf' of Shakespearian legend. In a world that largely denied female authority, she had to rely upon other channels of influence like the various dukes of Somerset or the king's chief councillors for support. However, Maurer says the striking thing about Margaret's quest for power was 'not the extent to which she offended gender expectations, but the effort she made to at least appear to live up to them'.[30]

With Margaret safely in his power, King Edward's march to Coventry may have been triumphant, despite having to send out various commissions to raise more troops to go against his enemies. Edward may have considered the rebellion in Yorkshire a lot worse than that of 1469. However, on Monday 13 May, Henry Percy, Earl of Northumberland galloped through the gates of Coventry with a few of his retainers to inform Edward that the northern rising, instigated by the Nevilles, had petered out through lack of support, and that he, Percy, had everything under control.[31] Northumberland promised to return to his domains and keep order immediately. Undoubtedly, he was thankful to be back in his old position as earl once more, and after all the machinations of Warwick and Queen Margaret, Edward hoped he could look forward to a lasting peace in England. How wrong he was. At the same time the king was discussing the north with Henry Percy, the City of London was under attack.

7

Bridges of London

In Southwark, at Blackheath, and Kingston eke,
The Bastard and his meanie in the country about,
Many great men in London they made seek,
Man, wife and child they durst not rout.[1]

☘

While Edward IV was occupied elsewhere in England, events were moving at pace south of London. Sometime on the morning of Friday 10 May 1471, a rider appeared on Blackheath, where Fauconberg's rebel army had camped for the night. No doubt, the messenger was stopped by sentries, and when he requested to see Thomas Fauconberg, he was likely shocked by the sea of tents occupying the open heathland. If the messenger was a military herald, he would have been well placed to take stock of the situation. The number of smoking fires and tents stretching into the distance may have given him an approximation of the rebel strength, but if the lords and city fathers in London were expecting a few hundred rebels up in arms, they were sadly mistaken. Indeed, to anyone viewing the rebel camp on the distinctive ridge south-east of London, then called *Bleak Heath*, it must have looked like the occupants of a whole town or city had blocked the London road.[2]

After being taken into camp, the messenger handed Fauconberg a letter from the Lord Mayor, John Stockton, backed by his council and lords, who had deliberated Thomas's requests at the Guildhall for at least a day. However, a far more important note from Edward IV was also enclosed with the mayor's letter, which carried more weight than anyone in the rebel army could imagine. As such, the messenger or herald may have waited for an immediate reply, but when Fauconberg had read both letters and digested their contents, he likely needed time to think and consult with his captains before an answer. Indeed, the contents of the letters may have come as a complete shock to Thomas and his followers, as events so far west were fresh news, as opposed to what was common knowledge in or around London, such as the defeat and death of the Earl of Warwick at Barnet on 14 April.

Mayor Stockton's letter was long and wordy, to say the least, but it is worth repeating here (with only slight abridgements) as it contains a flavour of the atmosphere in London at the time and shows the confidence of the city fathers before the siege. This confidence is betrayed by repeated warnings from the mayor about Fauconberg's rising, although this is tempered by promises of fair treatment if he stood down his forces and submitted to King Edward. No doubt the mayor's letter was also intended to delay the rebels until the king returned to the city, and although it is a formal enough reply to Fauconberg's requests, given on 8 May at Sittingbourne, the message betrays a latent fear of the rebels if they gained entry to the city:

> Worshipful Sir, we received your letters written at Sittingbourne the eighth day of the present month of May, by which we understand [it has] come unto your knowledge that if you and your fellowship should come unto the City of London, like as you write you intend to do, that you would rifle and despoil the said city. [Also] you desire us by the said letter that we should give no credence to such [a] surmise, saying and taking [heed] of God that you never intended so to do, praying us to suffer you and your said fellowship to pass through the said City of London upon your journey to perform and execute such things as in your said letters being more largely expressed. Sir, we let you know that when the king, King Edward the Fourth, our sovereign lord, after his great victory upon Easter Day last passed beside Barnet, departed out of the said City of London, he charged and commanded us upon our allegiance that we should keep the same [city] safely and surely on his behalf, not suffering any person of what degree, condition, or estate or gathering, or making assemblies of any people contrary to his laws without [the] authority of his high commandment

to enter therein, for the which cause and many other we [dare not] or will [not] suffer you to pass through the same city, letting you know for certain that we understand that if you and your said fellowship should come and enter into the same, that your said fellowship would be of like condition, or as like disposition [to those] in time passed as by sundry precedents it appeareth unto us right largely [that] it should not lie in your power to let your said fellowship [refrain] from despoilage and robbery. Wherefore, we advise you for that love and service that we have [given] unto that noble knight, your father and our good lord, whose steps we [hope] that you should follow. And for [that] favour that we have borne and bear unto you for the good disposition and virtue that in time passed we have known to be in you, that you spare and abstain yourself from such [an] unlawful gathering and assembling of people the which if you so do we [will] not only give unto you great honour and worship, but also to your prevail and cause the king [will] rather be your good and gracious lord.

More, our sir, we have received a proclamation sent from you in which we understand that you, by the commandment of Henry, late king of this realm, Margaret, late queen and Edward, late called prince by the advice of the Earl of Warwick, whom you supposed to be alive as we [have] been informed and other, [that] you be ordained Captain of the Navy of England and men of war both by the sea and by land. Right worshipful sir, we marvel greatly that you, being a man of such great wisdom and discretion, should be deceived by simple sayings and feigned tales [and] we certify you upon our worship and truth that both the said Edward, late called prince, and the Earl of Warwick be slain and dead for we know for certain, not only by the report of men of credence both of this city and by or which were with the said Earl of Warwick on the field when he and his brother Marquis Montagu were slain, but also by open lying of their bodies in the Church of Pauls [for] the space of two days which many of us did see and understand for certain to be the bodies of the said Earl of Warwick and Marquis.

Also sir, the said Edward late called prince, the Earl of Devonshire, Lord John of Somerset, Lord Wenlock, Sir Edmond Hampden, Sir Robert Whityngham, Sir John Lewknor [and] John Delves with many more were slain upon Saturday last passed at Tewkesbury, and the Duke of Somerset, the Lord of Saint John's, Sir Gerveys of Clifton,

Sir Thomas Gresham with [many more] to the number of twelve persons [were] taken and beheaded on Monday last passed as we [have] been certainly informed at Tewkesbury aforesaid where God gave the king our said sovereign lord the victory. [We also] certainly understand, not only by letters signed with our said sovereign lord's own hand, whereof we send you a copy herein enclosed, but by writings sent from lords and gentry there being present unto diverse and many persons and men of worship. And how, and in what manner and form, the said Edward late called prince [was] taken and slain wherefore we friendly exhort and stir you not only to abstain yourself from such unlawful gatherings and assemblies of people and giving faith and credence to any simple feigned and forged tales contrary to [the] truth as it is rehearsed, but also to take, accept, and obey the king, King Edward the Fourth, for your sovereign lord [and] the great victories afore rehearsed which God has given him by his mighty power considered like all the lords spiritual and temporal of this land, and we have also agreed for to do, and you so doing shall cause the king rather to be your good [lord] and thereby you shall eschew great jeopardies, perils and inconveniences that might eschew [from] the contrary. And also, you shall not only have our good wills and benevolence in all things that hereafter you shall have to do between us, but also, we shall be [arbiter] to the king's highness trusting that by our prayer he shall be unto you [a] good and gracious lord. Letting you know for certain that you nor your host shall not come within the said city. Written in London in the Guildhall the ninth day of May.

To the worshipful sir, Thomas Fauconberg
By the mayor, aldermen, sheriffs, common council,
master wardens of crafts and constables of the City of London.[3]

King Edward's original signed note written soon after the executions at Tewkesbury on 6 May has not survived. However, an analysis of the mayor's letter gives a good indication of what it contained. According to the evidence, the mood in London three days later and the fact that the city fathers were fairly confident of their position after the king's victory prove their hopes were high that the rebels might disperse and return to their homes. On the council's advice, even the Archbishop of Canterbury had written to Fauconberg warning him of the moral and religious consequences of attacking the city. But the chances that Thomas would change his original plans were slight now his demands had also been refused by the Commonality.[4]

In his letter, the mayor firstly acknowledges Fauconberg's message on 8 May and his fears that the rebels might pillage London if given access. He also seems worried that he might be blamed if the city is looted and points out that Fauconberg would likely deny all responsibility for this if his men ran amok in the streets. The mayor then adopts a firmer approach and warns of the promise he and the lords in the city gave Edward IV when he marched out of London to face Queen Margaret in the west. He also reminds Fauconberg about the anarchy that resulted when rebels had been allowed into the city in the past, namely during Cade's rebellion and the Kentish rising of 1470. He firmly believes that Fauconberg is not powerful enough to stop this kind of random pillaging if he and his army are allowed to pass freely through the city, and it is this, rather than any other excuse, that is reiterated throughout the letter, which otherwise would have been just a firm reprimand.

Next, the mayor adopts a more personal tone by mentioning Fauconberg's father, William, 'that noble knight and our good lord' whose example Thomas should follow. He then applauds Thomas's previous 'good disposition and virtue' and advises him to abstain from his present course of action, take Edward IV for his king and accept his mercy. The mayor understands that Fauconberg may have been led astray by others like Warwick and his promise of dubious appointments to office – namely that of being 'Captain of the Navy of England and men of war both by the sea and by land'. He reminds Thomas that Warwick and his brother Montagu are dead and that their bodies have been displayed at St Paul's for all to see. The mayor marvels at Fauconberg's gullibility considering his 'great wisdom' and warns him that he has been deceived by 'feigned and forged tales'. Whether the mayor thinks Fauconberg is unaware that the Earl of Warwick is dead is debatable, but surely, a month after the battle of Barnet, the mayor cannot think that Thomas is so out of touch. However, what the mayor has to say next in his letter may have come as a complete bombshell to Fauconberg as news had only just arrived in London about the battle of Tewkesbury, and this news becomes the pivotal point of the mayor's argument.

The copy letter from Edward IV containing information about the battle, the casualties and the executions at Tewkesbury must have been sent after Monday 6 May (considering the content), and the mayor decides to use this new information to strike fear into Fauconberg and crush his willingness to rebel. With Prince Edward slain, King Henry's dynastic isolation must have hit Fauconberg hard, and the mayor asks Thomas, yet again, to refrain from rebellion and pillage by abandoning his cause. He cleverly warns him of the repercussions of his illegal 'gatherings', using the threat of Edward's ruthless executions at Tewkesbury as an effective deterrent. After this statement, Fauconberg is warned of the 'great jeopardies, perils and inconveniences' that might 'eschew' from his actions, although the mayor softens this threat with a promise that he will mediate with the king, saying that Edward 'will be a good and gracious lord' to Fauconberg if he submits and his forces disperse. The mayor then reiterates again that under no circumstances will Thomas and his host be allowed into the city, and this final statement is backed by the full weight of the city fathers and the Yorkist lords who were no doubt present at the Guildhall when the mayor's letter was drafted.

As for Thomas Fauconberg's response, he had a large army on Blackheath awaiting orders, and he knew wasting time would prove detrimental to his plans and damage morale. No doubt Thomas was enraged by the mayor's words, and this is apparent in *The Great Chronicle of London*, which may have echoed Fauconberg's lost response (if he made any) to the mayor and lords in the city:

> With the which answer, [Fauconberg] was not a little contented but swore many great oaths that he would pass that way [through London] in spite of the mayor and all his power and that he would rule the city by the space of a day and a night at his pleasure, and upon that vow so made, he called his lewd council unto him and took their advice how he might best assail the city.[5]

The massive Essex rising was no doubt nearing London by now, and some of Fauconberg's fleet, loaded with artillery and troops, had sailed from Blackwall and Radcliffe to St Katherine's Wharf and were also awaiting orders. However, time was running out, and although no one in the rebel army knew the whereabouts of Edward's forces, there was no need to hold back the rebellion with protracted negotiations. If Thomas could attack quickly in concert with his other forces, London might fall, and his mission, originally foreseen by Warwick but now spurred on by thoughts of Edward's return, would succeed if the city could be taken and Henry VI freed. The *Arrivall* points out that both Mayor Stockton and Thomas Fauconberg knew that some Londoners were also secret Lancastrians and others were known criminals waiting for a chance to fill their pockets:

> [A] great number of persons within the city were rather disposed to have helped to have such mischief wrought than to defend it; some, for they were maliciously disposed, and were, in their hearts, partial to the Earl of Warwick's quarrel, and to the party of Henry, wherefore [they] were many; some, were poor; some, men's servants and men's apprentices, [who] would have been right glad of a common robbery, to the intent they might largely have put their hands in rich men's coffers.[6]

However, here, the story of the siege of London divides opinion among contemporary writers and historians. One school of thought is that Fauconberg immediately attacked the city in force. Another, supported by contemporary chronicles, says that Thomas and the rebels first marched west to Kingston Bridge, 10 miles away, hoping to threaten London and Westminster by crossing the Thames higher upriver. The pro-Yorkist *Arrivall* is confident about this manoeuvre and that Fauconberg left some of his ships below the Tower of London as a deterrent (although they could hardly sail up the Thames because of London Bridge and the Tower defences). The author also points out that this was a clever ruse to 'destroy Westminster and then the suburbs of London and do their utmost against the city, revenging that their entry was denied them and their passage'.[7] The pro-Lancastrian *Warkworth's Chronicle* agreed with this course of events in principle, and despite several unconnected aspects of the story, the author hints at an interesting meeting between Lord Scales (Earl Rivers) and Fauconberg near or on Kingston Bridge:

> The Lord Scales [Earl Rivers], and diverse other of King Edward's counsel that were in London, saw that the Bastard and his host went westward and that it should be a greater jeopardy to King Edward than was Barnet field or Tewkesbury field, in so much as when the

field of Tewkesbury was done, his host was departed from [it]. Wherefore they [Rivers] promised the Bastard, and diverse others that were about him, and especially to one Nicholas Faunt, Mayor of Canterbury, that he should entreat him to turn homeward again.[8]

Aside from the brave stance by Rivers, his words were hardly a persuasive rebuff to thousands of armed men ready to attack London. Therefore, it is more likely that the earl warned Fauconberg and Faunt that his brother-in-law Edward was marching towards them with a large force and that they should return home now or face the consequences of treason, especially the Mayor of Canterbury, Nicholas Faunt, who should have known better. However, the pro-Yorkist *Arrivall* makes this rebuff by Earl Rivers much more transparent by explaining the probable thinking behind Fauconberg's retreat back to Southwark:

> The Bastard had certain knowledge that the king [Edward] was greatly assisted with all the lords of the realm in substance, [a] great number of noblemen, and other, in greater numbers than [at] any time he had had before. They [Fauconberg and Faunt] greatly fearing [the king's] high courage and knighthood, and the great victories that God had sent him returned again, and came before London, and showed themselves in whole battle in Saint George's Fields. And [they did] this for diverse considerations; for one, they doubted greatly the recounter of the king; also, the multitude of them came rather for robbing than for revenging by way of battle; they doubted, also, to assail the city on that other side of Thames, for in case they might not prevail, they of London should likely stop them [on] their way homeward unto their country [Kent]. And for to divide their host, some upon the one side of London and some upon the other side, they thought it folly, for as much as, with few folks, they might have broken the bridges after them, and stopped their passage.[9]

In St George's Fields

Reading between the lines, it is plain to see what is plausible and what is supposition or bias in the sources. Quite clearly, the rebels wanted to cross Kingston Bridge for a specific reason, bearing in mind that the rationale for Fauconberg's rebellion was to release Henry VI from the Tower, not encounter Edward IV in open battle. Evidently, Fauconberg commanded a considerable force, certainly more than a few thousand men, and this is noted in *Warkworth's Chronicle*, but without King Henry in their ranks, Lancastrian sympathies could not hope to be resurrected or sustained in the city. In short, Fauconberg doubted his chances of victory against Edward after speaking to Earl Rivers. However, as discussed previously, some rebels were pressed men, yet others were prone to robbing rather than fighting a battle. And lastly, if Fauconberg envisaged an assault on the city via Westminster, this might have proved extremely dangerous if the Yorkists had managed to cut them off on the wrong side of the Thames. Earl Rivers may also have arrived in strength at Kingston Bridge to dissuade Fauconberg or even fight a battle there – a fact supported by C.L. Scofield, who points out that the *Issues Rolls* indicate that barges (or balingers with oars) loaded with troops were sent upriver by Earl Rivers to prevent the rebels from crossing the Thames at Kingston.[10] Either way, burning Westminster may not have been Fauconberg's prime intention. Circumventing London from the east would have made this possible if this was his main aim. Therefore, this conclusion brings us back to the first scenario mentioned earlier – that on 12 May, prior to his march to Kingston, Fauconberg marched from Blackheath with his whole force and directly attacked London Bridge with fire and sword, an event that was mentioned in the pro-Lancastrian *Warkworth's Chronicle*:

> But then the Lord Scales [Earl Rivers], who King Edward had left to keep the city, with the mayor and aldermen, would not suffer the said Bastard to come into the city for they had the understanding that Prince Edward was dead, and all his host discomfited. Wherefore the Bastard loosed his guns into the city and burnt at Aldgate and at London Bridge; for the which burning, the commons of London where sore grieved, and greatly moved against them: for if they had not burnt, the commons of the city would have let them in, in spite of [Earl Rivers], the mayor and all his brethren. Wherefore the Bastard and all his host went over [the Thames] at Kingston Bridge, ten mile westward.[11]

The conclusion, therefore, is that London Bridge was attacked first on 12 May, and when this did not succeed, Fauconberg diverted his attention to Kingston for reasons that will become clear shortly. Additional evidence for this frontal assault is given in records derived from Journal 8, folio 7, in the London Metropolitan Archives, which read almost as an eyewitness account similar to that given in *The Great Chronicle of London*, which will be mentioned later:

> Be it remembered that the mayor and aldermen, with the assent of the Common Council, fortified the banks of the river Thames from Castle Baynard as far as the Tower of London with men at arms, bombards, and other implements of war to prevent an attack by the seamen who had brought a large fleet of ships near the Tower, and the said bank was held by the aldermen and the rest of the citizens in great numbers. Be it remembered also that on Sunday, the twelfth day of May in the eleventh year of Edward IV [1471], Kentish seamen and other rebels of the lord the king made an attack upon London Bridge and on the new gate there, and [they] set fire to divers houses called beer houses near the hospital of Saint Katherine.[12]

As mentioned earlier, Jack Cade and his rebels had assaulted London Bridge in the past, and the new gate (called the Great Stone Gate) was a substantial construction. Like the bridge itself, the approach was lined with shops and houses adjoining Southwark, and it would be wrong to think that the gate was left undefended. The gatehouse would have become a veritable death trap of falling arrows and incendiary devices when Fauconberg and his men attacked. The burning of the gate may have cost many lives. Indeed, Fauconberg's assault failed, according to sources, and the rebels were forced back through Southwark, licking their wounds. The smoking houses before the gate may have signalled to the rebels on the opposite bank of the Thames to fire the suburbs near St Katherine's Hospital. Beer houses and inns of Dutch and Flemish traders had been targets before in 1470, and according to the above evidence, they seem to have become targets again, probably at the instigation of Sir Geoffrey Gate, who had used terrorism in the past to try and bring about widespread panic in the city.

In retrospect, the above attack was a method of testing the defences and making a point to the city fathers that the rebels meant business. It may also have been a way of holding the rebel army together and encouraging looting. However, we do not know the exact details of this attack from any source, other than that its failure at London Bridge caused Fauconberg to rethink his strategy. In the end, Fauconberg marched his 'whole host' westwards in an attempt to cross Kingston Bridge and burn Westminster.[13] But what stopped him from doing this? A 10-mile march to Kingston from Southwark was not a leisurely stroll with an army of belligerent rebels wondering what was in store for them. Therefore, Fauconberg and his advisors must have had an excellent reason to lead thousands of men from Southwark to Kingston Bridge and back again in an attempt to cross the Thames. Clearly, the answer lies in the movements of Edward IV and what news Earl Rivers and Fauconberg knew of this, considering the limitations of messengers and medieval communication in 1471.

On 12 May, Edward IV was still in Coventry, over 90 miles away, but it is unlikely Fauconberg would have known this with any certainty. However, we know from the mayor's letter that London and Earl Rivers had received other news from the king that he was remustering an army in the Midlands and intending to march on London as soon as possible. Therefore, when *Warkworth's Chronicle* says Rivers met Fauconberg at Kingston, he may have fooled Thomas into believing the king was closer than he thought. On 14 May, according to the *Arrivall*, Edward 'appointed a notable, and a well-chosen, fellowship out of his host, and sent them unto the City of London, afore his coming, to the number of fifteen hundred men'.[14] Edward did not depart with his main force until the next day, but the truth of the matter is that Rivers may have been bluffing when he and Fauconberg met at Kingston. However, according to *Warkworth's Chronicle*, Thomas was unsure of Edward's location 'and for as much as fair words and promises makes fools feign, the Bastard commanded all his host to turn to Blackheath again',[15] which proves going against Edward was not Fauconberg's main intention at all. Indeed, he was probably more determined than ever to begin the siege in earnest and free King Henry before Edward's vaward arrived on the scene.

By the evening of 13 May, Fauconberg and his army were back before London and, more precisely, encamped at St George's Fields (then also called Southwark Fields), a large open space usually set aside for pasture and in some places prone to flooding since Roman times. Here from Southwark, Fauconberg would conduct the main assault on London using all three forces at his disposal:

So that upon the fourteenth day of May, the said Bastard being lodged in Southwark sent certain captains of his, of which one name Spicing was sent to Aldgate with a multitude of Essex men, and another named Quentin, a butcher, was sent unto Bishopsgate with another sort, and two others unto Aldersgate and Cripplegate, but the most number were at Aldgate and Bishopsgate, the which were charged to fire the houses about the gates and to make their assaults all at one time.[16]

As discussed, Spicing and Quentin were veterans of the 1470 rebellion, therefore, they may have been the most stubborn of all the insurgents. They may have fought in France, or they may have been men who were notorious barrack room lawyers. Quentin was, we are told, a butcher by trade, but other than this, we have no clue to either men's characters or their politics other than the fact they were rebels.

It will be recalled that on 12 May Fauconberg's fleet of ships had already been ordered to sail up the Thames to unload their guns, powder and shot on the south bank ready to bombard the city. Hundreds of mariners, the 300 men of the Calais garrison under Sir George Brooke, Sir Geoffrey Gate and other soldiers who had joined the fleet at Sandwich had disembarked at St Katherine's Wharf on the opposite side of the river. They were well-armed, we are told, and soon the shoreline, with its inns, businesses and warehouses were in flames. By the morning of 14 May, the Essex men under Spicing were in position on the outskirts of Portsoken Ward east of the city, and Quentin led more Essex men towards Bishopsgate (London's northern bastion), protected by the filthy and deep moat called the Houndsditch. Fauconberg and his other captains of Kent, including Nicholas Faunt, Richard Lovelace, Aucher, Neville and the like, appeared before the already charred gates of London Bridge. The attack on 12 May had been unsuccessful, but preparations were again made to burn the houses adjacent to the Great Stone Gate and Southwark. Approximately 10,000 to 15,000 rebels likely encircled London that day and the Wars of the Roses had never seen the like before. Never had a walled town or city experienced a siege in the wars, and only Cade's revolt in 1450 had managed to cross the Thames in anger.

According to *The Great Chronicle of London*, the rebel cordon around the city extended intermittently to Cripplegate, more than a mile north from the Postern Gate opposite the Tower of London. The city was thoroughly sealed off in the east (Fauconberg's intended route to the Tower), and his ship's guns were being rolled along Bankside to fire indiscriminately across the Thames into the city streets. What must simple Londoners have thought about all the preparations near their homes and beyond the walls? No doubt they feared the worst and were looking to Mayor Stockton and the Yorkist lords for encouragement. Above all they may have blamed Henry VI or Edward IV for their predicament, while some Lancastrian supporters likely welcomed the rebellion. Such was the polarisation caused by the Wars of the Roses.

However, the mayor, his aldermen and the Yorkist nobles were ready to resist the attacks. They had not been idle while Fauconberg had been occupied with Earl Rivers at Kingston Bridge. Contemporary chronicles tell us that preparations for a stout defence had been going on for some days. The Tower defences had been strengthened and a large number of 'pipes' had been filled to make barricades along the Thames. Therefore, the Yorkist lords must have guessed by now that Fauconberg's *real* target was the saintly Henry VI and King Edward's family, who had likely been moved within the thick walls of the Tower, as they were briefly in 1470. The immured Henry VI was also placed in the same place for safety (and apparently, comfort), as recorded in the Guildhall records of October 1470, and this was likely the Lanthorn Tower:

> And be it remembered that the lord Henry the Sixth, who on the said Wednesday and for many years past had been confined in a certain cell (in quodam Argastulo) [as a prisoner] within the said Tower, was conducted by the said mayor and aldermen to a certain chamber adorned with handsome furniture which the said Queen Elizabeth had prepared and in which, being with a fire, she purposed being brought [a] bed.[17]

As for the queen and her young son Edward, Prince of Wales, fear for their safety must have been paramount to the Yorkist lords. Because Fauconberg had lied to the mayor that he intended to pass harmlessly through the city, those tasked with royal safety must have envisaged the worst-case scenario. No doubt King Henry would be set free if the rebels managed to enter the city, but if Edward's family were taken hostage, then this would have put the arriving Yorkists at a grave disadvantage:

But the mayor [Stockton], who long before had kept day watch and night watch, had garnished every place of the city where any peril should be, with guns and other defences of war, and made so strong bulwarks at every gate that he feared nothing, and over that [he] appointed certain aldermen with a competent number of said commoners to watch the said gates and other places both day and night, and appointed with the Lieutenant of the Tower that if they [the rebels] came to Aldgate that he should with his company issue out at the postern and set upon them on that side.[18]

As discussed, similar preparations were made along the banks of the Thames, as recorded by the author of *The Great Chronicle of London*, and armed men, guns and citizen militias had been ordered into position. These defensive measures form part of several contemporary accounts of the siege, which mention building outer walls near the Tower and furnishing the gates with redoubts protected by guns. If these fortifications extended along the river from Baynard's Castle to the Tower, as we are told in sources, this would have covered some 2,000 yards of waterfront – not the sort of defence you would want to organise with men and artillery if Fauconberg's rebellion was insignificant.

To help achieve this deployment, the sheriffs of London had each appointed a hierarchy of helpers who organised the citizens by wards into a fighting force or militia. These officers, according to John Stow, included sixteen sergeants per sheriff. Every sergeant had a yeoman and six clerks, including a secondary, a clerk of the papers and four other clerks besides under-sheriffs, their stewards, butlers and porters. In fact, the system constituted a carefully structured body of men who reported higher up to each of the twenty-six aldermen under the Lord Mayor, who, in turn, were responsible for thousands of citizens and potential levies.[19] Additionally, the professional soldiers of the Tower garrison under Earl Rivers, Lord Duras, Lord Dudley and other Yorkist lords had their retinues with them in the city. The Earl of Essex, Henry Bourchier, Edward IV's treasurer, also had his household men with him in London, and he was given command of Bishopsgate, according to chronicles and a popular ballad of the time.[20]

No doubt, thousands of citizens from the wards outside the city walls fled from their homes into London and elsewhere to escape the rebels and their indiscriminate pillaging. Without a thought to the lives of innocent men, women and children, the city's suburbs were quickly overrun by those rebels who chose to plunder rather than uphold their grievances by storming the city. Foreign merchants who owned inns and beer houses saw their livelihoods destroyed before their eyes, and now it was the turn of Londoners to face the rebels, who undoubtedly remembered the looting and killings of Jack Cade's rebellion in 1450.

It is a well-known fact in any era where there is war or revolution, there will also be indiscriminate rape, burning and pillaging of property, and on 3 July 1450, Cade's rebels, after securing London Bridge, first set about arresting and executing Henry VI's chief ministers without trial, then running riot through the city streets. Heads were soon displayed on pikes, and widespread looting began in earnest. No doubt, it was the 'wretched' pressed and idle elements among the rebels who decided to take advantage of the situation in 1450, and the threat was the same in 1471 on a much wider scale:

Much sorrow and shame the wretches they wrought,
Fair places they burnt on the water side.
Their mischievous deeds availed them nought,
Shamefully they wrought, and so them betide,
They would not leave their malice, but therein abide.[21]

Despite pillaging homes and killing innocent civilians in the suburbs, the rebels were now ready to assault London in force. Most likely, the main attacks were heralded by a signal of some kind, as we are told the siege was to be conducted 'all at once'. Sources do not document this signal, but the most likely visible beacon to launch a simultaneous attack was the burning of Southwark and London Bridge. However, another signal was undoubtedly the deafening rebel gunfire that erupted across the Thames, aimed at the city and its terrified population.

Portrait of Henry VI dressed in a simple blue robe and chaperon in the journal of Swabian knight Georg von Ehingen, c.1481. (Württemberg State Library)

Edward IV redrawn from an original painted c.1510. Taken from *The Chronicles of the White Rose of York*, published in 1843. (Author's collection)

The heraldic banner of William Neville, Lord Fauconberg, later Earl of Kent (c.1405–63). (Geoffrey Wheeler/Author)

The field known as Bloody Meadow (or Bloody Furlong) near Tewkesbury, where many Lancastrians perished in battle on 4 May 1471. (Author)

Line drawing of Richard, Duke of Gloucester's standard depicting his white boar badge and Yorkist suns and roses. The standard would have been parted and fringed with murrey and blue. (Geoffrey Wheeler)

One of the earliest depictions of old London Bridge, from a drawing by Antonie van den Wyngaerde, c.1544. The 'starlings' are clearly visible. (Bodleian Library)

Motto and signature of Anthony Woodville, Earl Rivers (1440–83): *M. Nulle la Vault, A Rivieres (Nothing is worth it, A Rivers)*. (Redrawn by the Author)

Detail of Aldgate from *Civitas Londinium* or *The Agas Map*, first printed from woodblocks *c.*1561 and attributed to the surveyor Ralph Agas (*c.*1540–1621). (© London Metropolitan Archives, City of London)

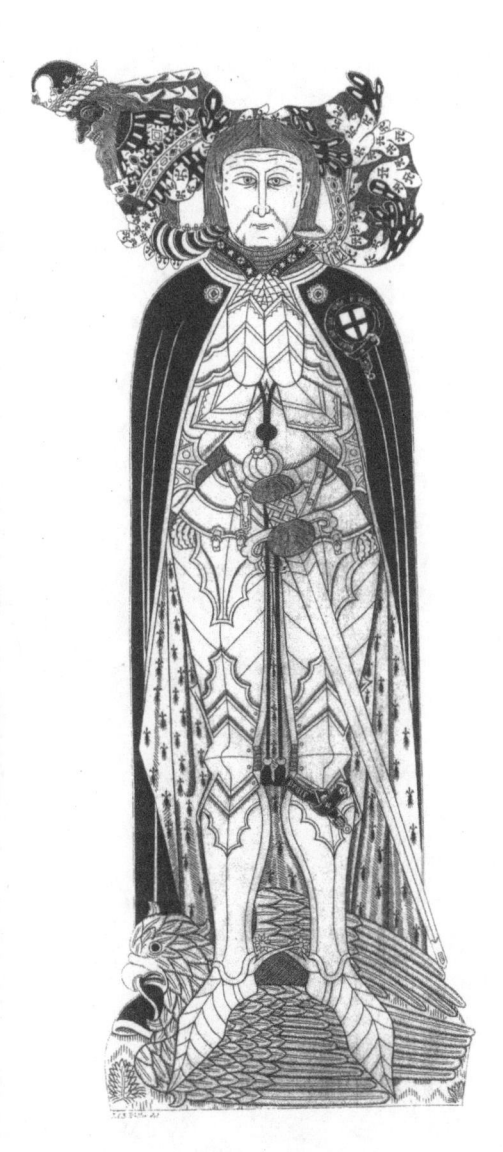

Brass effigy of Henry Bourchier, Earl of Essex (*c*.1404–83), Little Easton Church, Essex. (Geoffrey Wheeler)

Sir Thomas Urswick, Recorder of London (*c*.1415–79). Memorial brass effigy from the Church of Saints Peter and Paul, Dagenham. (Redrawn by the Author)

A letter from the Bastard of Fauconberg to the Mayor and Aldermen of London, 8 May 1471. (© London Metropolitan Archives, City of London, COL/CC/10/10/008, Journal 8, folio 4b)

Manuscript depiction of the Bastard of Fauconberg's attack on London. (Redrawn from Besançon MS.1168 folio 8 by Geoffrey Wheeler)

Contemporary woodcut of soldiers using handguns at a fifteenth-century siege, from the Rudicum Novitiorum, German School, 1475. (Redrawn by the Author)

Early foundations of the Postern Gate from which Anthony, Earl Rivers launched his surprise attack on 14 May 1471. (Author)

An early depiction of the Tower, with old London Bridge in the background. The Wakefield Tower is obscured by St Thomas's Tower and the Lanthorn Tower is located far right. (British Library, Royal MS 16 F II, folio 73r, redrawn by Geoffrey Wheeler)

Gatehouse of Middleham Castle (North Yorkshire), where Thomas Fauconberg was executed by Richard, Duke of Gloucester in September 1471. (Author)

A drawing attributed to Henry VI's effigy, tomb chest and achievements, showing the king bearded. Probably made c.1583–1606. (Bodleian Library, Ms. Bod. 277, folio 376v, Geoffrey Wheeler)

A section of the Canterbury Roll, naming those from the city who were involved in Fauconberg's rebellion of May 1471. (Reproduced courtesy of the Chapter of Canterbury, CCA-CC/WOODRUFF/56/1)

8

Bombardment

At London Bridge, another assault they made again,
With gunpowder and wildfire and straw [they] stroke,
From the gate to the drawbridge, they burnt down plain,
That ten miles [away] men might see the smoke.[1]

✧

Artillery in the Wars of the Roses, and certainly by 1471, had reached a technological peak, but this science (compared with guns of the next century) was far from exact. All types of field guns were used in the civil wars, and heavy artillery such as bombards, had helped reduce the walls of Bamburgh Castle in July 1464. Older forms of ordnance had become redundant, and generally, lighter, more manoeuvrable field pieces of the Burgundian type were being made and preferred on the march and the battlefield. Handguns were also being widely used in the wars to different degrees of effectiveness. But apart from this, European artillery did not undergo any striking changes between 1400 and 1471 other than to offer commanders a greater variety of guns. Moreover, artillery of various kinds and calibres, such as those used at Barnet and Tewkesbury, were thought useful to supplement the more general use of archery in large numbers. Therefore, it would be right to assume range rather than shooting capabilities dictated this decision, and that the potential for large-scale casualties and disarray in battle still rested with the much tried and tested English warbow.

The size, shape and manoeuvrability of artillery determined its use, and all types of guns were made and stored in London, specifically at the Tower and various foundries to the north-east of the city and on the banks of the River Thames. English towns such as Kenilworth and cities like Coventry also had supplies of artillery. Kenilworth Castle was used to stockpile guns for the Lancastrian government, and Stephen Clampard, esquire to the king, was paid £5 for transporting various pieces to the castle in October 1456. The following January, John Judde, Master of the King's Ordnance, was paid for bringing twenty-four new *serpentine* guns and other equipment to Kenilworth, although storage was becoming an issue.[2] In the summer of 1469, Coventry's armaments included a *serpentine* with one chamber, two *fowlers*, a gun with three chambers, a great gun also with three chambers and four handguns, according to the *Coventry Leet Book*.[3] Coastal towns like Dover also acquired ordnance, and some ships were equipped with guns to use against pirates and to pursue naval warfare. The Paston family of Norfolk owned a personal stock of artillery at Caister Castle. John Howard's arsenal included several cannons and handguns, and this was a fashionable trend among nobles who could afford to purchase them. Therefore, gun ownership in the Wars of the Roses was not restricted to the Crown, and according to surviving inventories, artillery was a common feature of armies who were looking to defend prepared positions, as at Dartford in 1453, Ludford Bridge in 1459 and Northampton the following year. The Earl of Warwick used artillery and handguns at the (second) battle of St Albans in 1461 and placed ordnance across Bernards Heath to defend the Yorkist position.[4] Edward IV used field artillery to disperse Sir Robert Welles and his Lincolnshire rebels at Losecote Field in 1470, proving that artillery was an effective shock and awe weapon of the period.

The word 'cannon' was not a well-used description in the civil wars, but this description *was* applied to various forms of nondescript artillery. Generally, each field gun had its own name and size depending on the type of shot used. Names helped categorise guns, and barrels varied from 1 to 18ft long, weighing anything up to 4,000lb. Barrels were generally made from wrought iron, and breech loaders held a charge in a removable chamber to make reloading easier. Smaller wrought-iron guns of the period were cast from iron, brass and bronze, and most were made to order from foundries. The categorisation of gun types in the fifteenth century was also sometimes dictated by their place of origin or historical nomenclature, and no rules seem to have been observed by designers, hence their troublesome and dangerous history.

Bombards, some with barrels up to 18ft long, were the largest and heaviest muzzle- and breech-loading guns of the fifteenth century. They fired 300–950lb stone balls that were usually transported on carts or moved by water and were assembled *in situ* for siege warfare. Usually, a bombard took time to entrench and position correctly, and their rate of fire was extremely slow (only a few shots a day). A type of gun described as a *veuglaire* was smaller than a bombard and was used for similar purposes, and a *fowler* (apparently made of forged, not cast iron) could be between 3 and 10ft long with a calibre of 2 to 10in. A type of mortar, known as a *pestereau*, with a large-diameter wrought-iron barrel is also recorded in some siege accounts, while at the other end of the scale, *culverines* (initially made in Germany) had barrels of 2 to 4 ft in length with a calibre of only 1 to 2in.

Smaller *culverines* were fitted with wooden stocks, and some were known as *culverines à main*, a hand-held muzzle-loader and the forerunner of the arquebus or hackbut (hooked gun) of the late fifteenth century. These handguns were essentially iron tubes firing stone or lead bullets, and we hear of their use in Wars of the Roses battles where they achieved varied success and failure in the hands of mercenaries, Flemings and the like. In the siege of London, it is recorded that the rebels used them to try and gain access to Aldgate. In fact, the two handgunners climbing scaling ladders in the *Arrivall* most likely illustrate the professional soldiers of the Calais garrison commanded by George Brooke and Walter Wrottesley.[5]

The guns called *serpentines* were commonly found on board medieval ships, and when used on the battlefield mounted on a gun carriage, they were highly effective and manoeuvrable. Distinctive for their long breech-loading iron or copper alloy barrels, they fired a 2- to 6in stone or lead ball. A curved elevating device helped to vary their range, and their wheels were iron-tyred, not unlike a modern field gun. It was usual for ships to carry up to a dozen or so pieces of artillery along with a stock of shot and gunpowder, and in 1479, Lord Howard reported two of his ships had been captured with up to sixteen *serpentines* on board.[6]

Wrought-iron swivel guns were also mounted on the forecastles and rearcastles of ships, and the presence of multi-barrelled devices known as *ribaudequins* proves that the variety of artillery pieces was only limited by the imagination and the science of gunpowder (not an exact art by any means). Considering the primitive nature of medieval artillery, it was common for guns to explode, given a crudely shaped cannon ball or inferior barrel casting. The mention of carts used for transportation, even in 1475, also proves that heavy artillery was difficult to deploy on the battlefield. Heavy guns needed teams of horses and oxen to pull them during the march or ships to convey them from place to place. In Edward IV's French expedition of 1475, specific lifting gear was requisitioned by the Controller of the Ordnance, William Rosse, to load and unload various guns. Teams of all types of workers accompanied the army on campaign, and all the above kinds of artillery are mentioned in Edward's roll of arms, along with a stockpile of saltpetre and sulphur to make gunpowder, and iron and lead to make shot.[7]

It is documented that all types of guns were positioned at various points on the banks of the River Thames by both sides during Fauconberg's rebellion. Although the interesting point here is that sources say the rebels unloaded these from their ships, along with stores of armaments (and shot) that otherwise would not have been available in such large quantities by a medieval army on the march:

> The Bastard and his fellowship, thus returned from Kingston Bridge purposing to execute their great rancour and malice against the City of London, and that in all haste, to the intent they might have their prey afore the king's coming, which they thought not to abide, and to carry away in their ships, which were ready to attend for the same intent of robbery, but a mile or two from the said city. Wherefore they assailed the city with great violence, with shot of guns, such as they had brought out of their ships, in great number, and laid them on length [along] the water side, straight over against the city, where they prevailed nothing, for the citizens again-ward in divers places [had] laid ordinance, and made so sharp shot against them, that they durst not abide in any place along the water side.[8]

It is recorded that Fauconberg had at least forty-three ships in his fleet at the end of his campaign (the *Arrivall* mentions forty-seven at Sandwich).[9] But we also know that most of these vessels were sent up the Thames to Blackwall and Radcliffe. Therefore, if a ship could carry at least a dozen guns, according to John Howard's estimates, then Fauconberg may have been able to call upon 200 guns (probably *serpentines*) in the siege – a formidable arsenal of artillery and unlike anything witnessed on an English medieval battlefield. However, given the unlikelihood that Fauconberg unloaded or used heavy artillery (as this would have taken time to position on the south bank of the Thames) he was clearly disadvantaged, according to the sources. The citizens of London no doubt had larger guns on the banks of the Thames provided by the Tower arsenal, which would have been well stocked for such an eventuality. As mentioned earlier, the Londoners had plenty of time to prepare a position before the rebel assault, while Fauconberg had no choice but to improvise. His guns were of a lighter calibre, therefore, the exchange of fire across the Thames must have been furious, although the advantage was clearly with the defenders according to the *Arrivall*.

As for other missile weapons, there is a good reason to believe the warbow was also effective across the Thames, and this is reflected in a political ballad of the day:

> At London Bridge, they made assault, shame to see,
> The outer gate on the bridge they set on fire,
> Into London shot arrows without pity,
> With guns they were bet, that some lay in the mire.[10]

To explain the effect of medieval archery on the city, it is necessary to judge the width of the Thames in the late fifteenth century, and thus, the range of the warbow can be compared to this figure. The best way to estimate this distance is to consider the total length of London Bridge (measured at 309 yards) and determine if this figure compares with the effective range of the standard medieval 120lb warbow and arrow. According to modern research, fully documented in *The Great Warbow* and practically applied by S. Stanley in ballistic tests, this proves the shoreline *was* well within range, as sources record.[11] However, arrows may have been largely ineffective since it is also recorded the Londoners set up several forms of barricade along the Thames, including the 'pipes' mentioned earlier. As for edging nearer the north bank, recent research concerning London Bridge by D. Gerhold indicates that the nineteen arches and 'starlings' (piers) often created a waterfall effect under the bridge, so much so that the water levels upstream and downstream differed as much as 5ft.[12] Therefore, archers would not have been able to reduce their range because the river was at its capacity upstream most of the time in spring. However, downstream, past London Bridge, where the river was slightly lower, archery would have been highly effective due to the narrowing width of the Thames – although it is likely the Tower would have covered this eventuality with a clear field of fire. Therefore, sources can verify that archery was employed during the siege of London, but Fauconberg may have concentrated most of his archers and guns west of the bridge on Bankside, where there was little or no cover.

Generally, even smaller-calibre guns, such as *serpentines*, had a range of over 1,000 yards – much more than the distance required to shoot over the Thames with a bow and arrow. Still, larger pieces, such as those taken from the Tower, would have been more effective, although slower to reload as scouring barrels after firing was often time-consuming. Occasionally, the recoil of wheeled guns like *serpentines* could split mountings or shatter gun carriages on both sides, killing operators in the process, and it is generally assumed that faulty shot or imperfect gun castings accounted for many unwanted explosions. Likewise, the highly sensitive mix of gunpowder, stored in waxed bags for safety, was another hazard to gunners who manned artillery pieces. An imperfect balance of ingredients could cause unwanted detonations, and various grocers (who traded in saltpetre due to their contacts with the spice trade) were not regulated. The only way to control the mix of gunpowder was to solidify it into 'cakes' using urine. However, gravity generally tended to separate the ingredients according to their weight, hence the preponderance of explosions and deaths due to misfires that are variously recorded during the Wars of the Roses.[13]

As for sieges, they were uncommon in the civil wars and had never occurred against a populated town or city. Therefore, the unique scene before London must have greatly concerned the inhabitants. The bombardment may not have lasted long, judging by the timeframe of the siege, but the horror and significance of it cannot be ignored. In short, the battle across the Thames would have become a scene of smoke and fire. Acrid smells of sulphur and charcoal would have filled the air, and dead and wounded would have soon mounted on both sides. Undoubtedly, some damage was done to the city as rebel gunstones hammered into waterfront buildings, warehouses and defences. Innocent citizens were likely killed in the streets, and the detonation of hundreds of guns would have caused significant panic across London. However, according to contemporary evidence, Fauconberg received the worst of this bombardment, and he quickly decided to abandon his guns and switch tactics back to Southwark, where he hoped to resume his attack on the Great Stone Gate:

> Wherefore The Bastard purveyed another means to annoy and grieve the said city sore and therefore ordained a great fellowship to set fire upon the bridge, and to burn the houses upon [it] and thereby to make them an open way into the said city. [But] their burning at the bridge profited them nothing; albeit they burnt many houses to the number of sixty, the citizens had set such ordinance in their way that, though all the way had been opened, it had been too hard for them to have entered by that way, but upon their lives. The mayor, aldermen, and worshipful citizens of the city were in good array and set to every part, where was needed, a great fellowship, well ordered and ordained, for to withstand the malice of the aforesaid rebels.[14]

As described earlier, Fauconberg's first attempt to destroy the Great Stone Gate had failed on 12 May, and they were beaten back. Some houses surrounding the southern end of the bridge were destroyed as a result, and no doubt the rebel assault had badly damaged the gate itself. However, the defenders had retreated further along the bridge, and on 14 May the rebels managed to reach the second gatehouse, called the Drawbridge Tower, located a third of the way across London Bridge. Here, the mayor, aldermen and citizens stood fast behind their next line of defence – a gatehouse with two towers and a drawbridge – and this soon became the site of a desperate battle for supremacy.

Historians have estimated the roadway across London Bridge as being 15ft wide (enough room for two carts to pass), but the entrance to the Great Stone Gate was even narrower, forcing traders with transport to pay a toll. Beyond this gate, houses and shops were built on the bridge, forming a street, beyond which a 'military area' (clear of housing) led to the Drawbridge Tower, which overlooked it.[15] The drawbridge was only raised to allow shipping to pass along the Thames. Therefore, it may have been Fauconberg's intention to keep this intact so that he could cross with his men afterwards. However, we are told that houses were burning on the bridge and in Southwark during the siege, so this may have been the last chance to drive the defenders back and enter the city. Either way, Fauconberg and his captains led thousands of rebels forward through belching smoke, flames, falling gunstones and arrows. And this time they took the Great Stone Gate and ran at the drawbridge, undoubtedly accompanied by archers and mariners wheeling field guns behind them.[16] Their hope 'to make them an open way into the said city' may have looked brighter, and to their credit a third of the bridge had been crossed successfully. But all now depended on assaulting the Drawbridge Tower using fire and sword, and by all accounts, the defenders had plenty of fight in them to meet Fauconberg's spirited assault.

With gunpowder and wildfire

The first bridge assault may have been costly for the rebels. But after the burning of sixty buildings at the southern end of the crossing, it may have looked like the whole of London Bridge was on fire. It has been estimated that 140 houses and shops stood on the bridge at one time or another, and the 1471 fires could have caused at least a third of these to fall into the Thames. Many buildings had been standing since the beginning of the century, and the actual plots dated back to 1358, according to D. Gerhold.[17] However, the rest of the bridge remained intact, and the Drawbridge Tower was no doubt defended with every available man to hand. A gap of at least 30ft lay before the raised drawbridge, and this was the next obstacle the rebels tried to assault.

Fauconberg attempted to push forward, we are told by *The Great London Chronicle*, using archers, artillery and wildfire, but the citizens were so well provided with both that even if the passage had been entirely open, the rebels would 'have had a hard entering that way'. John Stow recalls in his *Survey* that Fauconberg 'burned the [stone] gate and all the houses to the drawbridge' and one of the 'bravest defenders of the bridge was Ralph Jocelyne, alderman and draper, who afterwards was made a Knight of the Bath and Lord Mayor of London' in 1477.[18] Therefore, it may have been that a Yorkist sally from the gatehouse drove the rebels back once they were weakened by artillery, and Jocelyne likely led this charge, such was his notoriety in later years. The city fathers may have feared that Fauconberg would set fire to the gatehouse itself and the houses behind it, thereby causing more damage to the bridge and cutting the defenders off from the city. However, the contemporary *Croyland Chronicle* tells us there was a desperate fight on the bridge, and the rebels were steadily pushed back across the military area towards burning buildings and the Great Stone Gate:

> The vestiges of their misdeeds are even yet to be seen upon the said bridge [1598], as they burned all the houses which lay between the drawbridge and the outer gate that looks towards the High Street of Southwark, and which had been built at a vast expense. God, however, being unwilling that a city so renowned, and the capital of the whole kingdom of England, should be delivered into the hands of such wretches, to be plundered by them, gave to the Londoners stout hearts, which prompted them to offer resistance on the day of the battle.[19]

Given the religious and political bias of the *Croyland Chronicle*, it is hardly surprising that the author attributed the winning of the bridge to the work of God. However, it is more likely that Fauconberg's assaults would never have succeeded while the fear and notoriety of the rebels were uppermost in the minds of the Londoners. Thousands of marauding ruffians pillaging their way through the streets and burning homes and businesses provided an excellent incentive for the citizens to fight vigorously. Also, only so many rebels could be brought to bear on the narrow and exposed bridgehead. Destroying the bridge entirely with artillery was counterproductive to Fauconberg's plan of simultaneously entering the city from the south and east. Therefore, as casualties mounted and rebel resistance began to waver, the Londoners gained confidence, and maybe with the aid of cavalry, they lowered the drawbridge, charged and eventually pushed Fauconberg's men back. Swarming into the still-burning suburbs of Southwark, the citizens chased the rebels through the streets and along the banks of the Thames, killing hundreds.

Fauconberg escaped the rout towards Blackheath, we are told. But now his only hope was that the assaults on the city gates by the Essex rebels were having better luck, or all was lost. He may have joined the Essex men, as some chroniclers mention him leading the rebels during their attacks on the city gates. However, despite his penchant for action and throwing caution to the wind, Fauconberg could not be in two places at once. The second assault on London Bridge and the city gates clearly happened at the same time (probably eleven o'clock) on 14 May.[20] Therefore, Fauconberg must have been in Southwark, not Portsoken Ward to the east, given that he had handed command of the Essex rebels to Spicing and Quentin that same morning.

However, despite two attacks, London Bridge had proved a formidable obstacle to take, and despite leaving behind a scene of destruction never witnessed on such a scale before, the Kentish rebels had been no match for citizens with a die-hard incentive. In fact, Fauconberg may have planned his escape long before the rebels broke ranks on the bridge, as there is little contemporary evidence that puts Thomas with the Essex rebels battling for Aldgate, Bishopsgate and the other points of entry. Therefore, Fauconberg's name may have been simply associated with his rebellion in a collective fashion rather than a way of locating the assaults he led personally.

Meanwhile, in the Midlands, as the siege of London was raging, Edward IV was oblivious to the danger to his throne. As mentioned earlier, he was still recruiting at Coventry on 14 May and thankful that the northern rebellion instigated by the Nevilles had come to nothing. However, after receiving another urgent messenger from London, Edward sent out a mounted detachment of men-at-arms before his intended march south so that at least a show of strength might arrive in the city before him. According to the well-informed author of the *Arrivall*:

> This [messenger] moved the king greatly to haste him towards [London], but it was needful that he came there furnished with as great, or greater, host than he had at any time since his coming into the land. Nonetheless, for that such [an] army might not be prepared so soon as the said fourteenth day of May, he appointed a notable, and a well-chosen, fellowship out of his host, and sent them unto the City of London, afore his coming, to the number of fifteen hundred men,

to be seen for the comfort of the queen, the lords, and the citizens. And [he] himself departed out of Coventry towards London the fifteenth day of May.[21]

In retrospect, there was little King Edward could do other than this. The wheel of fortune was turning quickly, and the clock was ticking. He now knew the seriousness of Fauconberg's rebellion, and it is hard not to imagine he may have changed his attitude towards Henry VI at this time. It would have been strange if Edward thought his prisoner was still no threat to his throne with London besieged. Henry VI was the root cause of the rebellion, and now Edward could do little to protect Queen Elizabeth and his young heir, the Prince of Wales. If the rebels managed to free Henry VI from the Tower and set up a new power-base in London, attracting closet Lancastrians to their cause, Edward's throne and his family would be in grave danger. Therefore, Henry was becoming a major problem to Edward despite his anonymity. He was no threat while the Yorkists ruled and governed England, but King Henry had too often become a clarion call to arms despite his otherworldly and untouchable holiness. In fact, his very *existence* attracted Lancastrian sympathisers, even though his heir had been killed at Tewkesbury and Queen Margaret was a shadow of her former self.

It is highly likely the ex-king could hear (and maybe see) what was happening across the river from his chamber in the Tower in May 1471. Although it is not known with any certainty if Henry was entirely sane after being incarcerated for such a long time, what is certain is that he was still alive and being adequately looked after by his Yorkist captors. Apart from some periods of shoddy treatment, King Henry had been provided for since his incarceration in the Tower in 1465. Various payments had been made to his keepers, who provided for his basic daily needs as ordered by Edward IV. Henry was not starved or thrown into a deep dungeon to rot like other prisoners. In fact, he had plenty of time to devote to his beloved religious pursuits in a small makeshift chapel (if he was kept in the Lanthorn Tower as contemporary sources indicate). As discussed, there was furniture and a bed in his room, he was clothed, fed, watered and had time to compose several prayers. To prove this point, the *Issues Rolls* of Edward IV record generous payments to Henry's gaolers dating from at least 29 September 1465, not long after the king was captured in the north.

These payments continued despite several major upheavals in government, including Warwick's rebellions, and when the siege of London was raging outside Henry's window, money was in hand to last until 25 May 1471:

[1465] In money paid at different times for costs and expenses of Henry Windsor, late de facto et non jure King of England, being in the Tower of London, by the hands of Thomas Grey and Richard Hatfield ...

[13 May 1468] To William Kimberly, a chaplain attending, by the king's command, in the Tower of London, there daily performing divine service before Henry, late de facto et non de jure King of England ... without any fee or reward for his attendance ...

[13 May 1469] To Thomas Grey, esquire. In money paid to his own hands, in advance, as well for the expenses and diet of Henry VI, late de facto et non de jure King of England, being in the Tower of London, as for the expenses and diet of the said Thomas and others dwelling within the said Tower for safe custody of the said Henry ...

[24 June 1471] To Sir Richard Radcliffe, esquire.[22] In money paid to his own hands, for the expenses of Henry, late de facto et non de jure King of England, then within the Tower; viz., on the 23rd day of April last past ...

[1471] To Robert Cousin, to provide robes, beds, and other necessaries, for Henry of Windsor, in the Tower of London ... [23]

[1471] To Robert Radcliffe and William Sayer, esquires. In money paid, etc., as well for their wages and daily provision, as for the diet and wages of thirty-six other persons ... attending at the Tower for the safe custody of the said Henry, viz., for seven days, the first day commencing on the 29th day of April in the 11th year of the present king ...

[1471] To William Sayer, esquire. In money paid to him in advance, for the diet of the said Henry and eleven persons attending the Tower for his safe custody ...

[1471] To William Sayer, esquire. In money paid to him for the expenses and diet of the said Henry and ten persons, attending in the Tower for the custody of the said Henry; viz., for fourteen days, the first day beginning the 11th May last past ... [24]

William Sayer (or Sayre) of Copford near Colchester was a Lieutenant of the Tower and had been a servant of Edward IV for at least ten years. His service correlates with the information in the *Issues Rolls* above, although the accounting period postdates May 1471 (as might be expected) as Henry's keepers were paid in arrears.[25] As a purveyor and gaoler, William's service was not limited to the ex-king's basic needs, but he was one of the last to attend the king before his death. There are several other payments to him (only) for attending to the 'late' king during his confinement, proving that Henry was taken care of while safely closeted away under guard in the Tower. Edward IV undoubtedly approved Henry's safe keeping as his security was paramount while dealing with Queen Margaret and her son in the west. Therefore, it is quite striking that King Edward was so accommodating to his counterpart, unless he had other plans for Henry on his return to London.

Most likely, Henry VI was psychologically distressed while he was confined in the Tower. His daily routines of mass and prayer were observed as they had always been, according to the sources, but no doubt Henry was suffering mentally due to his long spells of imprisonment since 1465. As documented, William Kimberly, a chaplain attending Henry's spiritual needs by Edward's command, was employed between 1465 and 1467. As can be seen, he was paid for his services in 1468, and he may have continued to attend the king unpaid at the time of the siege, although there is no record of this in the *Issues Rolls*.[26] Henry was closely guarded by servants of King Edward, who came and went, but other than this, he was likely isolated, and only a glimpse of Henry's character can be extracted from the contemporary record. Poignantly, he is mentioned in *John Blacman's Memoir* while he was in confinement, and this odd digression betrays something of Henry's feelings about the divine rule of kings and his God-given right to rule as he wished. It also expresses his concern for his subjects despite being imprisoned, and explains that there was at least one window in his apartments from which he could see the Tower moat:

When the king was shut up in the Tower, he saw a woman on his right hand from his window trying to drown a little child, and [he] warned her by a messenger not to commit such a crime and sin hateful to God; and she, rebuked by this reproof, desisted from the deed she had begun. Also, when this King Henry was asked during his imprisonment in the Tower why he had unjustly claimed and possessed the crown of England for so many years, he would answer thus: 'My father was King of England, and peaceably possessed the crown for the whole time of his reign. And his father and my grandfather were kings of the same realm. And I, a child in the cradle, was peaceably and without any protest crowned and approved as king by the whole realm, and wore the crown of England some forty years, and each and all of my lords did me royal homage and plighted me their faith, as was also done to my predecessors. Wherefore I too can say with the psalmist: The lot is fallen unto me in a fair ground: yea, I have a goodly heritage. For my right help is of the Lord, who preserveth them that are true of heart.'[27]

However, apart from the portrayal of a 'saintly' and accidental king whose crown was thrust upon him, according to John Blacman, the above first-hand knowledge reveals another hidden truth. If the above description of the window story is correct, this supports the theory that Henry VI was kept, and died, in the Lanthorn Tower (according to the Guildhall Records), as it was newly furnished by the queen, and the most advantageous place to view the Tower moat. The Wakefield Tower was (and still is) appreciably lower than the medieval Lanthorn Tower, and from the former, the outer moat is obscured by St Thomas's Tower and the outer curtain walls in front of it. Therefore, according to the evidence, this also proves the plaque denoting where Henry died in the Wakefield Tower is in the wrong place.[28]

As for the Bastard of Fauconberg's fate, his mission to rescue King Henry seemed doomed to failure. London Bridge, Southwark and some eastern suburbs of the city were in flames. It was probably not easy to see across the river, but Fauconberg's Kentish rebels, so full of themselves before the siege, were soon dispersed into the countryside. Some headed for Blackheath, including Fauconberg, and many rallied there, waiting to see what would happen next. However, it was clear that any further southern assaults on the city were now out of the question, and the fate of London rested with the Kentish captains Spicing and Quentin across the Thames. Here another great battle was raging. And at the same time as Fauconberg attacked London Bridge, at least two more large assaults were launched on the city walls and gates. As described earlier, thousands of Essex rebels had swarmed into Portsoken Ward looking for justice and tax breaks on their produce, and the siege of London was entering a new and desperate phase. In fact, the battle for the city was poised on a knife edge and the fighting was about to intensify beneath the formidable ramparts of Aldgate and Bishopsgate.

9

The Greatest Jeopardy

At Aldgate, they assaulted in an ill season,
They burnt fair houses, a pity it was to see,
Thus, these false men did open treason,
Supposing evermore to enter into the city,
God and good saints thereof have pity.[1]

✢

At some point before eleven o'clock on 14 May, Fauconberg had ordered Spicing and Quentin to attack the city gates from the east. And from the rebel ships at Blackwall and Radcliffe, professional soldiers of the Calais garrison (some carrying handguns), together with mariners dragging artillery, joined forces with the 3,000 to 5,000 Essex rebels gathering in Portsoken Ward and St Katherine's Wharf near the hospital of the same name.[2]

The *Arrivall* tells us this 'great fellowship' went over the Thames in Fauconberg's ships. However, it is more likely the rebel vessels only landed the 300 men of the Calais garrison, commanded by Sir George Brooke, Sir Walter Wrottesley and Sir Geoffrey Gate, rather than the whole Essex contingent, which had been gathering strength to the east of the city since at least the beginning of May. Undoubtedly, the Essex rebels would have marched overland from those parts of their county that saw King Edward's government as corrupt and unfair, and the Flemish beer houses and inns along the Thames became their first target. As explained, these were likely burnt on the orders of Sir Geoffrey Gate, who had focussed his attention on the same quarter during the Kentish rebellion of 1470. It was an act of terrorism that had worked well before to achieve Henry VI's 'readeption', and it was a direct economic slight on the city's merchant class. But either way, all the rebel forces were soon ordered to concentrate on the city gates while Fauconberg simultaneously assaulted London Bridge with the men of Kent.

No doubt, some of the Essex rebels were little more than peasants armed with billhooks, mattocks, clubs and any agricultural equipment with a blade they could lay their hands on. The Calais garrison provided the backbone, and its professional men-at-arms, wearing armour and equipped with poleaxes and swords, would have resembled a typical Wars of the Roses contingent. Fauconberg's sailors may have constructed scaling ladders to help them assault the walls, although there is no contemporary evidence of this apart from graphic depictions in the *Arrivall* and Besançon MS.1168.[3] However, aside from the apparent mob-handed approach of the Essex rebels, this eastern attack on the city would prove to be the most dangerous of the siege and extremely hard-fought, according to the written evidence.

On the north bank of the Thames, the man simply known as Spicing took command of half of the Essex men and led them towards Bishopsgate, and Quentin formed the other half beside St Botolph's Church, ready to assault Aldgate in force. We are told that makeshift bulwarks had been set up before the city gates, and they were likely manned by citizen militias equipped with artillery. Fields of fire had been previously cleared by Lord Dudley, Constable of the Tower, so guns could sweep the rebel attacks. Anthony Lord Rivers was in command of the Yorkist garrison at the Tower, and Henry Bourchier, Earl of Essex assumed responsibility for the defence of Bishopsgate. The Lord Mayor, John Stockton, the aldermen and other city wardens organised their militias at each gate and manned the city walls. According to contemporaries, Thomas Urswick, the City Recorder, and Robert Basset defended Aldgate while other officials took responsibility for their own wards, including that of London Bridge, which was at this time hard-pressed and partly in flames. Earl Rivers protected the royal family in the Tower and fortified the Postern Gate, the only other entrance to the city below Aldgate. However, with thousands of rebels massing to the east and north of the city walls, the threat of assault must have been a sight to snap anyone's nerves. The pro-Yorkist *Arrivall* agreed with the seriousness of the situation in London, clearly stating that the city 'as they all wrote, was likely to stand in the greatest jeopardy that [it] ever stood'.[4] However, experience was at hand, we are told:

> To the citizens and defence of the city came the Earl of Essex and many knights, squires, gentlemen, and yeomen, right well arrayed, who [showed] great diligence in ordering the citizens, first to prepare and ordain for the defence and surety of the said city and people thereof where it was necessary, and [second, to] prepare how and where they might best issue out upon [the rebels] and put them from their purpose. By which ordering of gentlemen and lord's servants in every part, the citizens were greatly encouraged to set sharply upon them with one whole intent, where else it had been likely they should not have willed to have done so much thereto as was done. For, as it is aforesaid, [a] great number of the city were there that with right good will would have been suffered to have fallen to mischief and robbery with the [rebels].[5]

Professional soldiers such as Henry Bourchier, Earl of Essex, Lord Duras, Lord Dinham, Sir John Scott and one of the king's esquires, Robert Radcliffe, supported Earl Rivers against the rebels, and some of these men would have commanded personal retainers who were hired by contracts of indenture. However, professional soldiering was not an ongoing career in the Wars of the Roses, and retainers were not soldiers indefinitely. Indeed, fighting was sporadic in the civil wars, and England did not have a standing army. Many retainers were sheriffs, justices of the peace and held other county offices to support their associations with great lords. Others were knights who served leading nobles in the hierarchy of feudalism that, in the fifteenth century, led to paid and unpaid service sealed by official contracts of indenture. Yet other veterans had served in France and may have been experienced in siege warfare. As for the citizen militias mixed in with the gentry, they needed additional support, or why else would the *Arrivall* mention their need for encouragement against what otherwise would have been an unruly mob clamouring for attention?[6]

Contrary to popular opinion, the Bastard of Fauconberg's rebellion was not wholly comprised of simple peasants from Kent, Essex, Surrey and parts of Sussex. It is clear from later indictments that competent soldiers (and captains) led them – some from the Calais garrison.[7] In the fifteenth century, the garrison played a pivotal role as a formidable mercenary force, shaping the outcome of battles and exerting influence abroad and in England. The strategic port town of Calais was a crucial English stronghold, and it served as a gateway for communication, the wool trade and military operations on the continent. Composed primarily of professional soldiers, the garrison was usually captained by a prominent noble or military commander. The captain was responsible for overseeing the day-to-day operations, maintaining discipline and ensuring the security of the last English stronghold in France. Many garrison soldiers were experienced veterans who had fought in previous conflicts. They were well versed in the art of war, were skilled in using various weapons, including artillery, and were in a constant state of military readiness. However, the garrison was also known to have fickle loyalties, often swayed by changing political winds. Given their status as mercenaries, soldiers were not bound by strong ties to a specific noble, House or cause. They were more inclined to support the king or lords who provided them with generous wages and benefits. As a result, the garrison's allegiance shifted throughout the Wars of the Roses as different factions vied for their support. Prompt and full payment was essential to prevent the soldiers from mutinying or seeking alternative employers. Indeed, some of their commanders were extremely mercenary, in the true sense of the word, and frequently supported rebellion to acquire wage arrears. For instance, in 1461, a Lancastrian garrison in Hammes Castle near Calais was besieged by one of the defenders of London, Lord Duras, Marshal of Calais. In July of the same year, Duras and others were empowered to negotiate the castle's surrender terms. Hammes was handed over at the end of the month only after the defenders had first received £250 – a large sum of money in 1461 – which was doubtless their way of recouping earnings when the throne had changed hands after the battle of Towton.[8]

An extensive list of some of the Calais men who fought at the siege of London can be gleaned from their subsequent pardons, recorded in the *Issues Rolls* from 9 August 1471. Along with the pardons of Sir Walter Wrottesley of Calais, knight, and Sir Geoffrey Gate, the Marshal of Calais (and merchant of the Staple), are the names of those who were employed to protect the port and the surrounding strongpoints of Hammes, Guisnes and Rysbank. Many of the garrison in August 1471 had acquired several aliases, while lower ranks are described only as 'soldeour'– a position that entitled them to be paid between 6d and 12d as a foot archer or horseman. Knights and men-at-arms were paid more, while important Calais officials were waged separately. The Master Porter (or the Receiver of Calais) was John Courtenay of Powderham Castle after the siege of London. Other soldiers were aldermen and clerks who could negotiate wages independently. A lieutenant could be paid as much as 2s per day.[9] However, only thirty-five of the garrison were given pardons out of a possible 300 men after Fauconberg's rebellion. Therefore, many soldiers may have evaded justice or, being too valuable to prosecute, continued their employment despite being treasonous, proving how invaluable the garrison town was to Yorkist and Lancastrian governments no matter how rebellious its soldiers became.[10]

However, it is apparent from a Londoner's scornful description of the 'peasants' in Fauconberg's army that the Essex men were the most ill-equipped and unruly of the rebels. As *Warkworth's Chronicle* records, no standard defensive equipment of the Wars of the Roses is mentioned. According to various chroniclers, no padded jacks (jackets) or brigandines (plated or studded coats) and no plate armour (harness) were worn by the Essex rebels. Their only defence appears to have been their anger against the mayor for their food tax woes. Their rallying cry seems to have been partly legitimate, but many rebels were no doubt intent on robbery and similar activities, although this may have been a biased Yorkist viewpoint.

Along with shipmen and mariners, they were likely the ones who led away fifty of the hundred or so oxen which a London butcher had accidentally left grazing in a meadow near the Tower. We are told that the meat was destined for the queen's household, but no doubt it was slaughtered and roasted by the rebels to accompany the ale they had recently looted from the Dutch inns on St Katherine's Wharf.[11] For this reason, one can only imagine the rebel resolve to face the arrows and gunstones shot from the city walls and bulwarks set up before the gates. Some were undoubtedly oblivious to the danger, and likely had little or no idea what a battle was like or the injuries that could result from arrows, artillery and bladed weapons. For those in London it was the same story, but the mayor, lords and citizens could only do their duty and wait with bated breath for the attacks to come. They were, after all, defending their families, homes and livelihoods against a rebel onslaught.

As previously discussed, the attacks on London Bridge and the city walls appear to have been well coordinated, and there was a spate of renewed arson by the rebels in and around the gates intended to entice the citizens from their defences and cause confusion:

> And afterwards, on the 14th day of May being Tuesday the eleventh year aforesaid, about eleven o'clock in the morning of the said Tuesday, the said Kentish seamen and other rebels made an attack with great force and set fire to thirteen tenements upon London bridge. The said Kentish seamen and other [Essex men] to the number of 5,000 persons also made an attack from the Thames upon the gates of Aldgate and Bishopsgate and set fire to divers tenements.[12]

The defenders under the Earl of Essex at Bishopsgate held their ground. We hear nothing in the sources about Aldersgate and Cripplegate other than that they were also attacked and burnt. But there may have been a temptation to break out by the citizens as the bulwarks were overrun and 'the citizens sallied out of the gate to make a stout resistance' against the rebels.[13] The fighting was desperate, we are told by *The Great London Chronicle*, and like all medieval battles, it would have been confused, with hardly any identification between friend or foe. According to the *Arrivall*, rebel archers and artillery located before Bishopsgate bombarded the city at will, killing many Londoners as they tried to prevent Spicing's men from setting fire to the gates:

> [This other] party went to Bishopsgate, hoping to have entered there by another assault, where they shot guns and arrows into the city and did much harm and hurt. And, at the last, set fire upon the gates, for to have burnt them, and so trusting to have entered at large.[14]

The situation became even more critical at Aldgate as the rebels pushed forward en masse towards the makeshift redoubt. The original writer of *The Great Chronicle of London* (compiled by Robert Fabyan) may have been an eyewitness to the siege as the author even recalled what type of defensive protection two of the officials wore when the rebels advanced and stormed the gatehouse:

> The Essex men assailed the gates upon the east and fired the houses near unto the said gates and won the bulwark at Aldgate and drove the citizens within the portcullis and pressed so fast after that five or six entered with the citizens, of which some were slain with the falling of the portcullis and the others were soon slain within the gate. Then [there] was a mighty shot of handguns and a sharp shot of arrows which did more hurt to the portcullis and to the stonework of the gate than to any of the enemy on either side. Then the alderman of that ward, being in a black jack or doublet of [studs] named Robert Basset, and with him the Recorder of the City called Mr [Thomas] Urswick likewise apparelled, commanded in the name of God and Saint George the portcullis to be up drawn.[15]

The Postern Gate

According to primary sources, Aldgate was equipped with a double portcullis that was instrumental in saving London. The original gatehouse had two towers, but there is no mention of a drawbridge, which seems consistent with other city gates apart from the Postern Gate, which Stow records bridged the Houndsditch near the Tower.[16] If the outwork before Aldgate was overrun by the rebels during the first assault, this further proves that the bulwarks were useless and that a desperate situation now faced the citizens and their leaders inside the walls. If the gatehouse was captured, the rebels would flood into the city, and their next target would be pillaging London at will. Freeing Henry VI would have been secondary to those rebels set on a crime spree, and this was, as we have seen, the main reason why most Londoners were willing to put their lives at risk.

The Ghent manuscript of the *Arrivall* also illustrates rebel handgunners climbing ladders to gain access to the city, and even though the sources mention the use of handguns in the siege, it is more likely that these were fired at the gate itself, as recorded by *The Great Chronicle of London*, and not from ladders propped against 18ft-high walls. The

Houndsditch (not depicted in the Ghent illustration) would have also hampered this operation. Indeed, the gate itself was the only eastern access to the city, thus making the ladders apocryphal and likely drawn by an artist without any idea of London topography.

The author of *The Great Chronicle of London* recalls that the Aldgate portcullis and stonework were damaged by guns when the rebels rushed the bastion, and the situation became so desperate and confused that the citizens were pushed back. As the rebels entered under the archway, some were separated from the rest and trapped between the two heavy wooden gates as they fell. Lacking support, they were soon butchered on the spot. Other rebels were crushed when the second portcullis fell on top of them, according to an eyewitness. However, the city was not out of danger yet, and one chronicle in particular makes it clear that some rebels succeeded in taking the gatehouse, causing the city fathers to call for reinforcements:

> For at the first brunt, when the rebels had won [the] said bulwark and some had entered in the gate, anon word was brought to the mayor that Aldgate was won and a great multitude of the rebels [had] entered, wherefore the mayor with the sheriffs which rode from gate to gate and place to place to see the ordering of the people, in all haste with a trumpet called the commons to him which might be spared, and so sped them unto the said gate.[17]

After the above order was given by Mayor Stockton (who quickly supported the gatehouse), the fallen portcullis was 'up drawn' by Robert Basset and Thomas Urswick, who then urged their men forward to eject the rebels. Now supported by additional reinforcements from the city, they pushed the rebels back 'the which was shortly done, and thereupon they issued out with their people and with sharp shot and fierce fight [they] put their enemies back as far as Saint Botolph's church'.[18]

Both colourful illustrations in the *Arrivall* and the Ghent Library manuscript depict this spirited charge from the gate by the defenders, albeit in a chivalric style, with both sides wearing full armour and riding horses, which can hardly have been the case. Arrows are flying, men with burning torches can be seen setting houses alight, handguns belch with smoke after being fired and rebels in the foreground are being speared to death by Basset and Urswick's men. The depiction has all the hallmarks of the siege condensed into one colourful and bloody tableau.[19] However, something else likely prompted the rebel retreat to St Botolph's Church, other than the courage of the defenders, and this involved a sally from the Postern Gate below Aldgate, recorded by the author of the *Arrivall*:

> And so, after the continuing of much shot of guns and arrows a great while upon both parties, the Earl Rivers, who was with the queen in the Tower of London, gathered unto him a fellowship right well chosen, and followed by four or five hundred men issued out at a postern upon them, and came upon the Kentish men being about the assaulting of Aldgate, and mightily laid upon them with arrows, and upon them [hand-to-hand], and so killed and took many of them, driving them from the same gate to the waterside. Yet nonetheless, in three places, were fires burning all at once. The mayor, aldermen, and many of the said city were anon in their harness and parted their fellowship into divers parts, as they thought most behoveful, but a great part of the citizens were at Aldgate, and with them many gentlemen and yeomen, which all made the defence [as] they best might, and shot many guns, and arrows, among them. But for them, the Kentish men spared [none] to assail at both the gates so that the said lord and citizens determined in themselves to form in good array and to issue out upon them and put them to flight and discomfiture.[20]

The *Croyland Chronicle* also recorded a similar story giving credit to Earl Rivers, who eased the pressure on the gatehouse by leading the attack from the Postern Gate, which took the rebels completely by surprise:

> This they were especially aided in doing by a sudden and unexpected sally, which was made by Antony, Earl Rivers, from the Tower of London. Falling at the head of his horsemen, upon the rear of the enemy while they were making furious assaults upon the gate above-mentioned, he afforded the Londoners an opportunity of opening the city gates and engaging hand-to-hand with the foe.[21]

Now attacked on both fronts, the rebels before Aldgate retreated, and it seems those at Bishopsgate did the same, hoping not to get cut off by

Earl Rivers and his men. The Earl of Essex led this counter-attack, we are told, from the northern gatehouse, and because of this concerted effort, the rebels finally broke ranks and fled:

> The Earl of Essex, and also the aldermen.
> At Bishopsgate together they met,
> And out there [they] sallied like manly men.
> They beat them down, no man might him let,
> Freshly on their enemies that day did they fight.[22]

In the fifteenth century, a flank or rear attack was good enough to win any medieval battle, and if it was part of a coordinated plan during the siege of London once the rebels were engaged, the credit for this victory must be attributed to Rivers, whose cavalry charge on unsuspecting footmen was intended to break the deadlock before Aldgate. However, it is more likely that Earl Rivers *supported* the main push from the two gates, which broke the rebels' morale and will to carry on with the siege.

As explained, the Postern Gate on the Tower moat's north bank was probably an insignificant bastion in 1440. It had fallen into disrepair due to its location at the southern end of the Houndsditch, and John Stow, in 1598, recorded that the gatehouse was never again built of stone, although its foundations can still be seen today. The Postern was in a sad state of repair in the sixteenth century 'built of timber, lath and loam' and it was likely in a similar condition in 1471 when only a drawbridge protected it from direct attack.[23] However, during the siege, it is inconceivable that a field of fire did not cover the gate from the nearby Tower ramparts, which no doubt dissuaded the rebels from attacking it in force. And this seems to have been why Rivers succeeded in surprising the rebels at Aldgate. In short, the charge was unforeseen.

The surprise sally from the gate by the earl won the battle for the Yorkists, according to the *Arrivall*, and it seems strangely fitting that the queen's brother should be the one to triumph against the odds. However, *The Great Chronicle of London* tells a story clearly aimed at inflating civic pride and the tenacity of one alderman in particular:

> By that time, the Lieutenant of the Tower [Rivers] was coming with a fresh company which discomforted the rebels in such wise that they

gave back more and more. Then the aforesaid Robert Basset laid on fast about him as he from the beginning had done and comforted his people in such manner that there was slain many of the said rebels and shortly after put [the rest] unto flight, whom the said Robert Basset with the other citizens chased unto Mile End and from thence some to Poplar, some to Stratford, some to Stepney and so unto every place two miles about those parts of the city. By reason of the chase, they slew many of the said rebels and took many more of them prisoners which chase was not only followed by the said Basset and his company but also by other aldermen and commoners who were deputed to keep other parts of the city.[24]

As in most battles of any era, and especially those of the Wars of the Roses, the heaviest casualties usually occurred in the rout. Even the men of the Calais garrison were caught up in the general retreat across country and back to Blackwall and Radcliffe, where Fauconberg's fleet was moored. Many rebels were killed trying to board their ships, we are told. Some drowned in the Thames as the rest set sail without them, and everyone from the city, including Rivers, the Earl of Essex, Ralph Jocelyn and Robert Basset, joined the pursuit of fleeing rebels who were now desperate to escape punishment for high treason.

It is variously estimated that up to a thousand men were killed in the siege and rout. However, this number can only be estimated as the figure was inflated, as usual, by various chroniclers. The pro-Yorkist *Arrivall* quotes that 'about 3,000 and more fell in the chase and [the citizens] slew more than 700 of them. Many were captured, and after hanged for treason; the remnant went to the waterside and took to their boats, and went to their ships, and over to the other side [of the Thames] again.'[25] Other rebels stood their ground and shot guns at the pursuing citizens, according to *Vitellius A XVI*.[26] It is also recorded some rebels were taken prisoner and 'ransomed like Frenchmen' – an interesting turn of phrase considering the brutality and unchivalrous nature of the Wars of the Roses.[27] Therefore, collateral damage and civic casualties may never be known for sure, although various indictments state the names and trades of certain rebels who suffered execution or fines for their treason.[28]

According to *The Great Chronicle of London*, the city officials were not about to offer mercy. The urban medieval poor became prime targets as they scrambled back to their homes in Essex, and it is recorded that Spicing and Quentin were captured and beheaded soon after the siege. Their severed heads were set on pikes above Aldgate, although this necessary evil may have coincided with the numerous hangings and executions of the rebels at various roadsides in Kent. As for the rest of the rebel leaders, on the other side of the Thames, Fauconberg, Nicholas Faunt and the rest of his Canterbury rebels had determined to stay put at Blackheath. Fauconberg still had a large fleet of ships, and while he may have been aware of the disasters at Aldgate and Bishopsgate soon after they happened, it appears he was not about to surrender despite the persistence of Ralph Jocelyne, who was still rounding up Kentish rebels who had not formed up with Fauconberg on the heath:

> In which past time the Bastard, who had assailed other places upon the waters side and little prevailed, hearing of the discomfiture of his accomplices, withdrew him toward his ships. Then Ralph Jocelyne, alderman, with a good band of men, followed him along the waters side and so chased him until he came beyond Radcliffe, and in his return homeward [he] encountered with such as had fled from Aldgate and slew and took many prisoners.[29]

However, despite the general rout, Thomas Fauconberg remained resolute despite the advice of Nicholas Faunt, the belligerent Mayor of Canterbury, who tried to persuade him to abandon his enterprise before he was apprehended and captured in the retreat. That Fauconberg was not captured proves there was still hope, and the fact that he managed to rally the rebels on Blackheath that evening demonstrates the point. Those who survived the Aldgate and Bishopsgate assaults were soon ferried across the Thames in ships, and it was almost as if a new attack on London was contemplated the next day. Clearly, some of Fauconberg's captains did not want to give up so easily either. They had all committed treason and were wanted men, and they may have persuaded many Kentish diehards to remain with them at Blackheath, including those who were later indicted for their part in the rebellion. Therefore, for the present at least, Thomas Fauconberg and what remained of his host occupied Blackheath for three days, during which time several messengers arrived from London.

Fauconberg's delay may have been intentional and provocative, but it was ill advised. The advance guard of King Edward's army, commanded by the Duke of Gloucester, was nearing London, and Fauconberg was probably made aware of this by Richmond Herald and other messengers, who rode into his camp and tried to negotiate terms. We do not know the exact dates the couriers were sent or arrived at Blackheath, but C.F. Richmond describes who they were and that their messages must have been read before Fauconberg's final retreat on 18 May, or he may have submitted to Edward's mercy sooner. Unfortunately, we can only guess what the letters said, as none have survived. Richmond Herald was paid for his services on 24 June 1471, and Earl Rivers sent a personal letter to Fauconberg carried by Robert Baxter, one of his servants, with surrender terms. This communication was followed by a third letter, from the Archbishop of Canterbury, advocating a peaceable settlement. However, this note and others were likely written to delay Fauconberg rather than strike religious fear into him and no doubt Thomas acted accordingly.[30]

Undoubtedly, Thomas's main concern was that King Edward was marching on London with a large army, and the Duke of Gloucester, with 1,500 men, was even closer. To delay meant Fauconberg would become isolated and captured along with his fleet in the Thames. But also, Thomas knew that to remain at Blackheath meant certain death when Gloucester reached the city. Therefore, he soon made plans to slip away from the rebels despite being offered a general pardon if he handed over his ships and himself to the king. Maybe Thomas was waiting for a more official legal document to arrive signed by Edward, although this cannot be confirmed. However, what is certain is that Fauconberg's large fleet was his main chance of escaping the headman's axe, and evidently, on 18 May, he fled from Blackheath, hoping to reach Sandwich. En route, he ordered his ships in the Thames to sail before pressing on with the Calais garrison to Rochester. The next day, Fauconberg, Sir Geoffrey Gate and Sir Thomas Wrottesley rode hard for the coast, where everyone except Thomas crossed to Calais. In short, Thomas was deserted by his followers, although he may have decided to await a final decision from King Edward at Sandwich before fleeing England for good.

As for the thousands of common rebels, they were left leaderless and had no alternative but to disperse back to their homes or go into hiding, fearing reprisals:

The Greatest Jeopardy

When the Kentishmen heard of that affray,
Like masterless men, they went away,
Early in the morning, or it were day,
Through corners and hedges resorted into Kent,
They vanished away as their tails had been brent.[31]

Meanwhile, in London, barrels of wine were issued to the defenders of the city and those who had chased the rebels back to their ships and as far as Mile End.[32] No doubt the still smoking capital was being attended to by the citizens. The houses on London Bridge and the suburbs were likely still on fire, but luckily, the citizens could now await the arrival of reinforcements led by the Duke of Gloucester, followed by King Edward with a massive force, to chastise the rebels.

As for the nobles, they could be happy with their victory and the rewards that might come with it. But the two-day siege had been a desperate affair that could have gone either way. If Aldgate or Bishopsgate had fallen and the rebels had run amok in the city, the siege would have been over, considering the size of Fauconberg's forces. King Henry would have been released from the Tower, and the Yorkists would have been put at a grave disadvantage. The repercussions would have been devastating for Edward and England. However, the fact that the Bastard of Fauconberg did not free Henry from captivity has prompted many historians to disregard the siege of London for hundreds of years, forgetting that it had dire consequences for Henry VI, who still awaited his fate in the Tower.

10

Crushing the Seed

Thy troubled life and great vexation,
With patience that thou had therein,
And thy constancy in contemplation,
Has made the Heaven for to win.[1]

⁜

The death of Henry VI in the Tower of London on the night of 21–22 May 1471 is one of those Wars of the Roses cold cases that historians have revisited many times. Indeed, for some writers, including Shakespeare, Richard, Duke of Gloucester's brutal murder of King Henry sits alongside his many other supposed crimes: namely the stabbing of Edward, Prince of Wales at the battle of Tewkesbury, the drowning of his brother Clarence in a barrel of wine in the Tower, the poisoning of his wife, Anne Neville, at Westminster, and the infamous suffocation of his two young nephews sometime in 1483. All these supposed 'murders' have their place in Tudor propaganda and Shakespearian myth, but none can be conclusively proven by contemporary sources. There is only probability, or as Horace Walpole suggested in 1768, historic doubts.[2] However, add to this list of murders Gloucester's judicial executions of Earl Rivers, Lord Grey and Sir Thomas Vaughan at Pontefract Castle in 1483, not to mention the sudden beheading of William Lord Hastings the same year, and Richard's supposed 'crimes' begin to resemble a black comedy, or more seriously, a character assassination intended to tarnish Gloucester's name and the House of York.

Thankfully, modern historians have successfully debunked most of the accusations against Richard, citing contemporary sources, and as for others, they would simply fail to stand up in court. Henry's son, Prince Edward, was 'taken fleeing to the town wards and slain in the field' at the battle of Tewkesbury, and not killed by Richard personally, as the Tudors would have us believe.[3] The deteriorating relationship between Edward IV and his brother Clarence was the main reason for the latter's execution in 1478. Clarence was about to commit treason again, we are told, and Domenico Mancini reported that it was Richard, not Edward, whose 'feelings moved by anguish' caused him not 'to dissimulate so well' after Clarence's demise. Richard was heard to say, 'that one day he would avenge his brother's death', a remark that (if true) lays blame directly on Edward IV, who had the authority to order Clarence's execution, whereas Richard did not.[4] As for Queen Anne, Richard's wife, she seems to have contracted a debilitating illness in March 1485. According to the *Croyland Chronicle*, Richard 'entirely shunned her bed, declaring that it was by the advice of his physicians that he did so', an indication of contagion rather than poisoning, one would think.[5] Lastly, the mystery of the Princes in the Tower is an ongoing case even today (and it is not the subject of this book), although detailed work by P. Langley likely proves the princes lived beyond Richard's death.[6] Therefore, this only leaves Gloucester's political executions and the murder of Henry VI to deal with, although controversy will always dog Richard's public persona while ever Shakespeare is played to the masses.

As Lord Protector, Richard had the authority to punish traitors after Edward's sudden death in 1483. The queen's family, the Woodvilles, were his main targets due to their political manoeuvring for power. Cause enough, one would think, to order any number of executions, including that of Earl Rivers, Grey, Vaughan and even Edward IV's best friend, Lord Hastings, if they were suspected of high treason. As we have seen, Anthony Earl Rivers had been the star of the siege of London, and Gloucester may have resented his celebrity, especially if he thought the earl was lauded for saving Edward IV's throne and earmarked for Admiral of England. However, Richard, as Lord Protector, seems to have reacted in a more level-headed manner against the Woodvilles in 1483 as they closed ranks around Edward's heir. The survival of the Yorkist dynasty was at stake, as it was in 1471 and during Buckingham's rebellion. Therefore, Richard acted accordingly, and not unlike any administrator would have done in the same situation. However, to trace his association with Henry VI's death, we must revisit Coventry on 14 May while Fauconberg's siege was raging in London.

After the battle of Tewkesbury, King Edward was relatively free of his main rivals. He had won a second great victory, but Kentish insurgency remained a constant threat to the Yorkist regime. Like other Yorkists, Richard likely blamed Henry VI for Fauconberg's rebellion, and knew all his brother's victories would count for nothing if the ex-king was recaptured. A host of secret Lancastrians would emerge from the woodwork ready to crush the Yorkist achievement with royal approval and this may have weighed on Gloucester's mind. However, Richard (then aged 18) may not have blamed Henry directly for living. Indeed, considering Gloucester's outwardly pious nature, he may have regarded the ex-king as, first and foremost, a deeply religious man, judging by his later actions regarding Henry's reburial at Windsor Castle in 1484. But apart from this, the shadow of an alternative king still hung over the House of York, and after many years of confinement, Henry VI remained a catalyst for civil war despite his frailty. Therefore, we may ask, did Richard have a deep-seated motive to kill Henry VI of his own volition when he arrived in London before his brother in May 1471?

Noting Richard's chivalrous character and his past service to Edward IV, it would have been out of character for him to disobey his brother. Indeed, up until 1471 he had served him faithfully. But according to sources, Richard was the king's choice to face Fauconberg's rebels first. Therefore, on 14 May at Coventry, he was commanded to lead the king's vaward that would ride to London, hoping to lift the siege. After being given this authority, the plan was for his brother Edward to march out the next day with the main Yorkist force, but it is certain Richard's detachment of approximately 1,500 men arrived in London well after the siege ended. If Gloucester was welcomed into the city on or about 16 May, he may have been surprised by the absence of rebels, and although news of his coming may have led to Thomas Fauconberg's flight from Blackheath a few days later, Richard may have felt robbed of personal victory.

After consulting with the Yorkist nobles and the Lord Mayor of London, Richard would have secured the city with his additional troops. He would definitely have visited Blackheath and ridden along

Crushing the Seed

the Thames to make sure the rebel host and Fauconberg's fleet had dispersed. No doubt he would have also shared news of Edward's victory at Tewkesbury with other Yorkist lords and Queen Elizabeth before commending the city fathers on their excellent work during the siege. Gloucester may have also visited Henry VI, still lodged under guard in the Lanthorn or Wakefield Tower, although how much the king was told about his son's death and the Lancastrian defeat at Tewkesbury cannot be confirmed. As previously stated, at least a dozen people attended Henry under the supervision of William Sayer and Robert Radcliffe. Therefore, it is not illogical to assume the ex-king may have heard rumours of the Lancastrian defeat while imprisoned, as according to the *Issues Rolls*, Sayer and Radcliffe received payments for Henry's attendants after the battle of Tewkesbury from 11 May 1471.[7] Other payments are recorded after this date, including one for 40s to Robert Radcliffe for Henry's expenses.[8] However, after this last entry, there is an awkward silence in the *Issues Rolls*, and instead, in the *Arrivall*, we hear only of King Edward's triumphal entry into London on 21 May, not about Henry's confinement:

> The king [Edward] this season, well accompanied and mightily with great lords, and in substance all the noblemen of the land, with many other able men, well arrayed for war, to the number of 30,000 horsemen, came to the City of London soon after the dissembling of the Kentish host, on the 21st day of May, the Tuesday, where he was honourably received [by] all the people, the mayor, aldermen, and many other worshipful men, citizens of the said city. At the meeting of them, the king dubbed knights, the mayor, the recorder, diverse aldermen, with other worshipful [officers] of the said City of London, which had manfully and honourably acquitted themselves against the Bastard and his cruel host, honouring, and rewarding them with the order of his good love and grace, for their true acquittal, as they had right well and truly deserved that time.[9]

Although the actual strength of Edward's relieving force in the *Arrivall* is highly doubtful, the king likely led a large army into London on the morning of 21 May.[10] The Duke of Clarence was with him, and other notable lords, along with Queen Margaret, who was conveyed behind them in a guarded carriage, still no doubt grief-stricken by her son's death and fearful for her own future.

King Edward was received by Mayor Stockton, the city's alderman and other officials, along with a great crowd of people who welcomed the king back to London. As noted above, Edward responded by knighting Stockton and almost half the aldermanic body 'in the field' (outside the city walls). Indeed, the king owed the newly dubbed knights his throne and kingdom. Anthony Earl Rivers and the lords in the city had provided much-needed support in the siege, but it was the city fathers who had organised the citizens and prepared the defences against the rebel attacks. *Warkworth's Chronicle* recorded that the knighting ceremony occurred on 22 May, whereas the *Arrivall* states that the investiture took place before Aldersgate on Tuesday 21 May, which is more believable given the *Arrivall* is likely an eyewitness account.

The king made knights of John Stockton, Ralph Verney, Richard Leigh, John Young, William Taylor, George Ireland, John Stoker, Matthew Philipp, William Hampton, Thomas Stalbrook, John Crosby and Thomas Urswick for their good service. Other officials may also have been knighted at the time, including Bartholomew James, John Ward and Robert Basset, who all accompanied the army through Aldersgate 'with trumpets and clarions' playing and banners waving, to the delight of the citizens who were no doubt glad to see King Edward in the city rather than the rebels.

At St Paul's, the king, along with the dukes of Gloucester, Clarence and many other nobles, knelt and made offerings to God, thanking him for their recent victories, and soon after, the king was reunited with Queen Elizabeth and his son.[11] All was well in London, it seemed. However, it is recorded in the *Arrivall* that on the same night Edward was celebrating his homecoming, the long-suffering Henry VI died in the Tower.

A glorious martyr

There is no mention in official documents of where Henry died, but the traditional site of the Wakefield Tower is marked today with a commemorative plaque set into the floor of the side chapel claiming, 'By

Tradition Henry VI died here, May 21st, 1471', proving very little. As expected, the main chroniclers who recorded Henry's fate are partisan about the manner and location of his death – the pro-Lancastrian *Warkworth's Chronicle* of July 1472 (and Tudor chroniclers) being the most damning, saying that Henry was cruelly murdered somewhere in the Tower:

> And the same night that King Edward came to London, King Henry, being inward in prison in the Tower of London, was put to death the 21st day of May, on a Tuesday night, between eleven and twelve of the clock, being then at the Tower, the Duke of Gloucester, brother to King Edward, and many other.[12]

Strangely, *The Great Chronicle of London* is silent about the king's death but later points to a possible murderer (Gloucester). However, events were confused in London, or the story was likely constrained until officially compiled. The author of the *Arrivall*, after stressing King Edward's dominance over the Lancastrians, naturally dismisses foul play and attributes Henry's death to something else, which at first seems hard to fathom, coincidental or suggests a cover-up:

> Queen Margaret, herself taken, was brought to the king, and in every party of England, where any commotion was begun for King Henry's party, anon they were rebuked, so that it appeared to every man [that] the said party was extinct and repressed forever, without any manner of hope or relief. The certainty of all which came to the knowledge of the said Henry, late called king, being in the Tower of London, not having, afore that, knowledge of the said matters, [which] he took to so great despite, ire, and indignation, that of pure displeasure and melancholy, he died the 23rd day of the month of May.[13]

Apart from the curious dating of the king's death by the *Arrivall*, the manner of it seems, at first, highly suspicious. Queen Margaret may have delivered all the details of Tewkesbury to her husband, but the idea of the king dying from pure 'displeasure and melancholy' at a later date is hard to swallow, given the alternatives. However, the fact that Henry had just heard about his son's death in battle and the destruction of his

House is shocking enough to warrant further explanation. But considering Henry's mental state and the possibility that his medical condition could have accelerated a fatal reaction, could the official cause of death be correct? Henry took the above news badly (and fatally), we are told by the *Arrivall*, and this is underlined by the statement that he flew into a rage that was totally out of character. He was filled with anger, indignation, displeasure and melancholy, and therefore, this reaction could have triggered a stroke or heart attack where before there was at least some hope of rescue. Of course, Henry may have also feared his own death was imminent, and if he collapsed from a seizure, he may have suffered a fractured skull, a condition that we will return to in due course. However, the same head injury is likely to have occurred if someone had murdered Henry – a line of enquiry that features in every other account of the king's death.

The author of *Warkworth's Chronicle* has it that Henry was simply 'put to death' in the Tower just before midnight on Tuesday 21 May 1471, meaning that the king was formally executed – not slaughtered in a knee-jerk reaction. In other words, it was planned regicide. Richard, Duke of Gloucester 'and many other' were present in the Tower, says the author, and the timings given in the chronicle are quite specific – a fact that cannot be ignored – even though it is well known that *Warkworth's Chronicle* was pro-Lancastrian in tone. As Constable of England, it is hardly surprising that Gloucester was named as the murderer, although interestingly, he is *not directly blamed*. The fact that others were present may also allude to a privately viewed execution, although this cannot be proven. However, what is certain is that the Duke of Gloucester's name is mentioned for a reason, and this clouds the issue further with historians and some Ricardians who wish to completely exonerate Gloucester and pass the blame onto Edward IV, who had the means, the authority and the motive to destroy the Lancastrian dynasty at its roots.

The Milanese ambassador to France, as early as 17 June 1471, also thought Edward IV was guilty, even though his sources may have been dubious:

> King Edward has not chosen to have the custody of King Henry any longer, although he was in some sense innocent, and there was no great fear about his proceedings, the prince, his son, and the Earl of

> Warwick being dead as well as all those who were for him and had any vigour, he has caused King Henry to be secretly assassinated in the Tower, where he was a prisoner. They say he has done the same to the queen, King Henry's wife ... he has, in short, chosen to crush the seed.[14]

Although Queen Margaret was most definitely *alive* at this time (and lived in exile afterwards), we can see from the above extract that the belief abroad was that Edward had ordered Henry's death to wipe out the House of Lancaster permanently. To 'crush the seed' was an apt description of the final solution to England's problems, and who in England would have blamed Edward for removing the biggest thorn in his side? Since at least 1465, when Henry was captured in the north, Edward had kept the ex-king alive despite several revolts and threats to his throne. The Bastard of Fauconberg may have caused the siege of London, but Henry had been the focus of his attacks. Also, the Earl of Warwick marched on London in April 1471 because he thought he could rule England through Henry. Queen Margaret sought to restore Henry to the throne after the battle of Tewkesbury so that her son Edward could rule after he died. Therefore, one would have thought it would have been remiss of Edward IV not to kill the ex-king when he had the chance. However, what would Edward gain by killing a man who was a powerless figurehead?

The contemporary writer and diplomat Philip de Commines, who had previously met Edward IV in exile, was more to the point, claiming the Duke of Gloucester 'immediately after the battle [of Tewkesbury] slew this poor King Henry with his own hand, or caused him to be carried into some private place and stood by while he was killed'.[15] Like most contemporary chroniclers, Commines was in two minds about Gloucester's involvement in Henry's death. Still, he also suggests that Henry may have been put to death by someone else, which need not have been mentioned if he was aiming to lay direct blame on Gloucester or King Edward for Henry's murder.

The taciturn historian John Rous, who died in 1492, was of a similar persuasion to Commines that Richard 'caused others to kill the holy man'.[16] Before 1485, he praises Gloucester, but in a later version of the *Rous Roll*, he identifies Richard as Henry's probable killer, meaning he, too, was unsure and was covering his tracks with the advent of the Tudors. If Edward IV could not be blamed for ordering Henry's death, and Richard was not tasked with the practicalities of a private execution (as Constable of England), then who else was involved? Indeed, who were the 'others' mentioned in the chronicles? Undoubtedly, the Constable of the Tower, the ageing Lord Dudley, would have known that someone was about to be executed on his watch. Was he present at Henry's execution? And who was employed as the executioner – one of his gaolers?

The opinionated continuator of the *Croyland Chronicle* provides some interesting evidence from a religious viewpoint about who Henry's murderer was. But the author is hopelessly vague about the 'tyrant' who 'martyred' the ex-king and leaves the mystery open to question:

> I would pass over in silence the fact that at this period King Henry was found dead in the Tower of London; may God spare and grant time for repentance to the person, whoever he was, who thus dared to lay sacrilegious hands upon the Lord's anointed! Hence, it is he who perpetrated this that has justly earned the title of tyrant, while he who thus suffered has gained that of a glorious martyr.[17]

Apart from the traditional meaning of 'tyrant', the word (*tyrannus* in Latin) also means ruffian, thug or hired bully in Middle English. Therefore, if others of lower status were tasked with Henry's execution and were still alive in 1486 (the date attributed to the above chronicle), this interpretation illuminates an even darker corner of British history that deserves further exploration. Both Edward IV and his brother were dead by 1485, therefore, neither the king nor Gloucester, according to the *Croyland Chronicle*, actually held the murder weapon, although repentance for the supposed 'tyrant' in purgatory is one thing to consider. However, it is clear the person or persons who attacked Henry were still alive when the author of the *Croyland Chronicle* put pen to paper. Therefore, we must look elsewhere for a culprit, sometime in Henry VII's reign.

We already know who may have been responsible for Henry's well-being in the Tower in May 1471 from payments included in the *Issues Rolls*. King Edward's gaolers were all staunch Yorkist supporters, and we know that at least thirty-six individuals attended Henry on 29 April, reducing to eleven and then ten men by 11 May. This last figure may have remained constant over the next ten days (up until 21 May), but the fact is that Henry's guards and servants were reducing. Therefore, were any of these men involved in the king's death? And if so, who wielded the murder weapon?

It will be remembered that Robert Radcliffe, esquire, a kinsman of Sir John Radcliffe, Lord Fitzwalter was among those sent by Earl Rivers to suppress Fauconberg's rising in Kent before it reached London. But aside from this, he was also responsible for King Henry's security along with William Sayer, esquire, who each saw to the king's well-being and daily requirements in the Tower. As discussed, Sayer was one of the last gaolers responsible for 'Henry of Windsor' *that can be dated*, but as mentioned earlier, there was another entry in the *Issues Rolls* before Henry's death that is particularly interesting:

> [1471] To Robert Radcliffe esquire in money delivered to him ... as an advance for the expenses of Henry late in deed and not in right King of England, being within the Tower; advanced by the writ – 40s. He will account.[18]

Despite the above being described as an *advance* given to Radcliffe, this was an exceptionally small payment compared to previous issues, and we may wonder if this was intentionally restricted for another reason.[19] On the other hand, Robert may have expected more money later, although there is no evidence of further payments in official documents. All we know for certain is that money was issued to William Sayer for Henry's expenses from 11 May for fourteen days until 25 May 1471, and that after this date payments disappear from the record. However, when Robert Radcliffe takes over Henry's custody and he receives an advance of 40s before Henry's death, he suddenly becomes a person of interest. Indeed, Robert swiftly rises in Yorkist ranks in 1471. He is appointed Master Porter of Calais, a position of some importance for an esquire, and later becomes closely associated with the Woodville family at court. In 1472, Radcliffe was rewarded with forfeited estates, and even though Edward IV did this openly for his military service rather than anything suspicious concerning Henry VI, we may question his appointments from then on:

21 March 1472. Grant to Robert Radcliffe, esquire, son of John Radcliffe, knight, and the Westminster heirs male of his body, for his good service beyond the seas and in battles in England, of all manors, lands, rents, reversions and services within the realm late of William Fyndern, esquire, son and heir of Thomas Fyndern, knight, and Katherine, his wife, and in the king's hands by the forfeiture of the said William in the field called Barnet Field, and all manors, lands, rents, reversions and services within the realm of which the said Katherine is seized or anyone else to her use and which should descend to the said William on her death.[20]

Robert Radcliffe also forged much deeper associations with Edward IV, and in April 1472 he married Margaret Welles, a half-sister of the king's uncle (and brother-in-law), Viscount Welles. He is also mentioned in the *Cely Letters* several times between 1478 and 1482 as the Keeper of the Town of Calais, a step up in military and political terms considering his lowly status.

However, when Henry VII usurped the throne from Richard III in 1485, Robert chose to attend his coronation, where he is described as a knight of Norfolk in a memoir of Henry VII's court.[21] Sir Robert Radcliffe was knighted at the battle of Stoke in 1487 and remained largely pro-Tudor after the failed rebellion of the pretender 'Lambert Simnel'. But when John Radcliffe, Lord Fitzwalter turned traitor in 1496, Robert offered his support to a second Yorkist pretender, Perkin Warbeck, who claimed to be Richard, Duke of York, the youngest of the two surviving Princes in the Tower. No doubt Lord Fitzwalter's loyalty to Edward IV had endured long after Richard III's death, and although Robert had fought for Henry VII at Stoke against Lambert Simnel (allegedly Edward V), if anyone could recognise a prince from a pauper, then the Radcliffes were well placed to do this in both instances.[22]

As discussed, Queen Elizabeth and the two princes had lived in the Tower during Edward's absence from London in 1471, and Robert likely knew the king's two sons quite well as Henry VI's gaoler in May of that year. The Radcliffes' willingness to risk their lives in the Warbeck rebellion (which also failed spectacularly) suggests renewed loyalty to York, but apart from this there is no further evidence later in their lives connected with Henry VI's death. Sir Robert Radcliffe was captured for his complicity in the Warbeck rebellion and beheaded on Tower Hill on 4 February 1496, and John Lord Fitzwalter was also charged with treason the following year after trying to escape from Guisnes, proving he was a staunch Yorkist to the end.[23]

As for the wider Radcliffe family, it is known that they were closely associated with Edward IV and Richard III for many years. For instance, John Radcliffe was the son of the infamous Lord Fitzwalter, who was killed fighting for Edward IV at the battle of Ferrybridge in 1461. Richard Radcliffe (the 'Rat' of the popular ballad) was a councillor of Richard III and was tasked with executing Earl Rivers, Grey and Vaughan at Pontefract Castle in 1483. Radcliffe died fighting for the king at Bosworth in 1485, but all that can be said from this evidence is that the Radcliffe family were loyal Yorkists for most of their lives. Therefore, the 'others' who served Richard of Gloucester at the Tower of London in May 1471 more than likely included Robert Radcliffe, the last of King Henry's keepers, and the one who may have benefited most from his execution (judging by later evidence of his rise).

However, before leaving this line of enquiry, every murder ideally needs a body to prove culpability, and when so-called experts failed to uncover scientific evidence about Henry VI's death in 1910, there remained only speculation. Indeed, this is still true today until permission can be obtained to open Henry's tomb and perform thorough forensic tests on his bones. A perfect chance was missed in 1910, but there again, the advanced technology available today had not been invented in the early twentieth century. Therefore, we must not condemn those early antiquarians who no doubt sought the truth about Henry's death with good faith, even though they failed in spectacular fashion.

Today, forensic analysis can be used to determine the minutiae of a violent death, and other scientific tests can track an individual's life story from bones using ancient DNA. Apart from radiocarbon dating and osteology to determine age, gender and the general health of remains, DNA testing can prove ancestry, isotopic analysis can determine where a person lived during their lifetime and dietary information can be extracted from chemical signatures in bone to determine their owner's status in society. Thus, a reasonably accurate picture of an individual's life and topographic identity can be built from samples of bone. However, as I said, these technological advances were all science fiction in 1910, and it is astonishing, given the investigators' credentials, how primitive the analysis of Henry VI's remains proved to be. In fact, more was recorded of the actual tomb chest in St George's Chapel, Windsor Castle, than the king's remains, which were the main reason for the investigation.

Henry of Windsor

The excavation at Windsor Castle unearthed a brick grave or vault containing a small lead chest under an arch where tradition said Henry VI was reinterred after being transferred by Richard III from Chertsey Abbey in 1484. Ironically, Henry's tomb in St George's Chapel was found almost opposite that of Edward IV, his nemesis. A formal investigation of the king's remains was sanctioned by King George V, and the grave was opened on Friday 4 November 1910. The investigation was led by W.H. St John Hope MA, and others, including Dr A. Macalister, Professor of Anatomy at the University of Cambridge, who was brought in to give 'expert' analysis of Henry's bones.

Once unearthed, the lead chest was found placed in the centre of Henry's grave among a great deal of building rubbish, but when it was removed, its dimensions were 3ft 5in long, 15in wide and about 1ft deep. The lid was slightly decayed and had sunk with the amount of masonry that had fallen on top of it. However, the sides of the chest were intact, the bottom was badly corroded and when the lid was removed, inside there was a wooden box, dark in colour, also in a state of decay:

> It was a narrow, rectangular box with a sliding lid, 3ft. 3½in. long, 10in. wide and about ½in. thick, but the sides and ends, which were about 9in. deep, as well as the bottom, were 1in. thick. After removal of the pieces of the lid, there was disclosed within the box a decayed mass of human bones, lying in no definite order, but mixed with the rotten remains of some material in which they were wrapped. There was also a certain amount of adipocere,[24] and dry rubbish from the grave which had fallen in through the rupture in the lid of the leaden chest.[25]

After this description was recorded, the bones were carefully removed by Professor Macalister, and his subsequent report provided an extremely brief anatomical précis of Henry's remains, summarised here equally briefly.

The bones he examined were those of a 'fairly strong man' aged 'between forty-five and fifty-five' who was at least '5ft. 9in. tall'. The individual's skull was 'thin and light' and was 'unfortunately much broken' although the professor commented that the skull was 'well-formed but small in proportion to the stature' of the man. The few teeth found attached to the skull were very much worn down, and a portion on one side of the lower jaw had gone missing 'sometime before death'. The body had been dismembered before it was put in the chest at Chertsey, and the professor claimed that the remains had been buried in the earth for some time before being exhumed. Macalister says this suggestion 'would account for them being in the decayed condition in which [they] were found'. However, the professor admitted the bones were so unsatisfactory that he could not come to trustworthy conclusions other than to say the individual's right arm was missing, which, in his words, accounted for 'the accidental enclosure of the left humerus of a small pig'.[26]

Unfortunately, the examination of such an important person as Henry VI was inconclusive and disappointing, but Macalister's pragmatic report was not helped by the comments of W.H. St John Hope, who gave his own personal view of the king's remains after they were returned to the grave sealed in a new box. Hope's remarks, published in *Archaeologia* 62 in 1911, record that the contents of the original wooden casket were somewhat moist on account of the spices that were used in 1471 to embalm Henry's body. He then references the payments recorded in the *Issues Rolls* to the individuals responsible for the king's burial rites and goes on to say that the wax, spices and linen cloth used to prepare the body for interment at Chertsey Abbey were the probable cause of dampness in the casket (despite the passage of four hundred years). Hope then notes that Henry's hair was 'brown in colour' and in one place 'apparently matted with blood' to the skull, which cannot be validated because no blood tests were recommended or recorded by Professor Macalister. Lastly, St John Hope confirms the reinterment of the king's bones at Windsor in an account roll of the Treasurer of the

College of Windsor and the story that Henry VII intended to move his uncle's remains to Westminster during his reign, a fact proven by his will.

St John Hope concluded there could be no doubt that the remains belonged to King Henry VI and that they were first buried in an 'ordinary grave' at Chertsey Abbey and then removed to St George's Chapel, although he fails to mention a date (see next chapter). He concludes his report by saying 'it seems to be established' that the bones were those of a man of about the king's age, and, so far as we know, of his personal characteristics (whatever these might have been). He claimed the remains belonged to someone who may have died a 'violent death' as is shown by the blood-clotted hair; that their condition was consistent with being buried in a coffin for some time; that care was taken to collect the bones and place them in a lead chest, suggesting the individual was of some importance; and lastly, that the remains were deposited in a place of honour in St George's Chapel, Windsor, in a vault especially made for that purpose, thus further confirming Henry's identity.

Without being too critical of the scientific evidence and restrictions in 1910, the report on Henry's bones remains doubtful. It appears at first glance that only Professor Macalister's comments can be trusted, although even these are anatomically disappointing. St John Hope's suggestion that Henry VI was murdered was never inferred by Macalister. The matted blood on Henry's skull was not seen or mentioned by him; the skull was smashed, and other than it being unusually thin, light and smaller than average, there were no conclusions about a probable cause of death. Macalister never suggested any medical reason for this, and with hindsight, the verdict was that the skull was more likely to have been crushed by the weight of building materials placed on top of it than by blunt force trauma. The professor noted that some of Henry's teeth were missing, and a pig bone was found in the casket. But the condition of the king's remains was so degraded, according to the professor, that the pig bone may have been 'picked up by accident' at Chertsey when Henry's body was exhumed and dismembered for transportation to Windsor (in 1484).[27]

Therefore, what are we to make of these findings, and how do they relate to Henry's mysterious death in the Tower? Did Edward IV formally execute the king? Was he secretly murdered by 'others' employed by the Duke of Gloucester? Did Gloucester stab Henry to death personally, as some chroniclers suggest? Or did the king die from other causes, which the 1910 investigation and the *Arrivall* partly reveal but which have never been taken seriously? The jury may still be out on Henry's death until his remains can be exhumed again and examined by experts using modern testing methods. But in the meantime, the evidence points to one of two conclusions that cannot be ignored: firstly, that King Edward ordered Henry VI's execution, and Gloucester organised this, or secondly, that Henry died from shock after learning of Tewkesbury, his son's death, Queen Margaret's capture and his own vulnerability once Edward returned to London and occupied the city.

It will be remembered we left the story of the siege of London with Edward IV returning to the city and knighting some of the defenders. But before this, we know the Duke of Gloucester, commanding a relief force, was the first to enter London. In fact, he arrived several days before Edward, mainly because his advance force likely had none of the restraints of a large marching army. We know the Lord Mayor of London, John Stockton, had been appraised of Edward's plans soon after Tewkesbury by letter, and the king no doubt wrote of his intentions to send Gloucester to his aid as soon as possible. According to the king's message, copied to Fauconberg, the mayor was also told the Prince of Wales was dead and that other Lancastrians had been executed after the battle. Therefore, was this news kept secret from Henry VI, or was he told immediately? As discussed previously, Henry was still alive on 11 May, according to the *Issues Rolls*, and Robert Radcliffe's advance payment confirms that the king was alive after this date despite growing rumours of Tewkesbury. However, the *Arrivall* and the chronicle of Jehan de Waurin tell us Henry died of 'grief and melancholy' immediately after he was told the tragic news of the battle, and according to *Warkworth's Chronicle*, this occurred between eleven and twelve o'clock on 21 May, soon after Edward IV returned to London with Queen Margaret. Therefore, apart from drawing the obvious conclusions of Edward's culpability, can we rule anything else out using the above chronology?

If King Henry was murdered by the Duke of Gloucester without orders from the king, as some chroniclers suggested, this could have been done when he returned to London before King Edward arrived in the city.[28] It is extremely unlikely the king commanded his brother to do this while still on the road, and Gloucester would not have acted of his own accord, fearing serious reprisals in London. On the other hand, 'others' may have been employed by Gloucester to do the job for him if Edward ordered Henry's death once he entered the city. However, the bones exhumed at Windsor in 1910 showed no apparent signs of violence apart from the inconclusive blood-matted hair and a loss of teeth, which cannot be proven either way. Also, as discussed, Professor Macalister did not mention blood in his report, and as for Henry's thin, light skull, this could have fractured if he fell on a hard stone surface, although, as explained, other things may have caused this to occur during the king's reburial. There is also the possibility that Henry was stabbed, smothered or strangled to death, leaving no tell-tale marks on his bones to further complicate the issue. But all things considered, the Duke of Gloucester seems to have had no personal reason for killing King Henry unless his brother ordered him to do so. In fact, Edward stood to gain if Henry consented to abdication rather than being assassinated, meaning that further uprisings and renewed civil war might be averted in the future.

As for the second possible cause of the king's death, it is known that Henry VI had an acute mental condition which also affected him physically. Therefore, it is possible the king suffered another massive seizure (caused by porphyria) that proved fatal on the night of 21 May. A stroke or heart attack would have caused him to collapse, and, in this case, his chances of survival would have been lessened by his fragile and light skull, as pointed out by Professor Macalister. Porphyria is a hereditary disease, and sufferers have a wide range of symptoms, including abdominal problems, difficulty breathing, loss of speech, paralysis, mental confusion and abnormally sensitive skin. Henry may have inherited this disease through the marriage of his father, Henry V, to Catherine of France. Catherine's father, Charles VI, had similar symptoms and sometimes imagined he was made of glass. Many other royals inherited the same condition, and the onset of porphyria not only explains Henry VI's bouts of madness and lapses into paralysis but also his memory loss.[29] For instance, the king could not remember the birth of his son, nor could he communicate with anyone in such a state, and he had other lapses of judgement and confusion in his reign that could be attributed to the disease. Thus, Henry could have died from the severe emotional shock of being told about Tewkesbury, the death of his only son, the capture of his wife and the utter destruction of the Lancastrian cause. Henry may also have been acutely aware that Edward IV could change his mind about him now he was master of England. It is recorded Henry felt 'safe' in the king's care after the battle of Barnet. Therefore, was the final nail in Henry's coffin the fear that he could no longer trust Edward? Did he lose faith in the safety and invisibility Edward provided? In short, was Henry tipped over the edge by a sudden stroke, causing him to collapse and die, whether from the stroke itself or from a fractured skull? And if it was Queen Margaret who told her husband the news of Tewkesbury in the Tower, was it her words that inadvertently killed him?

The Lancastrians and their chroniclers naturally state the Yorkists (and by implication Gloucester) cruelly murdered Henry, but if Henry was told first hand about the tragic consequences of Tewkesbury, and he was immediately filled with life-threatening anger and grief, as recorded in the *Arrivall*, then here is another possible reason for the king's mysterious death, free from any murderous intent.

Whatever the cause, Henry VI *was* certified dead by the morning of 22 May, and this is confirmed by the arrangements made for him to be 'chestyde' and exposed to public view at St Paul's on the Eve of the Ascension.[30] It was to be a grim day for the fallen House of Lancaster and an even worse few weeks for the rebels in Kent. On the same day Henry's coffin was conveyed to St Paul's, the Duke of Gloucester was ordered to leave London with a large force to hunt down Thomas Fauconberg and his navy at Sandwich – a task that would lead to betrayal and yet another clandestine execution.

11

The King's Right Arm

The Duke of Gloucester, that noble prince,
Young of age and victorious in battle,
To the honour of Hector that he might come,
Grace him follow, with fortune and good speed.[1]

☦

Henry VI was 49 when he died in the Tower of London, and apart from his mental instability and the physical symptoms associated with it, his life expectancy before 21 May was not, as far as we know, compromised. He might have looked forward to another ten years of life by upper-class medieval standards, despite being King of England since a child. Therefore, it is not surprising that Henry's funeral rites reflected veneration rather than acrimony towards the king. Some contemporary writers and historians suggested that Yorkist security at his funeral was in some way aggressive, but this clearly has no foundation. Guarding a deceased king's funeral cortège with soldiers bearing polearms was not unique in the Middle Ages, and martial display is common even today, proving that the Yorkists were not covering up a crime or fearful of Lancastrian reprisals in the city, but merely following tradition.

The Eve of the Ascension was 22 May in 1471, and before King Henry was laid in his coffin that day, his body, according to the *Issues Rolls*, was carefully embalmed, with no expense spared:

> To Hugh Brice. In money paid to his own hands, for so much money expended by him, as well as for wax, linen, spices, and other ordinary

expenses incurred for the burial of the said Henry of Windsor, who died in the Tower of London. And for wages and rewards to divers men carrying torches from the Tower aforesaid to the cathedral church of St Pauls, London, and from thence accompanying the body to Chertsey.[2]

Other money was paid out to servants of Edward IV for similar funeral items and obsequies. Master Richard Martin was paid for '28 ells (yards) of linen cloth of Holland' to wrap the king's corpse, and also for other services within the Tower 'at the last valediction of the said Henry'.[3] Money was paid to Chertsey Abbey on the day of the king's burial. Rewards were given to soldiers from the Tower garrison to guard Henry's corpse and for hiring barges with masters and sailors to row his coffin 12 miles up the Thames to Chertsey. Various payments were made to the brethren of the Holy Cross, the Carmelite Friars, the Austin Friars, the Friars Minors and the Friars Preachers to celebrate obsequies and masses in the city and at Chertsey Abbey. These payments came to well over £100 – a large sum of money by today's standards – proving this was not a clandestine funeral held by a guilty party but a public show of respect.[4] Henry visited and stayed at various religious houses during his reign and while he was on royal progress, including periods at Chertsey, proving that nothing sinister can be attached to Henry's interment there rather than at Westminster Abbey or some other royal mausoleum. Indeed, the king, in keeping with his religious asceticism, likely willed an ordinary grave (despite later accounts), and this was certainly not an attempt by Edward IV to bury Henry's memory in some out-of-the-way place where the ex-king might be soon forgotten.

After Henry's body was prepared and embalmed in the Tower on 22 May, there was a torchlit procession to St Paul's that night, and this is recorded in *The Great Chronicle of London*, whose anonymous author had Lancastrian sympathies, so much so that he was prepared to name the king's murderer:

> Upon Ascension Eve, the corpse of King Henry the Sixth was brought through Cornhill from the Tower with a great company of men of that place bearing weapons as if they should have led him to some place of execution. And so [they] conveyed him unto [St] Pauls, where

that night he was set in the body of the church against the image of our Lady of Grace open visaged, that he might be known, and upon the morning with a few torches he was brought to the waters side and from thence unto Chertsey and there buried, for whom shortly after God showed sundry miracles, [and] of whose death the common [saying] went that the Duke of Gloucester was not all guiltless.[5]

The pro-Lancastrian *Warkworth's Chronicle* also recorded Henry's funeral procession through London that day, although the wording was cleverly charged with homicidal bias and shock tactics, suggesting Henry was murdered. While the king's coffin was still raised on its catafalque in St Paul's, the chronicler says a strange phenomenon occurred, which soon became the basis for further anti-Yorkist propaganda:

And on the morrow [Henry VI] was brought to [St] Pauls, and his face was open so that every man might see him, and in his lying, he bled on the pavement there, and afterward at the Blackfriars [he] was brought, and there he bled new and fresh, and from there he was carried to Chertsey Abbey in a boat and buried in Our Lady Chapel.[6]

However shocking this sight was for onlookers, anatomically speaking, the presence of blood leaking from Henry's corpse is improbable. Henry had been dead for at least sixteen hours before these stains were spotted. Blood coagulates or 'pools' soon after death; therefore, this phenomenon must have been caused by something else.[7] An excessive build-up of spices and embalming fluids may have seeped through Henry's body and coffin as it was trundled through the streets of London. The stains on the ground would, no doubt, have been more visible when the body was stationary at St Paul's and later at Blackfriars before it was loaded onto a barge, but either way, it is unlikely to have been fresh blood.

In 1484, the common saying that Henry's corpse was found wholly intact when his coffin was opened at Chertsey is also evidence that the king's corpse was overly preserved rather than the result of a miracle, as some later writers recorded. The inconclusive discovery of Henry's tomb in 1910 mentions 'a certain amount of adipocere' in the wooden casket containing Henry's bones, suggesting the waxy residue was still in evidence. There were rotting pieces of fabric mixed in with the remains, and St John Hope records the decay of the original wooden casket so that a new one had to be made before reinterment. Therefore, the dramatic bloodletting story in *Warkworth's Chronicle* is suspect, along with the supposition that King Henry was stabbed to death (by Gloucester) without his brother's permission. However, if embalming fluids did leak out of Henry's coffin, this may have been due to a fractured skull – although proof of this would need to be established by modern analysis of his remains.

Meanwhile, on the same day Henry's body was being transferred to Chertsey Abbey for burial, his so-called murderer, Richard of Gloucester, was riding into Kent to apprehend the rebels. King Edward followed later that day, backed by an army, whereas Richard was explicitly directed towards Sandwich, where Thomas Fauconberg and several of his captains had taken refuge with their fleet. As previously discussed, some rebels had already been captured and imprisoned during the siege of London, but it is clear the return of the king's fleet was the main priority of the Yorkist regime. Fauconberg's ships were a crucial asset to England. During the siege, they had acted as a movable supply headquarters for the rebel attacks on London. Troops and artillery had been moved easily to where they were needed along the Thames embankment, and escape was made possible for some rebels and mariners when the siege failed. Now Fauconberg's large fleet was on standby once more at Sandwich, and no doubt the fear was that Thomas might escape to France and trade his ships with Louis XI for a friendly exile. The Calais garrison was also a worry for King Edward now they were leaderless. Indeed, it is no wonder Edward was quick to react soon after he returned to London, and if Fauconberg could not be dealt with by force, then his previous offers of pardon would be used as bait.

Contrary to historical opinion, the security of the Yorkist regime in 1471 was still at an extremely low ebb after the siege of London. King Edward had disposed of his enemies by winning two great victories at Barnet and Tewkesbury, but Fauconberg's rebellion was not the end of anti-Yorkist feeling, and most commentators feared a return to the unsavoury politics of Edward's rule in Kent and Essex. In fact, rebellion was so deep-seated that it had to be met with violence and executions. Most Yorkist writers and official chroniclers barely mention Fauconberg after the siege of London, apart from his eventual fate. The official *Arrivall* glosses over the brutal backlash aimed at restoring law and order. But *The Great Chronicle of London* sheds a ray of light on what happened soon after 23 May:

> Then shortly after [Henry's funeral] the king with a great band of men rode into Kent, and there caused enquiries to be made of the accessories of the aforesaid riot, where many were found culpable, of the which, such as were rich were hanged by the purse,[8] and others that were needy were hanged by the necks, by mean whereof the country was greatly impoverished and the king's coffers somewhat increased, and soon after was the head of the aforenamed Spicing sent unto London and commanded to be set upon Aldgate where it stood long after, and during this season of punishment of the Kentish men, many of the Essex men were hanged in the highway between London and Stratford, and their other captain called Quentin was hanged and headed and after his head was set upon Aldgate [beside] Spicing his fellow.[9]

Spicing and Quentin were captured shortly after the siege, but Nicholas Faunt, the rebel Mayor of Canterbury, was in the Tower awaiting the king's pleasure. He may have been tortured for information about his fellow rebels, as it is recorded that a list was found on him when he was caught naming various men in Canterbury who had joined or helped finance the rebellion. Therefore, many other rebels who had not marched on London also faced execution, and many went into hiding, fearing Yorkist reprisals. Rebels were also being hunted down and rounded up in Essex, where the Earl of Essex and Lord Dinham were active. The Duke of Gloucester, acting as Lord High Constable of England, and other judges like Sir John Scott presided over courts of oyer and terminer in Kent to root out traitors, and more than a hundred were indicted, of which eight of the ringleaders were hanged.[10] It was one of the largest recorded instances of oyer and terminer in the period, and rebels in Canterbury, Rochester, Maidstone and Blackheath were also captured and executed by the roadside.[11] It was an operation of military precision that punished almost anyone associated with Fauconberg's rebellion. Other rebels were fined heavily, but this was only the start of the hardships endured by some men in the south-east.

What mischief grows after insurrection!

In Canterbury, the commons were soon craving Edward IV's mercy. When the king arrived there on 26 May accompanied by Clarence, Norfolk, Suffolk, Rivers, Lord Hastings and other Yorkist lords, he began a thorough investigation into all those who had financed, helped and participated in the siege of London. The result was the aforementioned list of two hundred names who had been judged guilty or had helped the insurgency under compulsion. As discussed, the list still survives today in the Canterbury Cathedral Archives, and apart from the legal formalities, each of the convicted men is listed by their occupation. As mentioned, these individuals were not all ruffians or labourers looking to take advantage of the rebellion as a means to loot and pillage London. Some were high-ranking city officials, while others were described as captains, meaning they had acquired military experience. The case for Canterbury's rebellious nature was judged clear and compelling, and King Edward immediately sent for the mayor, Nicholas Faunt, who paid dearly for his part in the uprising, along with seven others (fifteen according to other accounts).[12] On 29 May, Faunt was brought from London on a newly purchased horse and saddle and was hanged, drawn and quartered at the Bull's Stake in the Buttermarket opposite Canterbury Cathedral.[13]

The list of guilty rebels was completed and amended sometime after Nicholas Faunt's execution, as he is described as 'late' in the document. But many of the insurgents were fined rather than executed, and this is similarly recorded in *Warkworth's Chronicle*, whose author clearly disagreed with the punishments:

> And immediately after that was the Lord Dinham and Sir John Fogg and diverse others made commissioners [who] sat upon all Kent, Sussex and Essex men that were at Blackheath, and upon many other that were not there; for some men paid 200 marks, some 100 pounds, and some more and some less so that it cost the poorest man 7s. which was not worth so much, but [they] were forced to sell such clothing as they had, and borrow the remainder, and laboured for it afterwards; and so the king had out of Kent much good and little love. Lo, what mischief grows after insurrection!'[14]

Over £2,000 (about £1 million by today's standards) was exacted from all concerned, and enquiries were extended into remote parts of Essex, Sussex, Surrey and the Cinque Ports to root out more rebels. Edward took away the liberties of those towns who had sent men and mariners to join Fauconberg in a bid to curb further rebellion, and some men received pardons as late as November 1471, such as William Sellow and others who are mentioned in a Canterbury charter dating from this period.[15] The king also feared reprisals from the Calais garrison and their captains, Sir Geoffrey Gate and Sir Walter Wrottesley, who had deserted Fauconberg after the siege. But more than anything, Edward wanted his navy returned so that his enemies had no means of repeating the tactics employed by the rebels. Some Lancastrian nobles were still at large, including the Earl of Oxford, his two brothers and Viscount Beaumont, who had fled after Barnet to seek refuge in Scotland. Other knights and landowners in Kent still retained their feelings for Lancaster, and now suspected Henry VI had been murdered. As a former Warwick supporter, Nicholas Faunt and others had been executed in Canterbury, and many, including Fauconberg, must have been nervously anticipating a similar fate. As discussed, they had previously been given a chance to save themselves from punishment. Now it seemed they might be captured and executed in the most horrible way for treason. However, when the Duke of Gloucester arrived at Sandwich, it seems Fauconberg was already prepared to make a deal:

> The said Bastard sent unto him [Gloucester] such means as best he could, humbly to sue for his grace and pardon, and them of his fellowship, and, by appointment, willed there to be delivered to the king's behove all his ships, and become his true liegemen, with as straight promise of true allegiance as could be devised for them to be made, which, after deliberation taken in that part, for certain great considerations, was granted. Wherefore the king sent thither his brother Richard, Duke of Gloucester, to receive them in his name, and all the ships, as he so did the 26th day of the same month, the king that time being at Canterbury.[16]

It will be remembered that at Blackheath Fauconberg had been visited by several messengers and heralds offering him pardon, and now, when it looked like all was lost, he swallowed his pride. Thomas finally took advantage of the king's offer by trading his ships for freedom, and this was agreed by Gloucester at Sandwich with a promise to take Fauconberg back into the king's confidence. The rebel ships would revert back to the king, and Gloucester, acting as Admiral of England, would seal the bargain with a pardon rather than a public beheading.

Most contemporary writers believed this was the end of Thomas Fauconberg's incredible story and that he or Edward IV betrayed his pardon at some point, but this was not the case. Most sources assume that Fauconberg was captured and executed in Southampton 'and his head sent to London and set upon the bridge'.[17] Some chroniclers said he was killed shortly after the siege of London, while others are unsure when and where he died.[18]

On 27 May 1471, the Duke of Gloucester received the submission of Fauconberg and his forty-seven ships. *Warkworth's Chronicle* records that Edward, after arriving at Sandwich, 'took the Bastard with him and returned again to London'. Thereafter, Fauconberg stayed in the city, or more precisely Westminster, until 14 June, when he was given safe conduct to travel north with the Duke of Gloucester, who was then Warden of Carlisle and the West March. Fauconberg had received a general pardon on 10 June, along with a host of other known rebels, including Robert Neville, who was acquitted on 4 June. After a long list of men receiving their pardons in 1471, the record briefly states:

> 10 June. The like to Thomas Fauconberg, esquire, alias 'gentleman' of all Westminster, of offences against the statutes of cloths and capes committed by him before 22 May.[19]

The 'cloths and capes' referred to the practice of giving livery and maintenance during the Wars of the Roses. As discussed earlier, the feudal system bound every man to his master, meaning that a retainer would wear his lord's livery colours and fight for him, and in return, he would be maintained with wages or services in kind. Military service for protection in the law courts and the battlefield could be dangerous to the king if abused, and Fauconberg's offence was that he had instigated this practice illegally when he had raised men in the southern shires. Edward IV had legislated in 1468 that livery and maintenance was forbidden by law, except for domestic servants, estate officials and legal advisors. However, this law was largely ignored. Many nobles still recruited their tenants and retainers throughout the civil wars (and after), and it seems Edward used this wording as a practical way of issuing Fauconberg's pardon without drawing attention to the fact that he forgave a rebel who had committed treason and deserved to die.

Meanwhile, in Kent and the Cinque Ports, men were still being punished for their part in the rebellion. A rebel and traitor called 'Black Barre' was captured and thrown into gaol in Sandwich. The mayor received a letter on 11 June from the king that he was to be tried immediately and then, without delay, executed as an example to all others who might rebel against him. However, Robert Cook (the Mayor of Sandwich) was offered a pardon, although the Earl of Arundel took command of the port, becoming warden in 1472. Sir Geoffrey Gate and his companions at Calais soon submitted to Lord Hastings when commanded, and they all received pardons for their part in the siege of London. Even soldiers of the garrison were forgiven by King Edward, according to the *Issues Rolls*, and *The Great Chronicle of London* records what became of some of Fauconberg's mariners:[20]

> The last day of May, King Edward came out of Kent and pardoned the Bastard of Fauconberg and all his shipmen at Sandwich where were delivered to the king the navy of forty seven ships great and small, and of shipmen to the number of eight or nine hundred [who] dispersed into diverse places.[21]

For this reason, when Fauconberg accompanied Gloucester northwards into Yorkshire, he must have been unaware that anything was wrong with how he had been given his freedom and re-entered the king's service. According to the Burgundian chronicler Jehan de Waurin, Fauconberg 'came and went with Gloucester's other servants without being constrained or harmed' and no doubt Thomas felt comparatively safe at Middleham Castle, or he would have escaped to Scotland where other Lancastrians were exiled. Edward had pardoned many rebels, and they soon became Yorkist supporters. It had been the king's policy in the civil wars to be lenient on occasion, and this same policy was followed in 1471 to a degree. He badly needed support, but Fauconberg was still a rebel at heart and probably could not forgive and forget Warwick's death. He was after all a Neville, and according to Waurin, he was back at sea in the summer of 1471, although why remains a mystery.[22]

It seems Fauconberg had no rebellious intentions, and there is no proof at this time or later that he committed any crime. John Paston (the younger), who had fought on the Lancastrian side at Barnet, received his pardon on 17 July but he was unsure how or why Fauconberg had been captured. He later explained in a letter dated 15 September 1471 that 'I understand that Bastard Fauconberg is [either] headed or like to be, and his brother both; some men say he would have deserved it, and some say nay', a clear indication that Thomas and William Fauconberg were under arrest by this date and well-known personalities.[23] However, in another letter dated 28 September, Sir John Paston (senior) was more specific about events and reveals that only Thomas's brother had managed to escape from his captors:

> Item, Thomas Fauconberg, his head was yesterday set upon London Bridge looking into Kent ward, and men say that his brother was sore hurt and escaped to sanctuary to Beverley.[24]

Most sources agree the Fauconberg brothers were captured as their ship weighed anchor in Southampton, which, if nothing else, explains the confusion in some other chronicles that this was the place where Thomas was executed. Although the evidence is not specific about why the brothers were arrested again, we know they were not at Middleham Castle when this happened. The brothers may have simply been found guilty of deserting their posts and going to sea without authority. However, a more likely reason is the Yorkists feared the brothers might aid exiled Lancastrians like the Earl of Oxford or even Jasper or Henry Tudor, who were still beyond government control, and this caused them to act when Thomas finally docked at Southampton. Here Fauconberg was judged a dangerous and unpredictable man, so much so that his pardon was revoked on 11 September when the king ordered Robert Cousin and John Cole to seize his goods as a traitor.[25] It seems Edward IV had decided to change his mind about pardoning his former enemies and followed a similar course of action to Tewkesbury. A few days later, we hear from John Paston that Thomas and William had been arrested, and by 28 September, Thomas's head was spiked on London Bridge for all to see. Therefore, what happened between these dates to change Edward's mind and make him go against his word, and where was Fauconberg executed?

Southampton should have been where the brothers were put to death for treason if they were found guilty. But it seems Edward had decided that neither the south of England nor London was a suitable place for the Fauconberg brothers to finally pay for causing him so much trouble. Why resort to such clandestine tactics? Probably because Kent and the southern shires were still a hotbed of revolt, and yet another rebellion, using Fauconberg's execution as an excuse, was the last thing Edward needed in London. Clearly, his promise of a pardon for Fauconberg was a means to persuade him to surrender his navy intact and create a breathing space. He was prepared to let Thomas live only if he behaved himself. He could not afford to risk his throne yet again, especially to a man who had a Neville way of encouraging thousands to revolt. Therefore, the Bastard had to die, and the king would use his good 'right arm' to execute his will.

The 18-year-old Duke of Gloucester was, no doubt, ready to follow his brother's orders as before. After all, Fauconberg had been his opposite number when it came to commanding the king's navy, and Richard, like most nobles of his age, was eager to serve. It is strange that Fauconberg still wielded so much power in the land that the king feared a public execution in London, and this begs the question why Fauconberg was such an enigmatic figure. What were his feelings when he placed his head on the block at Middleham Castle, where his execution took place? What had he hoped to gain by rousing thousands of rebels to free Henry VI from the Tower? Were the economic and social conditions in Kent, Essex and other counties so volatile and amenable to Warwick's propaganda that the rebellion would have happened anyway without Thomas's leadership? Nothing could stop the siege of London when the die was cast, even the news of Tewkesbury and Edward's march on the capital. However, at the end of his life, Fauconberg was a rebel to the last. According to *The Paston Letters*, there was a fight and a flight. His brother William was wounded and managed to escape across country to sanctuary at Beverley Minster, whereas Thomas was left to face the axe. When the Duke of Gloucester ordered Fauconberg's execution to proceed, no doubt Thomas thought Richard was merely carrying out his orders as Constable of England and not pleasing himself.

After claiming sanctuary at Beverley Minster, Thomas's brother may have gone into permanent hiding, but we know that in October 1477, he received a pardon for all his offences, which may have been a sign that Edward did not see William as a threat without his brother.[26] However, what we do know for sure is that the king paid 30*s* for Henry Cappe to convey Thomas's head back to London where, according to *The Great Chronicle of London*, it was 'there upon the bridge pitched upon a stake or pole where it stood long after'.[27]

So ended the life of the Bastard of Fauconberg, son of Lord Fauconberg, Earl of Kent, a loyal supporter of Edward IV and probably the man chiefly responsible for the king's victory at Towton and the winning of his throne. The irony is inescapable, even though Thomas was a bastard child and not noble in any way. Illegitimate children were at a disadvantage in medieval England. Some bastards entered the church, and some did well through marriage. Others became soldiers, and a few made it into the history books, like Thomas Fauconberg. Very few led thousands of men into battle, laid siege to London for two days and terrorised the seas as a pirate in charge of a large navy of well-equipped warships. Thomas Fauconberg was vilified after his death, and even today, he is regarded as a medieval rebel. But what of the man he tried to save from the Tower? What influence did he have on history after his death? The memory of 'Henry of Windsor' casts a long enigmatic shadow, it seems, and his saintly afterlife goes on and on, even to the gates of Rome.

12

The Saint King

Here, over the martyr-king, the marble weeps,
And, fast beside him, once-feared Edward sleeps,
The grave unites: where e'en the great find rest,
And blended lie the oppressor and the oppressed![1]

✥

On the last day of August 1481, an ageing miller called Richard Queston was looking after his grandson, a boy of 4 years old, at his water mill at Westwell near Canterbury. While the miller was working, his grandson went outside to play, but when the boy was called in, there was no answer. The miller shouted his name several times and frantically searched for the boy, but still, there was no sign of him until the miller saw that he had fallen beneath the water wheel.

The boy was motionless in the deep trough. Only his outstretched hands were visible, and his grandfather failed to reach him despite seeking help from neighbours. Soon, a large crowd gathered at the mill, and when the miller saw no hope for the boy, he was grief-stricken. No one dared jump into the water to retrieve the body. Some tried to stop the wheel from turning, to no avail, but at last, a bystander who was bolder than the rest pulled the body from the mill race with an iron hook and laid it on the bank.

When the boy's parents arrived, they were inconsolable, and many of the townsfolk offered up prayers for the dead boy's soul. However, the minute the crowd invoked God, the Virgin Mary and especially King Henry VI, the boy began to move. He opened his eyes, and it was proclaimed a miracle. Subsequently, as the story goes, the boy grew to full age, and the saving of his life was wholly attributed to Henry VI. At the time, the king had been dead for ten years, but this was not the first occasion Henry had been acclaimed as a religious icon. The crowd clearly knew of the dead king's powers, and in later years, the story became so famous it was one of the many miracles investigated by Rome to determine Henry VI's canonisation in the Tudor period.[2]

It is said that as early as 1473, an image of the king was being venerated at York Minster, and in 1478, Edward IV tried to prevent pilgrims from visiting Chertsey Abbey and Henry's tomb for similar reasons. The Abbot of Chertsey, understandably fearful of Edward's wrath, did his best to discourage any adoration at Henry's tomb. But still, pilgrims continued to make journeys from all over England, and some attested to miracles there by the 'martyred king'. Rumours had already circulated that Henry may have been murdered by the Duke of Gloucester rather than 'officially' having died of melancholy in the Tower of London. And this stigma of a saintly king who had suffered innumerable vicissitudes in life plagued Edward for at least ten years until his death at Westminster in April 1483.

As for Richard, Duke of Gloucester, the presumed murderer of Henry VI, he had plenty to occupy his time in the years after the siege of London and before his brother Edward died. While rumours about King Henry's death were still circulating in England, there is no evidence Richard was troubled by these accusations or the miracles at Chertsey. The Duke of Gloucester was too busy keeping order as Constable of England and later Lord of the North. In 1475, he took part in his brother's abortive invasion of France and later became Warden of the West Marches towards Scotland. He also became Admiral of England and was well regarded by the citizens of York, a city where his brother had never been liked. In 1482, Richard retook the border town of Berwick as part of the English invasion of Scotland, and by the end of the year, he was one of the most powerful nobles in the kingdom. Therefore, due to his various commitments to the Crown, Richard was employed elsewhere in England during the latter part of Edward IV's reign until his brother died suddenly and his 12-year-old son was summoned to succeed him as Edward V.

Gloucester's role in northern England may explain his rare appearances at court, but no doubt the spectre of his supposed 'crime' against

Henry VI was problematic when he visited London on state business. Henry was still widely popular as a religious icon, and out of the hundreds of miracles being performed at Chertsey and later at Windsor, fifty were reported from devotees who had travelled from Kent, Sussex and Essex – three counties where rebellion still simmered under the surface. Eighty-five miracles were reported by pilgrims who had travelled from abroad, and many of the cures were visited on small children. But when Edward IV died and Gloucester usurped the throne from the 'bastardised' Edward V as Richard III, widespread support was hard to muster. Both York and Lancaster had to be appeased in some way, and Richard formulated a plan involving Henry VI that was similar to that of Henry V when he removed the body of Richard II from Langley to Westminster Abbey in 1413.

Following this precedent, Richard III had the remains of Henry VI dug up at Chertsey in 1484, and after dismemberment, these were put in the same lead coffin St John Hope and his colleagues opened in 1910. Richard likely believed that reinterring them at Windsor Castle, Henry's birthplace, would show a measure of contrition on his part, rebuild his reputation with dissident Lancastrian lords and also make a tidy profit. Access would be given to Henry's tomb; pilgrims would offer money and place candles in return for a cure to whatever ailed them, and this might also show that the Yorkist regime was innocent of Henry's murder. The new tomb of Henry VI would be directly opposite that of Edward IV to stimulate feelings of accord, while the grave of another miracle worker, Master John Shorne, would be close by for added credibility if any were needed.[3]

As will be remembered, it was said that when Henry's body was dug up at Chertsey, it was found perfectly preserved, and this furthered claims that the king was in some way 'divine' and worthy of sainthood. Pilgrimages were extremely popular in the medieval world, but actual miracles performed at Henry's tomb were rare. Those attributed to 'Holy King Henry' occurred after the event (or were evoked by those who could not travel to Windsor), and most were surrounded by mythology. Some sufferers were revived on their deathbeds at home, while others attributed their recovery to Henry VI, but a cure never came for most people. However, the cult of the 'Blessed Henry' increased in popularity. Ordinary people understood the rumours about the ex-king's persecution and suffering during his lifetime, and once his body was removed from Chertsey to Windsor, Henry's cures became renowned. His image began to appear on pilgrim badges, tokens, statues and depictions in stained glass. Large frescoes of him were painted on church walls and rood screens across England, and it seemed Henry had become more famous dead than alive.[4]

But all this time, the cult of Henry VI remained a lingering threat to the Yorkist regime, and for this reason, Richard III's original plan of contrition and reburial backfired. However, the king's public displays of piety and good nature continued. It is variously recorded Richard made reburial and religious forgiveness his watchword – especially when making amends for his brother's transgressions – and even though this never helped elevate his popularity as a good king, Richard sought to rebuild the Yorkist achievement when it was at its lowest ebb.[5] He had many enemies at home and abroad. The Tudors were threatening his tottering throne from a safe distance, and some nobles in England were once again invoking rebellion and civil war as a means to advancement. No doubt Richard III tried to amend his perceived character during his short reign, but he was no different, and no worse, than most fifteenth-century English nobles raised in the Wars of the Roses. Survival was everything if his position was threatened, and a medieval king had to be ruthless. However, when Richard was killed in battle near Bosworth in 1485, a change of dynasty meant that Henry Tudor could wipe away the stain of the Yorkist kings and conjure up another political angle for his uncle's tomb at Windsor. Although his methods were half-hearted and lacked proper finance, Henry VII also realised a saintly King Henry VI could work to his advantage, and he set about promoting his uncle's canonisation with three popes, who deemed that testimonies were needed first to establish truth from legend.

Henry VII first petitioned for his uncle's sainthood sometime before 1492, but canonisation was a long process, and Rome was not to be hurried in its decision. A miracle had to be compelling, and apart from proving recoveries from madness, blindness, deafness, sickness including the plague, epilepsy, lameness and a whole host of other ailments common in medieval life, the claims had to circumnavigate unavoidable administrative delays such as the death of popes and ecclesiastical commissioners. Exhaustive enquiries took a long time to complete, and each miracle had to be recorded and evaluated. Scepticism was a big part of the process, and those who came forward and attested to miracles were mainly charlatans. For instance, in 1489, a girl of 3 called Beatrice was pinned to the ground by a huge tree trunk that had fallen on top of her in a storm. Henry's intercession brought her back to life.[6] Two poor carters from Caversham were almost deprived of their livelihood when their cart overturned, destroying barrels of wine. They invoked Henry's help, and he graciously provided restitution.[7] A farmer trying to complete his ploughing in a thunderstorm was struck by lightning and left for dead, but Henry revived him after 126 days.[8] Henry was also instrumental in saving a man unjustly sentenced to hang by putting his 'holy' hand between the noose and his neck. And when an evil spirit in the shape of a black dog attacked a traveller, it was only scared off when the man called out for Henry's help.[9]

There were at least 172 recorded miracles, and 445 cases were reported at Windsor alone between 1484 and 1500. About 77 miracles were subsequently investigated, and 23 of these were deemed acceptable to the pope's emissaries. In 1543, it was recorded that a large collection of wax images, candles, crutches and personal garments were overflowing the tomb at Windsor, and a choirman, Robert Testwood, could not refrain from admonishing the offerings as idolatrous.[10] However, thousands of visitors still prostrated themselves at Henry's altar, wore a red velvet cap that was supposed to cure headaches, and even Henry VIII offered at the king's tomb on 10 June 1529, the Tudor king adopting the Lancastrian cause to blacken the Yorkist age and the civil wars.[11]

In his lifetime, Henry VII made plans for a complete refurbishment of St George's Chapel, and he intended to move the dead king's remains yet again to a new tomb. But this only caused a storm of controversy between the abbots of Chertsey and Westminster, who each revived a prior claim to Henry VI's bones. The king's council were brought in to adjudicate, and eyewitnesses were summoned to prove that Henry, while still alive, had chosen to be buried at Westminster and not Chertsey. According to the claims, Henry had even selected the spot where he was to be interred, and permission was granted in 1504 to remove the king's bones from Windsor to where a new chapel was being built at Westminster. Drawings of the king's tomb depicted him bearded and dressed in armour, and in his will, Henry VII also planned to be buried alongside his uncle, so great was his interest. However, when Henry died in 1509, his namesake was still not deemed worthy of sainthood. Therefore, his body remained at Windsor, where it still resides today.

Henry VI was never canonised, although he was regarded as a saint by countless devotees of his cult, and in time, his failings as a monarch were soon forgotten. Henry VI's ghost had managed to outlive the memory of his contemporaries and the Wars of the Roses due to a life in the shadows. Fortune's wheel had turned full circle again, it seemed. The dark ages so eagerly portrayed by Shakespeare had to be set in stark contrast to the pretended light of Tudor stability. The fact that Edward IV had achieved twelve years of peace in England soon after the siege of London was ignored. After September 1471, dynastic squabbles had run their course, and even though Edward had come out on top in the civil wars, the Tudors found it convenient to blame the Yorkists for killing Henry VI. They used the king's suffrage under Edward IV and Richard III as a conduit to legitimise their Beaufort lineage. And what could be better than a 'saint king' in the family to promote a direct link to the Almighty?

The Tudors used every means in their arsenal to blacken the age of the Wars of the Roses, even though the Yorkist kings were regarded as the true Plantagenet descendants of Edward III. Enemies were everywhere, and even Edward IV tried to transfer inward fears abroad. For three years after the siege of London, he courted Burgundy and Brittany to renew the Hundred Years War, and he almost succeeded in reviving the old rivalry with France in 1475. Edward's army of invasion was one of the finest to leave the shores of England. However, despite the king's enthusiasm, and contrary to the Duke of Gloucester's pressure to fight the French in the style of Agincourt, England never went to war. Edward was bought off by a tidy settlement that temporarily filled his exchequer, and no doubt Louis XI was also pleased he had avoided a conflict so easily.

But what of the rebels in Kent, Essex and other southern counties who had freely chosen or been press-ganged into joining the Bastard of Fauconberg's siege of London? What was the reason for their discontentment? And how alive was their unconquered spirit after 1471?

Invicta!

For generations, Kent was, and still is, the seaborne gateway to Europe. Its proximity to France is geographically unique and was more important in the medieval era when trade in wool and other commodities was essential. French raiding of the south coast was a common occurrence, and even ordinary people were aware of the political significance of Kent and its proximity to a host of enemies across the Channel. Men from Kent and Essex had been involved in all of England's conflicts abroad, especially in France during the Hundred Years War. And as discussed, Kent, in particular, was governed not by high-ranking nobles but by local landlords and minor gentry. The Kentish motto ever since the Norman Conquest had been 'Invicta' (meaning unconquered), and the feeling that the population was in some way different from the rest of England had stood the test of time. Throughout the medieval period, there had been at least one insurrection every generation in Kent, and therefore, the inhabitants were shaped by rebellion for one reason or another. High taxes, unfair customs, lack of defence against France and even plain old discontentment had regularly stirred up revolts in the county. Kent was England's spokesperson and common voice, but its hatred of corruption was not usually directed at the king. Leaders and peasants involved in popular revolts spoke of the 'Common Profit', the 'Common Weal' and later the 'Common Wealth' of the kingdom. These watchwords were used as war cries against the corruption of the king's ministers who had offended their county, and many high-ranking officials had been executed over the years for their misgovernance. Other counties like Essex, Surrey and Sussex followed Kent's leadership when they suffered from unfair taxes and economic pressures. Even rebels in Cornwall sought their support in 1497. Popular political poems of the Wars of the Roses displayed in public places invoked the war cry of Invicta regularly, and thousands answered the call for reform against those London officials who had taken advantage of their lofty positions:

Now is England all in fright,
Much people of conscience light,
Many knights and little of might,
Many laws and little right,

Many acts of parliament,
And few with true intent.[12]

Economic hardship, lack of security and general misgovernance were constantly stated in Kentish manifestoes, and this message was repeated time and time again down the centuries. It was also copied elsewhere in England, causing similar rebellions up and down the country. Kent was singled out for ridicule by those in London, even kings, who threatened to fence off and turn the county into a deer park because of its rebellious nature. London was initially sympathetic to the rebels who gained entry to the city in 1381 and 1450, but this changed when looting and violence were let loose in the streets. Never again would Londoners trust a Kentish uprising marching towards the city, and this was the rallying call of the citizens when Fauconberg attacked London in 1471. When the Earl of Warwick recruited the commons of Kent before significant battles of the Wars of the Roses, the incentive was to topple a corrupt government of one kind or another. In 1460, before the battle of Northampton, Kent was the first to send willing troops, whose main complaint was that they felt strongly about how they were being treated personally:

They lapped away the fat from me,
Me to mischief was their intent.
And never to me they would consent,
They which called you ever traitors untrue,
Until now the true commoners of Kent,
Be coming with you, falsehood to destroy,
And truth long exiled now to renew.[13]

In 1450, Jack Cade's men were prepared to sell their lives dearly for a cause they believed in. Their famous manifesto, expertly written on a folio sheet of paper, mentions twelve causes of England's economic distress. It was addressed to Henry VI's ministers, and in it, the rebels pointed an accusing finger at the king's corrupt government and explained why they, 'your true liegemen of Kent', had gathered to oppose the high and mighty men responsible. They sought help from God and King Henry to right the wrongs of the land and punish all those who had offended their county. Ten years later, in 1460, another ballad was meant to rouse the men of Kent despite its numerous meanderings and biblical quotations. But by this time, just posting a newsletter on the gates of Canterbury had become a sufficient provocation to invoke feelings of Invicta in the city:

Time has come falsehood to destroy,
Time to root out the weeds from the corn,
Time to burn the briers that trees annoy,
Time to pluck up the false hunter with his horn.[14]

As discussed, in 1470, Kentish rebels were yet again rampaging through Southwark, burning and pillaging houses and businesses to aid Warwick's coup and hasten King Edward's flight to Burgundy. When the Bastard of Fauconberg marched on London to free Henry VI, the same muster sites, entry points and attack strategy used for generations were employed to assault London. Rochester, Blackheath and London Bridge were the preferred routes into the city. And as a result, Southwark suffered the most, along with migrant populations, proving the rebels did not spare anyone if it promoted their aims. Kentish identity and suffrage were interchangeable feelings, reflected in the same language used in rebel manifestoes for generations. According to their viewpoint, the monarch was anointed by God and men who usurped his laws were traitors. It was the same in 1549 and 1554, although the story changed somewhat. During the latter predominantly religious rebellion, headed by Sir Thomas Wyatt, it is interesting that simmering Kentish unrest was the underlying recruitment tool used to recruit 4,000 men to march on London and battle their way along Fleet Street. It is also worth noting that Kingston Bridge was again used to try and outflank the city and its defenders.[15] Even more incredible is the story that another victim incarcerated in the Tower of London (Lady Jane Grey) was sacrificed because Queen Mary feared her popularity. Like Henry VI before her, Jane had become innocently associated with rebellion and tragically paid the price because she threatened the Tudor regime.

History proves Kent was always a bubbling cauldron of revolt, waiting for a champion to emerge from the ether. Thomas Fauconberg took advantage of Kent's ready-made army of malcontents in 1471, and the siege of London was the result. After the battle of Barnet, his unquestioning loyalty to his uncle, the Earl of Warwick, redoubled his efforts to attack the city despite the news of King Edward's victory at Tewkesbury. Warwick's death at Barnet only fanned the fires of discontent in Kent due to the earl's popularity in the county. The rebels had always responded vehemently in the past to the earl's carefully worded and 'beautiful speeches', and with his fleet of sailing ships, commanded by Fauconberg, and the Calais garrison in support, victory against Edward IV became a real possibility in 1471. Henry VI was the rightful king in the eyes of the rebels, and Edward IV was the corrupt usurper and lawbreaker who had offended their county. Essex, too, had risen against the king's economic pressures and unmanageable taxes on foodstuffs. The 'Common Weal' was threatened again, and because of Tewkesbury, time was running out to strike a blow for the commons. The siege almost succeeded, had it not been for fears in London that the city would be burnt and pillaged. The rebels pushed through Aldgate, and if they had been allowed to swarm into the rest of London, freeing Henry VI from the Tower, it would have been one of the biggest upsets in medieval history.

Unlike all-out war, rebellion is too easily forgotten, especially if it fails against the state. The victors tend to paper over the spilt blood and erase, or belittle, its leaders. Thus, the *absolute* truth is erased from memory. Time marches on, and in Fauconberg's case, his name has been, quite literally, bastardised in the historical record. No doubt he was a pirate and adventurer, but apart from this, who was Thomas Fauconberg, and why did he persist in his rebellion when he knew all hope was lost? Can we end this account of the siege and Henry VI's last days by revealing a concealed identity and why he was such a charismatic figure during the rebellion?

Above all, Thomas Fauconberg was loyal to Warwick and the Neville family even though the tendency today is maybe to portray him as an outcast due to the long shadow of his illegitimacy. However, as a bastard child of the well-renowned William Lord Fauconberg, Earl of Kent, Thomas was no ordinary sea captain. He was noted in some official documents as a 'gentleman', and although he was never knighted in his career, he received the freedom of the City of London, which he later stormed and burnt with careless abandon.[16] His buccaneering activities in the English Channel were no different from those of his father, uncle or the rest of those mariners who used their captaincies as a chance to commit crimes, sometimes against friendly nations. Fauconberg's seafaring freedom and battles on the high seas prove he was his own man and a ruthless enemy to anyone who opposed him. He was also a thief and an opportunist, and the scale of the siege of London proves he was undoubtedly an ambitious man loyal to Henry VI. His brother William (the other Bastard of Fauconberg) may have been cut from the same cloth. He, too, was earmarked for execution but was later pardoned for his crimes, and this likely points to a stark difference between the two brothers.

With most of the leading members of his family dead or put into exile, Thomas may have felt his life was prey only to time and occasion after Barnet, whereas William may have been only following his brother's example. Before the siege of London, Thomas claimed he was acting on Warwick's orders as his 'Captain of Kent', which can be seen in his dogged persistence to free Henry VI even after he learned of the battle of Tewkesbury. In his letter to the Commonality of London on 8 May 1471, Fauconberg stated he dearly wished to fight Edward 'with the help of Almighty God and the king's true commons'. He wanted 'to revenge his quarrel against the said usurper (Edward) and his adherents and to seek him in what parts he was willing [to fight] in the realm of England'.[17] But upon closer inspection, this willingness to confront Edward IV was only a ruse to enter London unopposed and capture Henry VI, thereby releasing closet Lancastrians and their adherents into the streets. Unfortunately, we have no record of Fauconberg's answer to the Lord Mayor of London when his request to march through the city was denied. Indeed, he may never have written a letter after hearing the shock news of Tewkesbury. But, if nothing else, this dogged perseverance tells us that Thomas, by this stage, was desperate and eager to avenge Warwick's death. To recapture King Henry, it was clear he would use any means at his disposal, including fabricating a pack of lies, and after the siege, he knew he had been caught up in a series of events that had a life of their own. Edward and his army were marching on London, and he was caught in a corner of England with only one escape route – the sea. That he did not escape abroad to France or elsewhere likely shows his true colours. It is hard to imagine what Fauconberg was thinking when he accepted Edward's offers of pardon and why he trusted the king to keep his word. Fauconberg was either stupid or had a trusting, almost cavalier attitude towards his enemies. On the other hand, he may have been a brave man. Thereafter, he was not content with helping those who had offered him an olive branch. He was put in the shadow by Richard, Duke of Gloucester as Admiral and paid the ultimate price at Middleham for breaking free of the duke's service. It was the only possible end to a tragic story. As Polydore Vergil so eloquently explained in his *Anglica Historia*, if the Bastard of Fauconberg's rebellion had been raised earlier and London had been seized, no doubt Edward IV would have encountered untold problems when he reached the outskirts of the city. Indeed, Fauconberg may have won the final battle and ousted Edward from England.

As for Edward's younger brother, Richard of Gloucester, this author suggests there is only one true verdict concerning his part in the death of Henry VI. If Henry did not die 'naturally' of a stroke or massive heart attack after hearing news about Tewkesbury (which we have no way of proving), then it is likely Richard *was* directly involved in Henry's assassination (or secret execution), acting as the king's right arm. It is highly unlikely Richard would have done this while his brother was still on the road to London. But after Edward arrived in the city on 21 May and established Yorkist rule, the king was likely in no mood to suffer fools gladly while there were secret Lancastrians waiting to rise against him.

Also, Edward's mind may have been made up by one salient point overlooked in this particular cold case. Queen Margaret presented a much bigger problem to Edward because she was likely a grieving and vengeful woman. Fauconberg's rebellion was over by 22 May, and executions of the ring leaders were already underway. But Henry's queen presented a greater threat than her husband. In the past, she had been the power behind the throne, and plenty of Lancastrian rebels would flock to her standard if King Henry was allowed to live. If Henry died, Margaret ceased to be a threat without her son to succeed, and she could be ransomed off to the highest bidder.[18] Therefore, Henry VI had to die, chiefly because of the danger of further rebellion and Margaret's presence in England, not because Henry directly threatened King Edward personally.

Richard, Duke of Gloucester was no doubt tasked with this private execution in his official capacity as Constable of England, and he likely procured 'others' in the Tower to shed the ex-king's blood, according to contemporary sources. It was a grim and soul-searching task to kill a king, but it is said Gloucester was in attendance while the task was completed. No doubt weakened mentally by his confinement, the holy man presented an easy target. And although we do not know exactly *how* Henry VI was executed, we can be sure the act was no knee-jerk reaction by Richard acting on his own volition.[19] Simply put, Edward IV had to secure the kingdom after Fauconberg's rebellion in his official capacity as king, and Gloucester had a job to do as Constable, no more, no less.

However, Henry's execution (for the same reasons explained above) had to be covered up to deflect Lancastrian reprisals in London, and the author of the *Arrivall* was on hand to do this by disseminating the news in brief throughout Europe in several translations of the *Short Arrivall*. According to the official line, Henry had died of 'outrage, anger, indignation, displeasure and melancholy' at the news of Tewkesbury and the death of his only son and heir. In short, the weakened king had suffered a massive seizure, and this sealed the fate of Lancaster for the time being and left England at peace, but without resolution, under Yorkist rule. The Duke of Clarence was the next to suffer execution, Mafia-style, for his undisclosed treason, which was, by anyone's reckoning, long overdue. If Richard of Gloucester also arranged his brother's private execution in the Tower 'in his official capacity' by order of the king and used 'others' to do the deed, then we might have some sympathy for his predicament. In short, Richard was the Constable of England, Edward was the king, and medieval kings had to be ruthless, as Richard was soon to find out during his reign when rebellion and dynastic revolution re-ignited again in 1485.

Epilogue

Of smooth and flattering speech, remember to take heed:
For truth in plain words may be told; of craft a lie hath need.[1]

✜

John Stow, the London antiquarian and historian, always protested never to have written anything for malice, fear or favour nor sought personal gain or vainglory from his work. And he displayed this need for plain truth (as far as he could) when he wrote his *Survey of London* in 1598. This work was the first and best topography of the capital, written by a man who had a deep interest in history and the city he loved. Above all, Stow's description of London is packed with detail, some landmarks being no different in his day from those seen by Fauconberg's rebels during the siege of London. Other localities in his *Survey* are readily identifiable on the famous *Civitas Londinium* or *Agas Map*, first printed from woodblocks in about 1561 and attributed to the surveyor Ralph Agas (c.1540–1621).[2] Earlier, Domenico Mancini also had a line or two to say about London in 1483 that conveyed a foreigner's view of the city during the reign of Richard III. However, today, Stow and Mancini's London and the last vestiges of the medieval city known during the Wars of the Roses have mostly disappeared beneath the march of modern development.

Unfortunately, only the Tower and traces of the original city defences remain to illustrate the story of the siege of London. Old London Bridge was finally demolished in 1831. The new bridge is not in the same place as the old (which was about 100ft downriver), and there is no tangible reminder of its grandeur today. Similarly, medieval Southwark is unrecognisable, apart from its much-renovated cathedral overshadowed by the all-consuming Shard. St Katherine's Wharf and hospital have been obliterated by the docks and a marina of the same name, and Portsoken Ward is only remembered in local elections, and not as a huge suburb with a diverse migrant population living 'without' the city walls. However, the original foundations of the early Postern Gate can still be seen adjacent to Tower Hill, and the London Wall can be traced north towards Aldgate and Bishopsgate. The scene of the battle of Aldgate is now lost beneath tarmac roads and office blocks too numerous to document. St Botolph's Church is surrounded by skyscrapers, and the Houndsditch, which John Stow severely criticised in his *Survey of London*, is the name of a single street rather than an open moat used for waste disposal and dead dogs.

All things considered, we are far removed from the reality of late fifteenth-century London. In fact, the medieval city, its daily life and its sights, sounds and smells might as well be located on the dark side of the moon. Therefore, we must use our imagination and the contemporary records when walking the battlefields of the siege. Even John Stow's work is only helpful to a point, even though it is incredible how much of medieval London was still standing in Stow's time before the Great Fire consumed it in the next century. However, we can at least imagine the topography of the siege and summon up a mind's eye view of London in 1471 using the chronicles, surviving archaeology and early maps.

Conflict archaeology is a discipline that has developed rapidly in the past twenty or so years, and it has become a specialised field that focuses on studying past conflicts, particularly battles and wars, using the material remains left behind in the landscape. The study combines elements of archaeology, history, anthropology and military mechanics to gain insights into the dynamics of armed conflict, the experiences of individuals involved and the broader socio-political context of a given point in time. Armed with this knowledge, we can reconstruct and interpret the physical evidence of battles to understand better the strategies, tactics, technologies and human interactions that shaped the outcomes of historical conflicts. However, most of the above disciplines cannot be applied in a built-up area like London. In short, we lack relevant archaeological evidence from Fauconberg's siege to form an opinion. We cannot excavate the areas of conflict for artefacts, and there are no human remains (or mass graves) to reconstruct the lived experiences of soldiers and civilians caught up in the siege. Therefore, it is challenging to reconstruct the fighting, confirm troop movements and identify killing zones that might better contribute to our understanding of the event.

However, thankfully there exist several early historical maps and drawings of London. We have descriptions of its medieval character and even models of some period structures. We can read the military histories of the Wars of the Roses to ascertain fighting methods and apply the contemporary chronicles and letters of the age. We can also use simple logic, which can be tested against the sources, to analyse what happened where, why, how and when in May 1471. We can even approach an interpretation of the personalities involved in the siege of London and how each one reacted to the crisis. In short, we can arrive at a factual account as a basis for further interpretation. The rest is for the reader to analyse and form a personal opinion about Fauconberg's rebellion and its significance in British history. As for the death, or murder, of Henry VI, I have presented the facts of the matter without 'malice, fear, or favour' (to paraphrase Stow). Illustrating the synergy between the king's death and the siege is key to unlocking the mystery. But it would be wrong of me not to form an opinion about this based on all the interdisciplinary evidence available.

How the demise of Henry VI was closely linked with Fauconberg's rebellion, and how regicide was the only way out to prevent a complete breakdown of law and order in the kingdom, are all central to our understanding of Edward IV's actions in 1471. An all-consuming and protracted British Civil War during the late fifteenth century (involving the entire population with devastating casualties) is hard to visualise today if we follow seventeenth-century precedents.[3] But by proportionally lowering the casualty rate to account for the medieval population during the Wars of the Roses, we can get a sense of the kind of widespread civil unrest that may have been visualised by Edward IV before he entered London on 21 May 1471. A lasting peace had to be established one way or another and a constantly warring or rebelling population, as opposed to intermittent noble bickering with private armies, was an unthinkable alternative. Such insurgency would have led to complete anarchy and a disaster of epic proportions if Henry VI had been allowed to live. The kingdom would have been paralysed, divided and likely open to foreign invasion. Therefore, the fear and actuality of protracted periods of rebellion, like that experienced in 1469–71, may have accelerated Edward IV to act more forcefully after the battle of Tewkesbury than at any other time in his reign. Removing the main agent and focus of insurgency in the Tower, callous as this may sound today, prevented the slaughterhouse, economic collapse and 'dark ages' that Shakespeare described so vividly in Queen Margaret's speech before Tewkesbury. That Edward used the Duke of Gloucester (in his official capacity) to execute Henry VI is irrelevant. Any other officer of the king would have been consigned to anonymity if he had been tasked with the deed. However, as it transpired, Gloucester's name was vilified in all but one chronicle.[4] Henry was a sitting target, and it would not have been hard for Gloucester to order 'others' in the Tower, like Robert Radcliffe, to execute the king in return for favouritism.

In the popular consciousness, Edward IV would be blamed for Henry's murder for centuries, the Duke of Gloucester more so. But the result was twelve years of unbroken peace in England. The Rose was thereafter considered one of the most ruthless and feared kings in medieval Europe. At times, he had shown leadership comparable to Henry V against his enemies, while in contrast, the Saint King had only achieved slight regard among the religious fraternity and those who sought to use him after he died for political reasons. Undoubtedly, Henry VI was a man ahead of his time in the humanitarian sense, even though he was a hopeless king. He was incredibly fortunate to achieve celebrity status after his death through miracle work, while others did not, and only the Bastard of Fauconberg might be worthy of our admiration for remaining loyal to what he believed in. By raising a widespread rebellion against a corrupt Yorkist regime and no doubt hoping to earn himself a proper place in medieval society, Thomas Fauconberg should be remembered today like countless other famous rebel leaders of British history. That he was not like Wat Tyler or Jack Cade is likely why he has failed to gain widespread popularity today, which I hope this work goes some way to putting right.

Overall, men like Warwick 'the Kingmaker' made Fauconberg famous for the wrong reasons. Before being betrayed and executed by the Duke of Gloucester, Thomas rebelled against authority, but after Warwick died there was no way out for him. He was deprived of his *true* identity as Neville influence waned in England. Fauconberg was a man who likely sought to prove his worth as a legitimate Neville in military terms during the Wars of the Roses, although this identity was always beyond his reach. He was an outsider, hence his affinity with the sea. And this is perhaps why Thomas succeeded so well in Kent, where local identity meant more than nobility, and community spirit reigned throughout the ages. By inciting ancient feelings of Invicta against corruption and greed, the Bastard of Fauconberg became Kent's champion. A population can only stand so much, and this was clearly felt in 1471 when the traditional gap between those who had and had not widened considerably to expose a wanton insurgency resulting in the death of a king.

Select Bibliography

Primary Sources

Archaeologia, Vols 29, 62 (1841).
Archaeologia Cantiana, Vols 10, 11, 47, 119, 122 (1876).
Calendar of Patent Rolls (CPR), 1452–61, Henry VI, Vol. 6, 1900.
Calendar of Patent Rolls (CPR), 1461–85, Edward IV, Henry VI, Edward V, Richard III, Vols 2–3, 1897–1901.
Calendar of Patent Roll (CPR), 1467–77, Edward IV, Henry VI, Vols 1–2, 1900.
Canterbury Cathedral Archives, CCA-CC/A/A/35.
Canterbury Cathedral Archives, CCA-CC/WOODRUFF/56/1.
Canterbury Cathedral Archives, Canterbury Chamberlain's Accounts, F/A 5, folio 91.
Exchequer of Receipt, Issue Rolls, E 403/844, m. 8. Easter Term, 11 Edward IV.
Fastolf Relation, College of Arms, Arundel MS 48, folio 342.
Julius E IV, *The Beauchamp Pageants*, British Library.
London Metropolitan Archives, City of London, folio 5, Journal 8, and folio 4b Journal 8.
MS. Arundel, British Museum, 28, folio 25.
The National Archives (TNA), E 403/844, mm. 5–8.
Nugae Antiquae, Sir John Harrington, 1769.
PRO. Exchequer, Warrants for Issue, E 404/74/3/1; E 404/74/3/108, 111.
Sandwich Old Black Book, folio 201.
Victorian County History, Middlesex and Kent.

Printed Sources

C.A.J. Armstrong, *The Usurpation of Richard the Third*, 1936.
T.M. Banta, 'Notices of the Sears Family', *The Searstan Family of Colchester England*, 1901.
F.P. Barnard, ed., *Edward IV's French Expedition of 1475*, 1975.
C.M. Barron, *London in the Later Middle Ages: Government and People, 1200–1500*, 2004.
A.B. Beaven, *The Aldermen of the City of London*, Vol. 2, 1908.
G. Bebbington, *London Street Names*, 1972.

Select Bibliography

C. Berry, *The Margins of Late Medieval London*, 2022.
A.W. Boardman, *The Medieval Soldier in the Wars of the Roses*, 2022.
—*St Albans 1455: The Anatomy of a Battle*, 2022.
—*Towton 1461: The Anatomy of a Battle*, 2022.
R. Britnell, 'Richard Duke of Gloucester and the Death of Thomas Fauconberg', *The Ricardian*, Vol. 10, 1991.
J. Bruce, ed., *Histoirie of the Arrivall of Edward IV, 1471*, 1838.
D. Burton, *Anthony Woodville: Sophisticate or Schemer?*, 2024.
A. Carson, ed., *Domenico Mancini de Occupatione Regni Anglie*, 2021.
F.C. Cass, *The Parish of Monken Hadley*, 1880.
G.E. Cokayne, *The Complete Peerage*, Vol. 5, 1826.
H. Cooper, ed., *Sir Thomas Malory, Le Morte D'Arthur*, 1998.
J.S. Davies, ed., *An English Chronicle of the Reigns of Richard II, Henry IV, Henry V and Henry VI*, 1856.
F. Devon, ed., *Issues of the Exchequer*, 1837.
W.H. Dunham, 'Lord Hasting's Indentured Retainers 1461–1483', *Transactions of the Connecticut Academy of Arts and Sciences*, 1955.
E. Dupont, ed., *Anchiennes Cronicques d'Engleterre*, Vol. 3, 1858–63.
E. Ekwall, *Street-Names of the City of London*, 1965.
H. Ellis, ed., *Raphael Holinshed, Chronicles of England, Scotland and Ireland*, 1808.
—*Edward Hall's Chronicle*, 1809.
—*R. Fabian, The New Chronicles of England and of France*, 1811.
—*Three Books of Polydore Vergil's English History*, 1844.
G. Eyre-Todd, ed., *Medieval Scottish Poetry*, 1892.
R. Firth-Green, ed., 'The Short of the Arrivall of Edward IV', *Speculum* 56, 2, 1981.
D. Flanders, *The Great Livery Companies of the City of London*, 1974.
P.W. Fleming, 'The Lovelace Dispute: Concepts of Property and Inheritance in Fifteenth-Century Kent', *Southern History*, 12, 1990.
G. Foard and A. Curry, *Bosworth 1485: A Battlefield Rediscovered*, 2013.
G. Foard and R. Morris, *The Archaeology of English Battlefields*, 2012.
G. Foard, T. Partida, S. Wilson, *The Barnet Battlefield Project*, 2018.
I. Friel, *The Good Ship: Ships, Shipbuilding and Technology in England 1200–1520*, 1995.
—*Henry V's Navy*, 2020.
W. Fulman, ed., *Rerum Anglicarum Scriptorum Veterum*, Vol. 1, 1684.
R. Furley, *Sir Thomas Wyatt's Rebellion A.D. 1554*, 1878.
J. Gairdner, ed., 'Gregory's Chronicle' in *The Historical Collections of a Citizen of London*, 1876.
—*Three Fifteenth-Century Chronicles*, Camden Society, 1880.
—*The Paston Letters*, Vol. 3, 1904.
D. Gerhold, *London Bridge and its Houses, c.1209–1761*, 2021.
A. Goodman, *The Wars of the Roses: Military Activity and English Society, 1452–97*, 1981.
A. Gransden, *Historical Writing in England II*, 1982.
R.A. Griffiths, *The Reign of King Henry VI*, 1981.
D. Grummitt, *The Calais Garrison: War and Military Service in England, 1346–1558*, 2008.
P.A. Haigh, *The Battle of Wakefield 1460*, 1996.

E. Hallam, ed., *Chronicles of the Wars of the Roses*, 1988.

J.O. Halliwell, ed., *A Chronicle of the First Thirteen Years of the Reign of King Edward the Fourth by John Warkworth*, 1839.

P.W. Hammond, *The Battles of Barnet and Tewkesbury*, 1990.

A. Hanham, *The Cely Letters 1472–1488*, 1975.

—'Henry VI and his Miracles', *The Ricardian*, Vol. 12, 2000.

—*Richard III and his Early Historians 1483–1535*, 1967.

W. and E. Hardy, eds, *Recueil des Chroniques et Anchiennes Istories de la Grant Bretaigne par Jehan de Waurin*, Vol. 5, 1891.

M.D. Harris, ed., *The Coventry Leet Book*, 1907.

I.M.W. Harvey, *Jack Cade's Rebellion of 1450*, 2017.

W. Herbert, *The History of the Twelve Great Livery Companies of London*, Vol. 1, 1837.

M.A. Hicks, *False, Fleeting, Perjur'd Clarence*, 1980.

—*Bastard Feudalism*, 1995.

—*Warwick the Kingmaker*, 1998.

S. Higginbotham, *The Woodvilles*, 2015.

A.B. Hinds, ed., *Calendar of State Papers and Manuscripts in the Archives and Collections of Milan*, Vol. 1, 1912.

G. Home, *Old London Bridge*, 1931.

W.H. St John Hope, 'The Discovery of the Remains of King Henry VI in St George's Chapel Windsor Castle', *Archaeologia*, Vol. 62, 1911.

R. Hope Robbins, ed., 'The Battle of Northampton', *Historical Poems of the XIVth and XVth Centuries*, 1959.

M. Ingram, *The Battle of Northampton 1460*, 2015.

P. Jackson, *London Bridge: A Visual History*, 2002.

M.R. James, ed., *Henry the Sixth, A Reprint of John Blacman's Memoir*, 1919.

L. Johnson, *Shadow King: The Life and Death of Henry VI*, 2019.

E.T. Jones and R. Stone, eds, *The World of the Newport Ship*, 2018.

M.K. Jones, *Bosworth 1485: Psychology of a Battle*, 2002.

A.L. Kaufman, *The Historical Literature of the Jack Cade Rebellion*, 2009.

M.L. Kekewich, C.F. Richmond, A. Sutton, L. Visser-Fuchs, and J. Watts, *The Politics of Fifteenth-Century England: John Vale's Book*, 1995.

A.J. Kempe, 'Notes on Battlefields and Military Works, No. 1 Barnet Field', *Gentleman's Magazine*, 1844.

C.L. Kingsford, ed., *The Chronicles of London*, 1905.

—'Extracts from the First Version of Hardyng's Chronicle', *English Historical Review*, 27, 1912.

H. Kleineke, 'Gerhard von Wesel's Newsletter from England 17 April 1471', *The Ricardian*, Vol. 16, 2006.

R. Knox and S. Leslie, *The Miracles of King Henry VI*, 1923.

P. Langley, *The Princes in the Tower*, 2023.

S. Lee, ed., *Dictionary of National Biography*, 1894–1900.

M. Lewis, *Richard III: Loyalty Binds Me*, 2020.

—*The Survival of the Princes in the Tower*, 2023.

H. Matthews, *The Legitimacy of Bastards: The Place of Illegitimate Children in Late Medieval England*, 2019.

Select Bibliography

H.E. Maurer, *Margaret of Anjou: Queenship and Power in Late Medieval England*, 2003.
M. Mercer, 'Lancastrian Loyalism in Kent During the Wars of the Roses', *Archaeologia Cantiana*, Vol. 119, 1999.
—'A Forgotten Kentish Rebellion, September–October 1470', *Archaeologia Cantiana*, Vol. 122, 2002.
G. Milne, *The Port of Medieval London*, 2003.
P. Murray Kendall, ed., *Richard III: The Great Debate*, 1965.
A.R. Myers, 'The Outbreak of War Between England and Burgundy in February 1471', *Bulletin of the Institute of Historical Research (BIHR)*, 33, 1960.
—*English Historical Documents, IV, 1327–1485*, 1969.
J.G. Nichols, ed., *Chronicle of the Rebellion in Lincolnshire 1470*, 1847.
A.J. Pearman, 'The Kentish Family of Lovelace', *Archaeologia Cantiana*, Vol. 10, 1876.
S.G. Potter, ed., J. Foxe, *The Book of Martyrs*, 1873.
I. Quintella, da Costa, *Annaes da Marinha Portugueza*, I, 1839.
J. Renouard, ed., *Chronique de Mathieu d'Escouchy, 1444–1461*, Vol. 1, 1863.
C.F. Richmond, 'Fauconberg's Kentish Rising of May 1471', *English Historical Review*, 1970.
H.T. Riley, ed., *The Croyland Abbey Chronicle*, 1854.
—*Registrum Abbatis Johannis Whethamstede*, 1, 1872.
G. Ropp, von der, ed., *Hanserecesse, 1431–1476*, Vol. 6, Leipzig, 1890.
S. Rose, *Medieval Naval Warfare 1000–1500*, 2001.
—*England's Medieval Navy 1066–1509*, 2013.
C. Ross, *Edward IV*, 1974.
—'Some "Servants and Lovers" of Richard in his Youth', *The Ricardian*, 55, 1976.
A.L. Rowse, *The Tower of London in the History of the Nation*, 1977.
G. McN. Rushforth, 'The Burials of Lancastrian Notables in Tewkesbury Abbey after the Battle, AD 1471', *Transactions of the Bristol and Gloucestershire Archaeological Society*, Vol. 47, 1925.
A.R. Scoble, ed., *The Memoirs of Philip de Commines*, Vol. 1, 1911.
C.L. Scofield, *The Life and Reign of Edward IV*, Vols 1–2, 1923.
J.B. Scott, ed., 'Letters Respecting Fauconberg's Kentish Rising in 1471', *Archaeologia Cantiana*, Vol. 11, 1877.
R.R. Sharpe, *London and the Kingdom*, Vols 1–3, 1894.
—*Calendar of Letter-Books of the City of London: Edward IV–Henry VII*, 1899–1912.
L.T. Smith ed., *The Itinerary of John Leland 1535–1543*, Part 8, 1909.
M.E. Smith, 'Henry VI's Medical Record', *The Ricardian*, 43, 1973.
R.D. Smith and K. DeVries, *The Artillery of the Dukes of Burgundy 1363–1477*, 2005.
D. Spencer, 'The Lancastrian Armament Programme of the 1450s and the Development of Field Guns', *The Ricardian*, 25, 2015.
—*Royal and Urban Gunpowder Weapons in Medieval England*, 2019.
L. Stephen, ed., *Dictionary of National Biography*, Vols 6–16, 1886–88.
J. Stevenson, ed., 'Annales Rerum Anglicarum', *Letters and Papers Illustrative of the Wars of the English in France*, Vol. 2, 1864.
J. Stow, *A Survey of London Written in the Year 1598*, 2009.
M. Stoyle, *Dissidence and Despair*, 1999.
J. Strachey, ed., *Rotuli Parliamentorum*, Vol. 5. 1783.

M. Strickland and R. Hardy, *The Great Warbow*, 2005.
A. Sutton, 'Sir Thomas Cook and his Troubles: An Investigation', *Guildhall Studies in London History*, Vol. 3, 1978.
J.W. Sutton, ed., *The Dicts and Sayings of the Philosophers*, 2006.
S. Sweetingburg, 'Those who Marched with Faunt: Reconstructing the Canterbury Rebels of 1471', *Southern History*, 39, 2017.
J.D. Taylor, *Sir Thomas Wyatt the Younger c.1521–1554 and Wyatt's Rebellion*, 2013.
A.H. Thomas and I.D. Thornley, eds, *The Great Chronicle of London*, 1938.
R. Thompson, *Chronicles of London Bridge*, 1827.
L. Visser-Fuchs. 'A Ricardian Riddle: The Casualty List of the Battle of Barnet', *The Ricardian*, Vol. 8, 100, 1988.
—'Edward IV's Memoir on Paper to Charles, Duke of Burgundy: The So-Called Short Version of the Arrival', *Nottingham Medieval Studies (NMS)*, 36, 1992.
G. Warner, ed., *The Libelle of Englyshe Polycye: A Poem on the Use of Sea Power 1436*, 1926.
P.J. Watson, 'A Review of the Sources for the Battle of Barnet, 14 April 1471', *The Ricardian*, Vol. 12, 2000–02.
C. Wedgewood and A.D. Holt, *History of Parliament: Biographies of the Members of the House of Commons, 1439–1509*, 1936.
D. Whipp, *The Medieval Postern Gate by the Tower of London*, Monograph Series, 2006.
W.J. White, 'The Death and Burial of Henry VI: A Review of the Facts and Theories, Part 1', *The Ricardian*, Vol. 5, 78, 1982.
G.A. Williams, *Medieval London: From Commune to Capital*, 1963.
B. Wolffe, *Henry VI*, 1981.
T. Wright, ed., *Political Poems and Songs Relating to English History*, Vol. 2, 1861.
Z. Zaller, *The Parliament of 1621*, 1971.

Notes

Introduction
1. W. Shakespeare, *Henry VI, Part 3*, Act 5, Scene 4.
2. See J. Bruce, ed., *Histoirie of the Arrivall of Edward IV, 1471*, 1838. The *Arrivall* was the official Yorkist (eyewitness) account of Edward IV's reclamation of the throne in 1471.
3. See A.H. Thomas and I.D. Thornley, eds, *The Great Chronicle of London*, 1938, pp. 218–21.
4. H. Ellis, ed., *Three Books of Polydore Vergil's English History*, 1844, pp. 153–4.
5. P.W. Hammond, *The Battles of Barnet and Tewkesbury*, 1990 and C.F. Richmond, 'Fauconberg's Kentish Rising of May 1471', *English Historical Review*, 1970.
6. See B. Wolffe, *Henry VI*, 1981 and R.A. Griffiths, *The Reign of King Henry VI*, 1981. See also L. Johnson, *Shadow King: The Life and Death of Henry VI*, 2019.
7. H. Cooper, ed., *Sir Thomas Malory, Le Morte D'Arthur*, 1998, p. 8.
8. Edward IV and the Earl of Warwick were the main contenders for power in 1471, but Henry VI claimed to be the rightful king.

Chapter 1
1. A poem said to be the work of Henry VI in captivity, 1465–71, cited in Sir John Harrington, *Nugae Antiquae*, 1769.
2. For a comparison of the two kings, see C.L. Kingsford, 'Extracts from the First Version of Hardyng's Chronicle', *English Historical Review*, 1912, pp. 744–5.
3. *Three Books of Polydore Vergil*, p. 70. See also the morality of the young Henry VI by Piero da Monte in R.A. Griffiths, *The Reign of King Henry VI*, p. 235.
4. James I's description of Henry VI cited by Z. Zaller, *The Parliament of 1621*, 1971, p. 69. See B. Wolffe, *Henry VI* and R.A. Griffiths, *The Reign of Henry VI*, for a more balanced view of the king.
5. For a new appraisal of Henry VI, see *Shadow King*.
6. J.S. Davies, ed., *An English Chronicle of the Reigns of Richard II, Henry IV, Henry V and Henry VI*, 1856, p. 79. See also H.T. Riley, ed., *The Croyland Abbey Chronicle*, 1854, p. 419 for England's plight in 1460.
7. Bastard feudalism was a system that allowed nobles to retain men in their service for pay. The term was first coined by C. Plummer in 1885.

8. See M.R. James, ed., *Henry the Sixth, A Reprint of John Blacman's Memoir*, 1919, pp. 37–8.
9. H.T. Riley, ed., *Registrum Abbatis Johannis Whethamstede*, 1, 1872, p. 247.
10. See Wolffe, *Henry VI*, pp. 125–32.
11. See Chapter 5, and I.M.W. Harvey, *Jack Cade's Rebellion of 1450*, 2017.
12. J. Gairdner, ed., *Three Fifteenth-Century Chronicles*, 1880, p. 94.
13. J.S. Davies, ed., *An English Chronicle*, pp. 79–80. The bastardry claim was likely Yorkist propaganda.
14. See H.E. Maurer, *Margaret of Anjou: Queenship and Power in Late Medieval England*, 2003, pp. 17–18.
15. For notes on porphyria, see M.E. Smith, 'Henry VI's Medical Record', *The Ricardian*, 1973, p. 14.
16. J. Strachey, ed., *Rotuli Parliamentorum*, Vol. 5, 1783, p. 241. This is another source of the bastardry claim, although this apathy could have been caused by Henry's illness.
17. See also M.A. Hicks, *Bastard Feudalism*, 1995, pp. 90–1.
18. J. Gairdner, ed., *The Paston Letters*, 1904, Vol. 3, p. 28.
19. See *Rotuli Parliamentorum*, Vol. 5, pp. 281–2.
20. Ibid., p. 348.
21. See H. Ellis, ed., *Edward Hall's Chronicle*, 1809 and H. Ellis, ed., *Raphael Holinshed, Chronicles of England, Scotland and Ireland*, 1808.
22. See A.W. Boardman, *The Medieval Soldier in the Wars of the Roses*, 2022 and A. Goodman, *The Wars of the Roses: Military Activity and English Society, 1452–97*, 1981.
23. For the battle, see M. Ingram, *The Battle of Northampton 1460*, 2015.
24. See P.A. Haigh, *The Battle of Wakefield 1460*, 1996.
25. J. Stevenson, ed., 'Annales Rerum Anglicarum', *Letters and Papers Illustrative of the Wars of the English in France*, Vol. 2, 1864, p. 775.
26. The fullest contemporary account of (second) St Albans is given in J. Gairdner, ed., 'Gregory's Chronicle' in *The Historical Collections of a Citizen of London*, 1876, pp. 213–14.
27. A.B. Hinds, ed., *Calendar of State Papers and Manuscripts in the Archives and Collections of Milan (CSPM)*, Vol. 1, 1912, p. 66. See also A.W. Boardman, *Towton 1461: The Anatomy of a Battle*, 2022.
28. *Towton 1461*, pp. 292–3.
29. For the war in the north, see 'Gregory's Chronicle', pp. 218–23 and J.O. Halliwell, ed., *A Chronicle of the First Thirteen Years of the Reign of King Edward the Fourth by John Warkworth*, 1839, pp. 36–9.
30. For Warwick's disaffection from Edward, see M.A. Hicks, *Warwick the Kingmaker*, 1998, pp. 255–79.
31. For the date of the battle, see M.D. Harris, ed., *The Coventry Leet Book*, 1907, p. 346. Sir Geoffrey Gate was Warwick's retainer and made governor of the Isle of Wight after the battle of Wakefield.
32. J.G. Nichols, ed., *Chronicle of the Rebellion in Lincolnshire 1470*, 1847, p. 112.
33. *The Great Chronicle of London*, p. 210. See also T. Hearne, ed., *Hearne's Fragment c.1470*, in *Chronicles of the White Rose of York*, 1845, p. 24.
34. For Clarence's betrayal, see C. Ross, *Edward IV*, 1974, p. 156.
35. L.T. Smith, ed., *The Itinerary of John Leland 1535–1543*, 1909, p. 105.
36. *CSPM*, p. 117.

37 *John Blacman*, pp. 39–40. See Chapter 3 for the attempt on the king's life.
38 Readeption: the word normally used to describe Henry VI's reign under Warwick.

Chapter 2

1 T. Wright, ed., *Political Poems and Songs Relating to English History*, Vol. 2, 1861, p. 271.
2 The Hanseatic League. The Anglo-Hanseatic trade war lasted from 1469 to 1474.
3 *Warkworth*, p. 11.
4 See Chapter 3 for Henry's attempted assassination.
5 A.R. Myers, *English Historical Documents, IV, 1327–1485*, 1969, p. 307.
6 For Warwick's letter, see A.R. Myers, 'The Outbreak of War Between England and Burgundy in February 1471', *BIHR*, 33, 1960, p. 115.
7 A.R. Scoble, ed., *The Memoirs of Philip de Commines*, 1911, Vol. 1, p. 339.
8 H. Kleineke, 'Gerhard von Wesel's Newsletter from England 17 April 1471', *The Ricardian*, Vol. 16, 2006, p. 7. It is unlikely Edward could muster 2,400 men.
9 *Warkworth*, p. 13.
10 Edward was called *The Rose of Rouen* in a political poem written in 1461. See *Archaeologia*, 29, pp. 343–7.
11 Northampton was won through treachery. Mortimer's Cross, Ferrybridge and Towton were three victories Edward should have lost but won because of weather conditions. Barnet and Tewkesbury were won due to mistakes by Edward's enemies.
12 The chance discovery of the skeleton was made by Sir Henry Emlyn while conducting renovations at Windsor.
13 W. Fulman, ed., *Rerum Anglicarum Scriptorum Veterum*, Vol. 1, 1684, p. 563.
14 See 'Gregory's Chronicle', p. 219. Apparently, Somerset shared Edward's bed regularly.
15 For a psychological view of the impact of Wakefield, see M.K. Jones, *Bosworth 1485: Psychology of a Battle*, 2002, pp. 39–56.
16 *Warkworth*, p. 36.
17 Towton claimed 28,000 lives (according to 'heralds') and the City of York sent 1,000 men to the battle. See *Towton 1461* and *Paston Letters*, Vol. 3, p. 268.
18 *Arrivall*, pp. 6–7.
19 Chroniclers determined that Warwick's army exceeded 20,000 men, a number that could never be contained within Coventry's walls. See *Arrivall*, p. 9 for a more realistic figure.
20 Ibid.
21 For Margaret's letter, see *Battles of Barnet and Tewkesbury*, p. 65 and E. Dupont, ed., *Anchiennes Cronicques d'Engleterre*, Vol. 3, 1858–63, p. 210.
22 Ibid., p. 11. For a biography of Clarence, see M.A. Hicks, *False, Fleeting, Perjur'd Clarence*, 1980.
23 *Arrivall*, p. 12.
24 The vision of the three suns (parhelion) was attributed by Edward to the Trinity.
25 The Duke of Somerset, the Earl of Devon and other Lancastrians were still in London.
26 *Arrivall*, pp. 13–14.
27 Ibid., p. 14.

28 *Warkworth*, p. 15.
29 See C.L. Scofield, *The Life and Reign of Edward IV*, Vol. 2, 1923, p. 576 and *Battles of Barnet and Tewkesbury*, p. 70.
30 *Great Chronicle of London*, p. 215.
31 See E. Hallam, ed., *Chronicles of the Wars of the Roses*, 1988, p. 244 and A. Gransden, *Historical Writing in England II*, 1982, pp. 292–3.
32 See L. Visser-Fuchs, 'Edward IV's Memoir on Paper to Charles, Duke of Burgundy: The So-Called Short Version of the Arrivall', *Nottingham Medieval Studies*, 36, 1992, p. 170.
33 For an alternative biography of Warwick, see *Warwick the Kingmaker*.

Chapter 3

1 G. Warner, ed., *The Libelle of Englyshe Polycye: A Poem on the Use of Sea Power 1436*, 1926, p. 53.
2 Fauconberg's father died in 1463 after which Thomas served the Earl of Warwick. See Chapter 6.
3 See 'Fauconberg's Kentish Rising of May 1471', p. 676 and I. da Costa Quintella, *Annaes da Marinha Portugueza*, Vol. 1, 1839, pp. 176–7.
4 CPR 1467–77, Vol. 2, 1900, p. 379.
5 See 'Fauconberg's Kentish Rising of May 1471', p. 676.
6 Griffiths, *Henry VI*, p. 423.
7 See H. Matthews, *The Legitimacy of Bastards: The Place of Illegitimate Children in Late Medieval England*, 2019.
8 For the Fauconberg lineage, see G.E. Cokayne, *The Complete Peerage*, Vol. 5, 1826, p. 276.
9 Ibid., pp. 276–85. Medieval English law maintained it was impossible for a man to rape his legal spouse and be prosecuted.
10 See J. Tait's biography in S. Lee, ed., *Dictionary of National Biography*, Vol. 40, 1894.
11 J. Renouard, ed., *Chronique de Mathieu d'Escouchy, 1444–1461*, Vol. 1, 1863, p. 166.
12 The *écu* was a French gold coin (comparable to an English crown) the value of which varied in the medieval period.
13 Griffiths, *Henry VI*, p. 406.
14 It is highly unlikely that Fauconberg was in France. See Fastolf Relation, College of Arms, *Arundel MS* 48, folio 342, in A.W. Boardman, *St Albans 1455: The Anatomy of a Battle*, 2023, p. 224–8.
15 R.R. Sharpe, *London and the Kingdom*, Vol. 1, 1894, p. 271. Journal 5, folios 152 and 175, Guildhall.
16 I. Friel, *Henry V's Navy*, 2020, pp. 58–60.
17 CPR 1452–61, Vol. 6, p. 438.
18 Livery and maintenance were ways of retaining manpower through mutual benefit.
19 Pont de Neullay (Newham Bridge), 23 April 1460.
20 See Goodman, *The Wars of the Roses*, pp. 32–3.
21 *An English Chronicle*, p. 93.
22 See Jehan de Waurin in *The Battle of Northampton*, p. 131.
23 See the battles of (second) St Albans, Ferrybridge and Towton in *Towton 1461* and 'The Rose of Rouen' in *Archaeologia*, 29.

24 See *Towton 1461*, pp. 179–82.
25 Thomas is usually styled 'Thomas Fauconberg' in records of the period or 'the bastard' after his death. He was titled 'gentleman' in official documents, although he was never knighted.
26 PRO. Exchequer, Warrants for Issue, E 404/74/3/1; E 404/74/3/108, 111.
27 CPR 1467–77, p. 250. Along with other ships belonging to Warwick.
28 Scofield, *Edward IV*, Vol. 1, p. 526.
29 *The Great Chronicle of London*, p. 211.
30 See Ibid., p. 19. Blind Chapelton (Blanche Appleton) was an area north-east of Mark Lane in Aldgate Ward. See also J. Stow, *A Survey of London Written in the Year 1598*, 2009, p. 141.
31 *Great Chronicle of London*, p. 211.
32 *John Blacman*, pp. 49–40.
33 Ibid.
34 See 'Fauconberg's Kentish Rising of May 1471', p. 675.
35 *Warkworth*, p. 19.
36 For more on ships during the period, see *The Medieval Soldier*, pp. 288–96.
37 See E.T. Jones and R. Stone, eds, *The World of the Newport Ship*, 2018.
38 For shipbuilding techniques and naval warfare, see *Henry V's Navy*; I. Friel, *The Good Ship: Ships, Shipbuilding and Technology in England 1200–1520*, 1995; S. Rose, *Medieval Naval Warfare 1000–1500*, 2001; S. Rose, *England's Medieval Navy 1066–1509*, 2013.
39 CPR 1467–77, p. 250.
40 Julius E IV, *The Beauchamp Pageants*, British Library. See also D. Brindley, *Richard Beauchamp: Medieval England's Greatest Knight*, 2001.
41 See Scofield, *Edward IV*, Vol. 2, p. 413. Issues Roll. Mich. 7 Edw. IV, 31 October 1467.
42 See CPR 1467–77, pp. 290–92.

Chapter 4
1 For a short pro-Yorkist depiction of Barnet, see *Political Poems*, p. 276.
2 *Paston Letters*, Vol. 5, pp. 99–103.
3 For an early account of the battle, see G. von der Ropp, ed., *Hanserecesse, 1431–1476*, Vol. 6, Leipzig, 1890 in 'Gerhard von Wesel's Newsletter from England 17 April 1471', pp. 7–10.
4 *Arrivall*, p. 18.
5 See John Speed's map of Middlesex and Hertfordshire 1611–12 for an approximation of the battlefield.
6 See G. Foard and R. Morris, *The Archaeology of English Battlefields*, 2012, and G. Foard and A. Curry, *Bosworth 1485: A Battlefield Rediscovered*, 2013.
7 *Warkworth*, p. 16 and *Great Chronicle of London*, p. 216.
8 See *Arrivall*; *Warkworth*; *Paston Letters*, Vol. 3; *Great Chronicle of London*. *Hanserecesse, 1431–1476*, Vol. 6. R. Firth Green, ed., 'The Short of the Arrival of Edward IV', *Speculum*, 56, 2, 1981.
9 For a breakdown of the armies at Barnet, see P.J. Watson, 'A Review of the Sources for the Battle of Barnet, 14 April 1471', *The Ricardian*, Vol. 12, 2000–02, pp. 51–4.
10 The various deployments are given in each of the main accounts.

11 'Gerhard von Wesel's Newsletter from England 17 April 1471', p. 9. Serpentine field guns had barrel elevation devices during this period.
12 Gloucester commanded the left at Tewkesbury. His men may have worn 'sun in splendour' badges similar to Oxford's star. See also *Warkworth*, p. 38.
13 For Gloucester's wounds, see L. Visser-Fuchs. 'A Ricardian Riddle: The Casualty List of the Battle of Barnet', *The Ricardian*, Vol. 8, 100, 1988, p. 12.
14 'Gerhard von Wesel's Newsletter from England 17 April 1471', p. 9.
15 See *Arrivall*, pp. 19–20 and the *Short Arrivall*, p. 328. The latter fails to mention Edward's prowess in arms.
16 *Warkworth*, p. 16.
17 Ibid., p. 17; *Paston Letters*, p. 100. For a list, see MS. Arundel, British Museum, 28, folio 25.
18 'Gerhard von Wesel's Newsletter from England 17 April 1471', p. 10. What an army 'looked like' was not necessarily its true strength.
19 Ibid.
20 *Political Poems*, p. 277.
21 *Paston Letters*, Vol. 5, p. 100.
22 For the history of this area and work by the University of Huddersfield from 2015 to 2018, see G. Foard, T. Partida, S. Wilson, *The Barnet Battlefield Project*, 2018; F.C. Cass, *The Parish of Monken Hadley*, 1880; A.J. Kempe, 'Notes on Battlefields and Military Works, No. 1 Barnet Field', *Gentleman's Magazine*, 1844; and *Victorian County History*, Middlesex, 1976.
23 'Notes on Battlefields and Military Works, No. 1 Barnet Field', p. 251.
24 *Great Chronicle of London*, p. 217.
25 *Commines*, Vol. 1, p. 201.
26 As opposed to his attitude in May 1471. See *CSPM*, Vol. 1, p. 157.
27 *Warkworth*, pp. 17–18.
28 *Arrivall*, pp. 25–6.
29 A medieval army could march 10–20 miles a day unless mounted or encumbered by artillery.
30 *Arrivall*, p. 28.
31 Ibid., pp. 28–9.
32 For this theory, compare *Arrivall* and the *Short Arrivall*.
33 *John Leland*, p. 162.
34 See the *Short Arrivall*.
35 See *Arrivall*; *Warkworth*; *Paston Letters*, Vol. 3; *John Leland*; the *Short Arrivall*.
36 *Battles of Barnet and Tewkesbury*, p. 95. For ratios of footmen to archers in the period, see *The Medieval Soldier*, pp. 125–6.
37 For Gloucester on the left at these battles, see also 'A Review of the Sources for the Battle of Barnet, 14 April 1471', pp. 61–2.
38 *Arrivall*, p. 29.
39 W.H. Dunham, 'Lord Hasting's Indentured Retainers 1461–1483', *Transactions of the Connecticut Academy of Arts and Sciences*, September 1955.
40 A week before Edward left Windsor more ordnance was commissioned. See CPR 1467–77, p. 259.
41 *Arrivall*, p. 175.

42 *Hall's Chronicle*, p. 301.
43 *Arrivall*, p. 29.
44 *Polydore Vergil*, p. 152.
45 Some 2,000 dead are recorded by modern sources, but no contemporary sources can confirm this figure.
46 *Warkworth*, p. 41. This may have looked like murder, but the Lancastrian leaders were rebels and had committed treason against Edward IV.
47 C. Ross, 'Some 'Servants and Lovers' of Richard in his Youth', *The Ricardian*, 55, 1976, pp. 2–3.
48 CPR 1467–77, p. 470.
49 Ibid., 1461–1485, Vol. 3, p. 60
50 *Paston Letters*, Vol. 5, pp. 104–5.
51 See G. McN. Rushforth, 'The Burials of Lancastrian Notables in Tewkesbury Abbey after the Battle, AD 1471', *Transactions of the Bristol and Gloucestershire Archaeological Society*, Vol. 47, 1925, pp. 131–48. A plan of the graves is included in the article.
52 *Arrivall*, p. 31.

Chapter 5

1 William Dunbar (1460–1520). G. Eyre-Todd, ed., *Medieval Scottish Poetry*, 1892, pp. 183–4.
2 Letter from Prospero di Camulio to Francesco Sforza, Duke of Milan in *CSPM*, p. 71–6.
3 There are at least four other meanings of Aldgate. But see G. Bebbington, *London Street Names*, 1972 and E. Ekwall, *Street-Names of the City of London*, 1965.
4 F. Devon, ed., *Issues of the Exchequer*, 1837, p. 495. Other walls were also built for defence against Fauconberg's rebels.
5 *Survey of London*, p. 124.
6 A.L. Rowse, *The Tower of London in the History of the Nation*, 1977. See also G. Milne, *The Port of Medieval London*, 2003.
7 *Survey of London*, p. 46. See also D. Whipp, *The Medieval Postern Gate by the Tower of London*, Monograph Series, 2006.
8 *Survey of London*, pp. 118–25.
9 Ibid., pp. 132–42.
10 See D. Gerhold, *London Bridge and its Houses, c.1209–1761*, 2021; G. Home, *Old London Bridge*, 1931; P. Jackson, *London Bridge: A Visual History*, 2002; chain barriers would have prevented Fauconberg's ships from sailing west beyond the bridge in May 1471.
11 A. Carson, ed., *Domenico Mancini de Occupatione Regni Anglie*, 2021, p. 71.
12 See R.R. Sharpe, ed., *Calendar of Letter-Books of the City of London: Edward IV–Henry VII*, 1899–1912, for an account of London's administration, business, debts, deeds and ordinances.
13 For the administration and fabric of London, see C.M. Barron, *London in the Later Middle Ages: Government and People, 1200–1500*, 2004; G.A. Williams, *Medieval London: From Commune to Capital*, 1963; C. Berry, *The Margins of Late Medieval London*, 2022.
14 For merchants and traders in London, see W. Herbert, *The History of the Twelve Great Livery Companies of London*, Vol. 1, 1837.

15 See *Great Chronicle of London*, pp. 213–21, *Calendar of Letter-Books*, pp. 91–100 and D. Flanders, *The Great Livery Companies of the City of London*, 1974.
16 A. Sutton, 'Sir Thomas Cook and his Troubles: An Investigation', *Guildhall Studies in London History*, Vol. 3, 1978, pp. 105–06.
17 Wat Tyler and Jack Cade gained entry into London in 1381 and 1450 due to a lack of corporate unity and party politics. This was not so for Fauconberg in 1471.
18 *History of the Twelve Great Livery Companies of London*, Vol. 1, p. 250.
19 Ibid., pp. 247–50.
20 A.B. Beaven, *The Aldermen of the City of London*, Vol. 2, 1908, p. 10; *Great Chronicle of London*, p. 227.
21 *DNB*, Vol. 58, pp. 56–7.
22 *Arrivall*, pp. 36–7.
23 *DNB*, Vol. 16, p. 108.
24 *Rotuli Parliamentorum*, Vol. 6, p. 129. See also *DNB*, Vol. 16, p. 247.
25 Ibid., Vol. 6, p. 10.
26 It was recorded that he was killed at Towton on 29 March 1461.
27 *Mancini*, p. 49. See also C.A.J. Armstrong, *The Usurpation of Richard the Third*, 1936, p. 83.
28 J.W. Sutton, ed., *The Dicts and Sayings of the Philosophers*, 2006. A prose text containing lore collected from biblical, classical and legendary philosophers.
29 For the Woodville family, see S. Higginbotham, *The Woodvilles*, 2015. For Earl Rivers, see D. Burton, *Anthony Woodville: Sophisticate or Schemer?* 2024 and *DNB*, Vol. 62, pp. 410–13.
30 CPR 1467–77, Vol. 2, p. 285.
31 *Issues of the Exchequer*, p. 494. The pound sign (£) developed from the letter *l*, the initial letter of the Latin word *libra*, meaning a pound of money.
32 Ibid. Many payments are entered onto the roll, including Lord Hastings and his men to take possession of Calais and Rysbank, dating the commission to before Tewkesbury as Hastings fought there with Edward IV.

Chapter 6

1 *Political Poems*, p. 279.
2 For Warwick's aims, see M.L. Kekewich, C.F. Richmond, A. Sutton, L. Visser-Fuchs and J. Watts, *The Politics of Fifteenth-Century England: John Vale's Book*, 1995, pp. 218–21.
3 See M. Stoyle, *Dissidence and Despair*, 1999, pp. 423–42.
4 See I.M.W. Harvey, *Jack Cade's Rebellion*; A.L. Kaufman, *The Historical Literature of the Jack Cade Rebellion*, 2009.
5 For the Beaufort influence in Kent, see M. Mercer, 'Lancastrian Loyalism in Kent During the Wars of the Roses', *Archaeologia Cantiana*, Vol. 119, 1999, pp. 221–44.
6 *Arrivall*, p. 33.
7 Canterbury was granted its City Charter in 1448 and the council acted as one with the mayor according to their indictments after the siege.
8 *Great Chronicle of London*, p. 218. A rover was a privateer or mariner, and the city records describe Fauconberg as one of these on many occasions.

9   See S. Sweetingburg, 'Those who Marched with Faunt: Reconstructing the Canterbury Rebels of 1471', *Southern History*, 39, 2017.
10 Canterbury Cathedral Archives, CCA-CC/WOODRUFF/56/1.
11 For a detailed discussion, see 'Fauconberg's Kentish Rising of May 1471', pp. 684–6. For an enquiry into the Surrey rebels, Kent and Essex, see CPR 1467–77, Vol. 2, pp. 300–03.
12 *Great Chronicle of London*, pp. 211–12.
13 M. Mercer, 'A Forgotten Kentish Rebellion, September–October 1470', *Archaeologia Cantiana*, Vol. 122, 2002, p. 148.
14 C. Wedgewood and A.D. Holt, *History of Parliament: Biographies of the Members of the House of Commons, 1439–1509*, 1936, pp. 102–03. See also PRO, KB 9/992/18.
15 For a more in-depth discussion, see 'A Forgotten Kentish Rebellion', pp. 143–52.
16 Canterbury Cathedral Archives, Canterbury Chamberlain's Accounts, F/A 5, folio 91.
17 'A Forgotten Kentish Rebellion', p. 148.
18 Ibid., p. 147.
19 Bergavenny/Abergavenny. The latter name and title were not officially adopted until 1730.
20 For the (second) battle of St Albans, see *Towton 1461*, p. 78.
21 A.J. Pearman, 'The Kentish Family of Lovelace', *Archaeologia Cantiana*, Vol. 10, 1876, p. 192.
22 See P.W. Fleming, 'The Lovelace Dispute: Concepts of Property and Inheritance in Fifteenth-Century Kent', *Southern History*, 12, 1990 and 'The Kentish Family of Lovelace', pp. 184–93.
23 For an alternative figure to the *Arrivall*, see *Warkworth*, p. 20.
24 Before writing this letter, Fauconberg would have known Warwick died on 14 April.
25 J.B. Scott, ed., 'Letters Respecting Fauconberg's Kentish Rising in 1471', in *Archaeologia Cantiana*, Vol. 11, 1877, pp. 359–60. Trans. from London Metropolitan Archives, City of London, folio 5 of Journal 8, and folio 4b of Journal 8 for the letter to the Commonality.
26 *Warkworth*, p. 20.
27 *The Great Chronicle of London*, p. 218.
28 *Arrivall*, p. 33.
29 Wars of the Roses armies were usually composed of half men-at-arms, retainers and their tenants, and half archers armed with the warbow. See *The Medieval Soldier*, p. 87.
30 Maurer, *Margaret of Anjou*, pp. 210–11.
31 See Scofield, *Edward IV*, Vol. 1, p. 589. See also Issue Rolls, Easter 11 Edward IV, 13 July.

Chapter 7

1   *Political Poems*, p. 277.
2   *Bleak Heath* (Blackheath) was known for its open aspect. Watling Street ran directly over the heath and Greenwich Park. The same area was used to muster rebel forces in 1381, 1450 and numerous other occasions.

3 'Letters Respecting Fauconberg's Kentish Rising in 1471', pp. 360–63. London Metropolitan Archives, City of London, folio 5 of Journal 8, and folio 4b of Journal 8.
4 See Scofield, *Edward IV*, Vol. 1, p. 591, citing Issues Roll, Easter 11 Edward IV, 24 June.
5 *Great Chronicle of London*, p. 219.
6 *Arrivall*, p. 34.
7 Ibid., p. 35.
8 *Warkworth*, p. 20.
9 *Arrivall*, p. 35.
10 See Scofield, *Edward IV*, Vol. 1, p. 592.
11 *Warkworth*, p. 19.
12 Latin translation from *London and the Kingdom*, Vol. 1, p. 392.
13 *Arrivall*, p. 35
14 Ibid., p. 34.
15 *Warkworth*, p. 20.
16 *Great Chronicle of London*, p. 219.
17 Latin translation from *London and the Kingdom*, Vol. 3, p. 386. See Journal 7, folios 223b–224. The Lanthorn Tower was traditionally the queen's residence in the royal apartments.
18 *Great Chronicle of London*, p. 219.
19 *Survey of London*, p. 413.
20 *Political Poems*, p. 278. There were also soldiers from the Calais garrison recruited by Richard Haute.
21 Ibid., p. 277.

Chapter 8

1 *Political Poems*, p. 278.
2 See D. Spencer, 'The Lancastrian Armament Programme of the 1450s and the Development of Field Guns', *The Ricardian*, 25, 2015.
3 *Coventry Leet Book*, p. 345.
4 See *Towton 1461*, pp. 74–5.
5 French version of *The Historie of the Arrivall of Edward IV*, MS 236, University of Ghent.
6 D. Spencer, *Royal and Urban Gunpowder Weapons in Medieval England*, 2019, p. 79.
7 F.P. Barnard, ed., *Edward IV's French Expedition of 1475*, 1975, pp. 141–2.
8 *Arrivall*, p. 35–6.
9 W. and E. Hardy, eds, *Recueil des Chroniques et Anchiennes Istories de la Grant Bretaigne par Jehan de Waurin*, Vol. 5, 1891, p. 675; ibid., p. 39.
10 *Political Poems*, p. 277.
11 M. Strickland and R. Hardy, *The Great Warbow*, 2005, p. 408–14.
12 *London Bridge and its Houses*, p. 4.
13 For guns misfiring at the (second) battle of St Albans in 1461, see 'Gregory's Chronicle', pp. 213–14.
14 *Arrivall*, p. 36.
15 For a detailed description of the bridge, see *London Bridge and its Houses*.

16 *Arrivall*, p. 36.
17 See *London Bridge and its Houses*, Chapter 3.
18 R. Thompson, *Chronicles of London Bridge*, 1827, pp. 287–8. Responsibility for the bridge had also been given to George Ireland and Thomas Stalbrook who were both aldermen of the city. See TNA, E 403/844, mm. 5–7.
19 *Croyland Chronicle*, p. 467.
20 *Battles of Barnet and Tewkesbury*, p. 108.
21 *Arrivall*, p. 34.
22 Likely a mistake for Robert Radcliffe, although he was not knighted in 1471.
23 This payment proves Henry was in the Lanthorn Tower, not the Wakefield Tower, if Journal 7, folios 223b–224 in *London and the Kingdom*, Vol. 3, p. 386 can be believed.
24 *Issues of the Exchequer*, pp. 489–97. Other payments are also recorded in the rolls.
25 T.M. Banta, 'Notices of the Sears Family', *The Searstan Family of Colchester England*, 1901, p. 6. See also W.J. White, 'The Death and Burial of Henry VI: A Review of the Facts and Theories, Part 1', *The Ricardian*, Vol. 5, 78, 1982, p. 71.
26 *Issues of the Exchequer*, p. 490.
27 *John Blacman*, pp. 43–4.
28 The Wakefield Tower was abandoned as a royal residence in *c.*1307 and it became a storehouse for official documents.

Chapter 9

1 *Political Poems*, p. 278.
2 *Arrivall*, p. 36.
3 See the Ghent Manuscript of the *Arrivall*, University Library, Ghent, MS. 236 and the *Nouvelles du Recouvrement par Edouard IV de son Royaume d'Angleterre*, Besançon, MS. 1168.
4 *Arrivall*, p. 34.
5 Ibid., pp. 36–7.
6 Ibid.
7 See 'Fauconberg's Kentish Rising of May 1471', p. 677.
8 A. Goodman, *The Wars of the Roses*, p. 56. See also D. Grummitt, *The Calais Garrison: War and Military Service in England, 1346–1558*, 2008.
9 *The Calais Garrison*, pp. 47–9.
10 CPR 1461–1485, Vol. 2, pp. 290–92.
11 Goodman, *The Wars of the Roses*, p. 217.
12 *London and the Kingdom*, Vol. 3, p. 271. Journal 8, folio 7, City of London, p. 391.
13 Ibid. But also see *Great Chronicle of London*, p. 219.
14 *Arrivall*, p. 36.
15 *Great Chronicle of London*, p. 219.
16 *Survey of London*, p. 48.
17 Ibid.
18 Ibid., p. 220.
19 See the Ghent Manuscript of the Arrivall, University Library, Ghent, MS. 236 and the Nouvelles du Recouvrement par Edouard IV de son Royaume d'Angleterre, Besançon, MS. 1168.

20 *Arrivall*, p. 37.
21 *Croyland Chronicle*, p. 467.
22 *Political Poems*, p. 278.
23 *Survey of London*, p. 46.
24 *Great Chronicle of London*, pp. 219–20.
25 *Arrivall*, p. 37.
26 C.L. Kingsford, ed., *The Chronicles of London*, 1905, p. 185.
27 Ibid. See also *The Medieval Soldier*, pp. 74–109, for chivalry in the wars and how it changed the code.
28 See Chapter 11 and Canterbury Cathedral Archives, CCA-CC/WOODRUFF/56/1
29 *Great Chronicle of London*, p. 220.
30 'Fauconberg's Kentish Rising of May 1471', citing P.R.O.E 403/844 under 29 May. See also *Issues of the Exchequer*, p. 591.
31 *Political Poems*, p. 279.
32 See *Issues of the Exchequer*, p. 495. Paid for 29 May.

Chapter 10

1 A prayer for Henry VI in English verse in *John Blacman*, p. 51.
2 See P. Murray Kendall, ed., *Richard III: The Great Debate*, 1965, p. 147.
3 *Arrivall*, p. 30.
4 *Mancini*, p. 45.
5 *Croyland Chronicle*, p. 499.
6 See P. Langley, *The Princes in the Tower*, 2023, and M. Lewis, *The Survival of the Princes in the Tower*, 2023.
7 The payments are recorded in *Issues of the Exchequer*, pp. 489–97.
8 Exchequer of Receipt, Issues Rolls (E 403), No. 844, m. 8. Issues of Easter Term, 11 Edward IV.
9 *Arrivall*, p. 38.
10 A contemporary ballad records King Edward had 8,000 infantry and 4,000 men-at-arms with him. *Political Poems*, p. 280.
11 Ibid., pp. 280–1.
12 *Warkworth*, p. 21.
13 *Arrivall*, p. 38. See also *Jehan de Waurin*, Vol. 5, p. 675.
14 *CSPM*, Vol. 1, p. 157.
15 *Commines*, Vol. 1, p. 201.
16 A. Hanham, *Richard III and his Early Historians 1483–1535*, 1967, p. 121.
17 *Croyland Chronicle*, p. 468.
18 Exchequer of Receipt, Issues Rolls (E 403), No. 844, m. 8. Issues of Easter Term, 11 Edward IV.
19 The sum of 40s in 1471 equates to approx. £1,368 in modern terms.
20 CPR 1471–76, Vol. 2, p. 336.
21 A. Hanham, ed., *The Cely Letters 1472–1488*, 1975, letters 42, 65 and 185. See *Paston Letters*, Vol. 6, p. 102, for Robert's knighthood at Stoke field. Also see E. Cavell, *A Memoir of the Court of Henry VII*, 2001, p. 325.
22 My research is ongoing regarding the Radcliffe connection.

23 See *Great Chronicle of London*, p. 257; *DNB*, Vol. 47, p. 128. Robert and John may have fought on opposite sides at the battle of Stoke in 1487 but both were implicated in the Warbeck rebellion.
24 Adipocere: a greyish waxy substance formed by the decomposition of soft tissue in dead bodies subjected to moisture.
25 W.H. St John Hope, 'The Discovery of the Remains of King Henry VI in St George's Chapel Windsor Castle', *Archaeologia*, Vol. 62, 1911, p. 536.
26 Ibid., pp. 536–7.
27 Ibid., p. 537. See also 'The Death and Burial of Henry VI', pp. 74–5.
28 *Commines*, p. 196; H. Ellis, ed., *R. Fabian: The New Chronicles of England and of France*, 1811, p. 662; *Polydore Vergil*, p. 156.
29 See 'Henry VI's Medical Record', pp. 14–15.
30 'Chestyde': put in a chest (coffin). *Issues of the Exchequer*, pp. 495–6.

Chapter 11

1 *Political Poems*, p. 280.
2 *Issues of the Exchequer*, pp. 495–6.
3 Ibid., p. 495.
4 Ibid., p. 496. Also see *Battles of Barnet and Tewkesbury*, p. 112.
5 *Great Chronicle of London*, p. 220. According to *Historical Writing in England II*, p. 233, the chronicle was written by several anonymous authors in the city and compiled by Robert Fabian.
6 *Warkworth*, p. 21.
7 Called 'livor mortis' in A.M. Christensen, E.J. Bortelink, N.V. Passalacqua, *Forensic Anthropology: Current Methods and Practice*, 2014, p. 122.
8 The term 'nether purs' is also slang for testicles or scrotum in Middle English. See the Prologue to Chaucer's *Wife of Bath*, and other stories of the period.
9 *Great Chronicle of London*, pp. 220–1.
10 'Oyer and terminer' was a term whereby commissioners were empowered to 'hear and determine' a criminal case in a court of law.
11 *Great Chronicle of London*, p. 220. In addition Sir John Scott was placed in command of Sandwich and Thomas Saintledger held Rochester for the Crown.
12 Ibid.
13 *Issues of the Exchequer*, p. 495.
14 *Warkworth*, pp. 21–2.
15 Charter of Edward IV, 3 November 1471. Canterbury Cathedral Archives CCA-CC/A/A/35.
16 *Arrivall*, p. 39.
17 *Chronicles of London*, p. 185.
18 See R. Britnell, 'Richard Duke of Gloucester and the Death of Thomas Fauconberg', *The Ricardian*, Vol. 10, 1991, pp. 174–83.
19 CPR 1471–1476, Vol. 2, p. 262.
20 'Fauconberg's Kentish Rising of May 1471', pp. 682–3.
21 *Great Chronicle of London*, p. 220.
22 *Jehan de Waurin*, Vol. 5, p. 675.

23 *Paston Letters*, Vol. 5, p. 109.
24 Ibid., p. 113.
25 CPR 1467–77, Vol. 2, p. 288.
26 CPR 1476–85, Vol. 2, p. 57.
27 *Great Chronicle of London*, p. 221.

Chapter 12

1 Alexander Pope, *Pastorals, Windsor Forest*, 1713. See Wolffe, *Henry VI*, p. 358.
2 R. Knox and S. Leslie, *The Miracles of King Henry VI*, 1923, pp. 35–9.
3 Master John Shorne was famous for enticing the devil into one of his boots.
4 See A. Hanham, 'Henry VI and his Miracles', *The Ricardian*, Vol. 12, 2000, pp. 638–52.
5 Richard ordered bones to be cleared from Towton battlefield because they had not been given a Christian burial by Edward IV. See *Towton 1461*, p. 256.
6 *The Miracles of King Henry VI*, pp. 51–2.
7 Ibid., pp. 100–02.
8 'Henry VI and his Miracles', p. 642.
9 Ibid., pp. 644–5.
10 S.G. Potter, ed., J. Foxe, *The Book of Martyrs*, 1873, p. 279.
11 Wolffe, *Henry VI*, pp. 355–6 and Griffiths, *Henry VI*, p. 354.
12 *Political Poems*, p. 152.
13 R. Hope Robbins, ed., 'The Battle of Northampton', *Historical Poems of the XIVth and XVth Centuries*, 1959, p. 213.
14 *An English Chronicle*, p. 93.
15 For more about these rebellions, see J.D. Taylor, *Sir Thomas Wyatt the Younger c.1521–1554 and Wyatt's Rebellion*, 2013; R. Furley, *Sir Thomas Wyatt's Rebellion A.D. 1554*, 1878.
16 CPR 1471–1476, Vol. 2, p. 262.
17 See London Metropolitan Archives, City of London, folio 5 of Journal 8, and folio 4b of Journal 8 for the letter to the mayor and aldermen.
18 Margaret was ransomed by Louis XI for 50,000 crowns at Rouen in 1476. She died in 1482.
19 For Gloucester stabbing Henry with a dagger, see *R. Fabian*, p. 662. With a sword, see *Polydore Vergil*, pp. 155–6.

Epilogue

1 *Survey of London*, p. 12.
2 For an online interactive map and encyclopaedia, see J. Jenstad, ed., *The Agas Map, The Map of Early Modern London*, Edition 7.0, 2022.
3 It is estimated that 250,000 people died in the British Civil Wars (1642–51), Ireland having the heaviest casualties.
4 *Arrivall*, p. 38.

Index

Act of Accord, 33, 47, 66
Agas Map, 233, 154
Aire, 44
Aldersgate, 104, 147, 108, 181, 194
Aldgate, 104–8, 112, 120, 144, 147, 149, 154, 163, 170, 175–7, 181–5, 187, 189, 212, 229, 234
Aldrich, Walter, 76
Alfonso V, King of Portugal, 58–9
Angers, 69, 72
Antoine, Bastard of Burgundy, 115, 117
archery, 87, 161, 165–6
artillery, 19, 35, 75, 78, 81–2, 84–5, 97, 106, 126, 130, 141, 149, 161–9, 176–7, 179–81
Artois, 44
attainder, 31–2
Aucher, Henry, 125–7, 129–30, 147
Audley, James Lord, 31

balinger, 76–7, 144
Bamburgh, 35, 161
Banbury, 51–2
Bankside, 148, 166
banners, 37, 83, 87, 93, 96, 99, 130, 132, 152, 194
Barnet, battle of, 10, 18, 56, 58, 78, 80–97, 100, 102, 111, 114–15, 118, 122, 125, 137, 140, 142, 161, 200, 207, 211, 214, 217, 228–30; battlefield chapel, 82, 87, 89; Deadman's Bottom, 82, 86, 89–90

Basset, Sir Robert, 110, 112, 177, 182–3, 186, 194
bastard feudalism, 25, 32, 121
Bath, 91
Baxter, Robert, 188
Bayford, 128–9
Baynard's Castle, 145, 149
Beauchamp, John, 89
Beauchamp Pageants, 76
Beauchamp, Sir Richard, 92
Beaufort, Edmund, Duke of Somerset, 27, 29–30, 46, 63
Beaufort, Edmund, Duke of Somerset (d. 1471), 55, 93, 95–6, 98–9, 101, 124, 138
Beaufort, Henry, Cardinal, 26
Beaufort, Henry, Duke of Somerset (d. 1464), 33, 35, 47, 65
Beaufort, Henry, Earl of Dorset, 30
Beaufort, Joan, 60
Beaumont, William Viscount, 84, 214
Berkeley, William Lord, 39
Bernards Heath, 128, 162
Berwick, 221
Beverley Minster, 217–19
Bishop's Palace, 54, 71
Bishopsgate, 104–5, 108, 111, 120, 147, 149, 170, 175, 177, 181, 184–5, 187, 189, 234
Black Barre, 216
Blackfriars, 104, 210

Blackheath, 78, 103, 130–2, 136, 141, 144, 146, 170, 174, 187–8, 192, 212–4, 228
Blackwall, 141, 165, 176, 186
Blacman, John, 25, 71–2, 174
Blanche Appleton, 70
Blore Heath, battle of, 31–2, 65, 113
Blount, Walter, Lord Mountjoy, 59
bombard, 145, 161, 163
Bordeaux, 114
Bosworth, battle of, 201, 223
Bourchier, Edward, 33
Bourchier, Henry, Earl of Essex, 114, 149, 155, 177–8
Bourchier, Humphrey, Lord Cromwell, 114
Bourchier, John, Lord Berners, 54, 57
Bourchier, Thomas, Archbishop of Canterbury, 54, 188
Brest, 67
Brice, Hugh, 208–9
Bristol, 91
British Civil Wars (1641–51), 31
Brittany, 45, 73, 225
Brooke, Sir George, 74, 78–9, 91, 122, 127, 147, 163, 176
Bruges, 42, 45
Bull's Stake, 213
Burgundy, 36, 38–9, 41–4, 48, 50–1, 57, 59, 71–3, 76, 97, 114–15, 117, 225, 228

Cade, Jack, 18, 26, 103, 119–21, 124, 128, 145, 150, 227, 236
Caen, 106
Caister Castle, 162
Calais, 24, 31–2, 44, 46–7, 56, 63, 65–6, 68–9, 103, 118, 129, 179–80, 199; Captain of, 58, 74, 114, 116, 179, 200, 216; garrison, 31–2, 59, 64–5, 73, 78, 96, 122, 124–5, 127–8, 133–4, 147, 163, 176–7, 179, 186, 188, 211, 214, 229
Canterbury, 24, 65, 78, 103, 118, 122–3, 126, 129–30, 187, 212–14, 220, 228
Canterbury Archives Roll, 123, 160, 213
Cappe, Henry, 219

caravel, 77
carrack, 77
Castillon, battle of, 28, 114
Catherine of Valois, Queen of England, 206
Caxton, William, 116
Cerne Abbey, 90
Charles VI, 206
Charles VII, 63
Charles, Duke of Burgundy, 38–9, 41–4, 46, 114
Cheltenham, 93
Chertsey Abbey, 24, 202–4, 209–11, 221–4
chivalry, 25, 33, 38, 44, 47, 116–17, 135, 186, 192
Cinque Ports, 65, 103, 122, 124, 214, 216
Clampard, Stephen, 162
Clarendon Palace, 28
Clifford, John Lord, 67
Clifford, Thomas, 49
Clifton, Sir Gerveys, 138
cog, 77
Cole, John, 217
College of Windsor, 204
Cologne, 84
Commines, Philip de, 44, 90, 197
commissions of array, 34, 50, 96, 134–5
Common Weal, 119, 226, 229
Cook, Robert, 216
Cook, Sir Thomas, 111
Cornhill, 209
Cornwall, 91, 120, 226
Cotswolds, 92
Courtenay, John, Earl of Devon, 55, 96, 99, 101, 138
Courtenay, Margaret, Countess of Devon, 101
Cousin, Robert, 172, 217
Coventry, 32, 51–3, 133–5, 87, 146, 162, 170–1, 192
Cripplegate, 108, 147, 181
Crosby, John, 110–11, 194
Crosby Place, 111
Crotoy, 62

Index

Culpepper, John, 117
culverines, 163

Dagenham, 112, 155
Dartford, 27, 30, 162
Dartmouth, 70
Daventry, 53
Delves, John, 138
Devon, 69, 91
Dinham, John Lord, 59, 118, 178, 212–13
Dintingdale, battle of, 34, 67
Doncaster, 50
Dover, 103, 122, 125, 162
Drawbridge Tower, 108, 167–8
Dymock, Sir Thomas, 37

Edgecote, battle of, 37, 115
Edmund, Earl of Rutland, 33
Edward I, 105
Edward II, 24
Edward III, 60, 114, 225
Edward IV, 9–10, 17–19, 32, 34, 40, 42, 48, 52, 55, 57–8, 66–7, 73, 77–8, 88, 103, 110–15, 140–1, 146, 151, 170, 200, 201–2, 215, 222, 225, 231, 235; character of, 37, 47, 56, 90, 100, 115, 119–20, 131, 135–6, 171, 173, 199, 217, 229; and Clarence, 191; and Henry VI, 196–8, 204–5, 207, 209, 221, 232, 236; military career of, 17–18, 32, 81, 83–4, 93, 96, 98, 108, 117, 144, 148, 162; and Warwick, 17–18, 32, 34, 36–9, 41, 51–2, 68–9, 74, 124
Edward of Lancaster, Prince of Wales, 27–8, 33, 38, 40, 47, 69, 72, 90, 92, 94–5, 98–9, 100–1, 190, 205
Edward V, 116, 171, 200–2
Elbys, John de, 59
Empingham (Losecote Field) battle of, 37–8, 162
Essex, 9, 78, 118–19, 122–4, 130, 132, 134, 141, 147, 170, 175–8, 180–2, 185–7, 211–14, 218, 222, 225–6, 229
Eton College, 26
Exeter, 70, 91

Fabyan, Robert, 181
Fauconberg, Joan, 61
Fauconberg, Thomas Lord, 61
Faunt, Nicholas, 77–8, 122–3, 143, 147, 187, 212–4
Ferrybridge, battle of, 34, 56, 67, 201
FitzAlan, Thomas, Earl of Arundel, 216
Flushing, 45, 60, 73
Fogge, Sir John, 121–2
foundries, 162
fowler, 163
France, 23, 26–8, 35–6, 38, 41–4, 46, 58, 60–3, 65, 69, 72, 90, 111, 113–14, 120, 147, 178–9, 196, 206, 211, 221, 225–6, 230
Francis II, Duke of Brittany, 45

galley, 77
Galliard de Durfort IV, Lord Duras, 112, 114, 117, 149, 178–9
Gastons, The, 93–4, 96, 98, 101
Gate, Sir Geoffrey, 37, 68, 70, 73–4, 78, 123, 125–7, 129–30, 145, 147, 176, 179, 188, 214, 216
George, Duke of Clarence, 19, 36–40, 42, 44, 50–1, 57, 68–70, 72–3, 85, 100, 125, 127–9, 190–1, 193–4, 213, 232; character of, 52, 71.
Gloucester, 92
Goodnestone, 128–9
Great Stone Gate, 107, 145, 147, 167–9
Gresham, Thomas, 139
Grey, Lady Jane, 228
Grey, Thomas, 172
Gruthuse, Louis Lord of, 42
Guildford, John, 125
Guildhall, 136, 139, 141, 148, 174
Guisborough Priory, 67
Guisnes, 65, 180, 201
gunpowder, 20, 81, 117–18, 161, 163–4, 166, 168

Hadley Green, 88–9
Hague, The, 42
Hall, Edward, 98

Hammes, 179–80
Hampden, Sir Edmond, 138
Hampton, Alice, 112
Hampton, John, 111
Hampton, Sir William, 110–11, 194
handguns, 45, 81, 85, 128, 157, 161–3, 176, 182–3
Hanseatic League, 45, 68
Harfleur, 62, 69
Harrington, Thomas, 33
Harrow, John, 33
Hastings, William Lord, 38, 42, 47, 50, 52, 57, 85–6, 97–8, 116, 190–1, 213, 216
Hatfield, Richard, 172
Haute, William, 117
Hedgeley Moor, battle of, 35
Henry III, 105
Henry IV, 50, 101
Henry V, 23, 40, 64, 113, 206, 222, 236
Henry VI, 18, 21, 23, 25–6, 33, 35, 38–40, 42, 44, 57, 60–3, 66–7, 69, 71–2, 79, 85–7, 91, 95–6, 102, 105–6, 114, 119, 121, 127–9, 132, 134, 142, 148, 151, 171–2, 182, 189, 210, 214, 218, 225, 229–30; character of, 23–4, 40, 54, 120, 236; medical condition of, 23, 25–6, 28, 40, 54, 173–4, 196, 206–8, 231; death of, 190–5, 199, 207–8, 231–2, 235; tomb of, 202–7, 221–2; miracles of, 24, 210, 220–4
Henry VII, 200, 204, 223–4
Henry VIII, 224
heralds, 35, 38, 94–5, 134, 136–7, 188, 214
Herbert, William, Earl of Pembroke, 37, 70
Hereford, 66
Hever, 128
Hexham, battle of, 35, 95
Holland, 41–2, 209
Holland, Henry, Duke of Exeter, 35, 43–4, 50–2, 55, 86
Holland, William, Bastard of Exeter, 33
Holy Trinity Priory, 107
Horne, Robert, 121
Hornsey Park, 85
Houndsditch, 104–5, 147, 182–3, 185, 234

Howard, John, Duke of Norfolk, 68, 100, 162, 165, 213
Hubbard, Richard, 76
Hull, 48
Humphrey, Duke of Gloucester, 26, 121
Hundred Years War, 28, 44, 60, 120, 124, 128, 225–6

Invicta, 226, 228, 237

Joan of Arc, 61
Jocelyne, Sir Ralph, 104, 110, 168–9, 187
John, Duke of Bedford, 26
John of Gaunt, 60
Judde, John, 162
Julian calendar, 41

Kenilworth, 162
Kent, 19–20, 39, 65, 69–70, 73–4, 78, 91, 102–3, 117–26, 128, 130–1, 133–4, 147, 177–8, 187, 189, 199, 207, 211–14, 216–19, 222, 225–30, 237.
Kentish Rebellion (1470), 19, 56, 70–1, 124–7, 130, 140, 145, 147, 177, 228
Kimberly, William, 172–3
King George V, 202
King's College Cambridge, 26
King's Lynn, 41, 50, 71
Kingston, 107, 136, 142–6, 148, 164, 228

Lambert Simnel, 200
Langley, 222
Langstrother, John, Prior of St John's, 71
Lanthorn Tower, 148, 158, 171, 174, 193
Le Conquet, 67
Leadenhall Street, 107
Leicester, 30, 50
Leigh, Richard, 110–11, 194
Leland, John, 94
Lewknor, Sir John, 138
Lincolnshire, 68, 111, 120, 162
livery jackets, 38, 64, 83, 85–6, 215
London Bridge, 104, 106–9, 120, 142, 144–7, 150, 153, 158, 161, 165–8, 170, 174–5, 177, 181, 189, 217–18, 228, 233

Index

London Wall, 104, 105, 234
London (see also specific entries), 233–5; administration of, 103, 108–18, 137–9; military structure of, 149, 178; travellers view of, 103–8
Louis XI, 38, 41–4, 55, 69, 71–2, 76, 211, 225
Love Day, 30
Lovelace, Richard, 126, 128–9, 147
Ludford Bridge, battle of, 32, 46, 56, 65, 96, 162
Ludlow, 31, 46

Maidstone, 212
Malmesbury, 92
Malory, Sir Thomas, 21, 40
Mancini, Domenico, 108, 115, 191, 233
Margaret of Anjou, Queen of England, 17, 27–9, 31–2, 38–41, 55, 66, 69, 71–2, 90–2, 95, 99, 101, 112, 124–5, 134–5, 138, 140, 171, 173, 193, 195, 197, 200, 205, 207, 231
Margaret of York, Duchess of Burgundy, 41, 51
Marks Manor, 112
Marshalsea, 126
Mary I, 228
Matilda, Queen of England, 216–18
Meaux, 62
Middleham, 159, 216, 231
Middlesex, 89
Mile End, 186, 189
Mill Avon, 99
Milton, 129
Moorgate, 108
Moote, John de La, 89
Morte D'Arthur, 21, 116
Mortimer's Cross, battle of, 34, 48, 53, 67, 96–7
Morton, John, 59

Nancy, battle of, 44
navy, 58–9, 72, 74–5, 78, 115, 138, 140, 207, 214, 216, 218–19
Nene, River, 33

Neville, Anne, Queen of England, 38, 69, 101, 190–1
Neville, Cecily, 44, 46
Neville, Edward, Lord Bergavenny, 117, 125, 127–8
Neville, George, Archbishop of York, 53–5, 57, 71
Neville, Isabel, 36
Neville, John Lord Montagu (Earl of Northumberland), 35, 37–8, 45, 50, 52, 55–6, 67, 69, 84, 86–8, 90, 138, 140
Neville, Ralph, Earl of Westmorland, 60–1
Neville, Richard, 125–7
Neville, Richard, Earl of Salisbury, 31–3, 46, 60, 63–5, 67, 76
Neville, Richard, Earl of Warwick, 9–10, 17–18, 31–2, 34–5, 39–40, 42–4, 46–7, 50–3, 55, 57, 62, 64–5, 67, 69–71, 73–4, 79–82, 84, 88–9, 115, 118, 125–7, 129, 135, 138, 140, 142, 162, 197, 227; character of, 55–6, 66, 115, 119, 122, 128, 236; split with Edward IV, 36–8, 41, 48, 68, navy of, 38, 45, 59–60, 63, 68, 72, 75–6; death of, 86–8, 90
Neville, Thomas, 33
Neville, Thomas, Bastard of Fauconberg, 18–21, 40, 42, 55, 58–71, 79, 90, 176, 187–9, 197, 205, 207, 211, 214–16; attacks on London, 103, 111, 117–19, 120–4, 127, 129–30, 133–4, 136–7, 139–48, 157–8, 166–75, 177, 227–9; character of, 230–1, 236–7; navy of, 72–4, 78, 164–5, 207; Letter to Commonality, 131–2, 156; execution of, 217–19
Neville, William, Bastard of Fauconberg, 61, 217–19, 230
Neville, William, Lord Fauconberg, Earl of Kent, 32, 60–8, 140, 152, 229
Newark, 50
Newcastle, 62
Newham Bridge, battle of, 65
Newport Ship, 74–5

261

Nibley Green, battle of, 39
Norfolk, 45, 100, 162, 200
Northampton, 53, 114
Northampton, battle of, 32, 47, 56, 66, 162, 227
Northumberland, 61, 67
Nottingham, 50

Ochoa, Martin, 64
Olney, 37
Orleans, 61

Paris, 107
Parr, Thomas, 33
Paston, Sir John, 80, 86, 89, 217
Paston, Sir John (senoir), 80, 217
Peasant's Revolt (1381), 120, 124
Percy, Henry, Earl of Northumberland, 44, 49–50, 135
Perkin Warbeck, 200–1
pestereau, 163
Picardy, 43
Pickering, James, 33
Pimlico House, 89
piracy, 42, 59–60, 63–4, 75
Plymouth, 70
Pole, William de la, Duke of Suffolk, 27
Pont L'Arche, 62
Pontefract, 33, 46, 50, 60, 128, 190, 201
Poplar, 186
porphyria, 28, 206
Porter, John, 68
Portsoken Ward, 104, 106, 147, 170, 175–6, 234
Portugal, 45, 58–9, 73, 77, 116
Postern Gate, 106, 147, 149, 158, 177, 182, 184–5, 234
Princes in the Tower, 191, 200
propaganda, 28, 31, 34, 56, 65, 70, 78, 91, 102, 119, 121–2, 190, 210, 218

Quentin, 126, 130, 147, 170, 175–7, 187, 212
Queston, Richard, 220

Radcliffe, 70, 125, 141, 165, 176, 186–7
Radcliffe, John, Lord Fitzwalter (d.1461), 201
Radcliffe, John, Lord Fitzwalter, 199, 200
Radcliffe (Ratcliffe), Sir Richard, 201
Radcliffe, Sir Robert, 118, 172, 178, 193, 199, 200–1, 236
Ravenspur, 45, 48
Rawlin, John, 76
Readeption, 9–10, 40, 42, 59, 69–70, 79, 96, 124, 177
retaining, 32, 49–50, 64, 70, 73, 126, 129, 135, 178, 215–16
Richard II, 24, 222
Richard, Duke of Gloucester (Richard III), 19, 38, 24, 42, 52, 57, 85–6, 88, 96–9, 100, 188–9, 192, 194, 201, 211, 221–2, 236; character of, 52, 100, 191, 204, 206–8, 218; and Fauconberg, 207, 211–12, 214–16, 219, 231; and Henry VI, 24, 193, 195–8, 202, 222–7, 210, 221, 231–3, 236
Richard, Duke of York, 27, 29–35, 45–7, 62–7, 96, 114, 128
Robin of Holderness, 37
Robin of Redesdale, 37
Rochester, 188, 212, 228, 103, 130
Rome, 219, 221, 223
Rose of Rouen, 45, 60, 91
Rosse, William, 164
Rotherham, John, Bishop of Rochester, 59
Rouen, 46
Rous, John, 197
Roxburgh, 62
Russell, John, 59
Rysbank, 180

St Albans, 55, 57, 84–5, 89–90
St Albans, battles of, 30–1, 33–4, 46, 48, 56, 63, 67, 95–6, 112, 128, 162
St Botolph's Church, 105, 177, 184, 234
St Clare, Abbey of, 105
St George's Chapel, 202, 204, 224
St George's Fields, 143, 146
St John, Chapel of, 105

St John's Field, 57, 84
St Katherine's Wharf, 70, 106, 141, 147, 176, 180, 234
St Katherine's, Hospital of, 106, 145
St Pancras Church, 111
St Paul's, 138, 209–10
St Thomas Becket, 24, 103, 107
St Thomas the Martyr, Hospital of, 126
St Thomas's Tower, 158, 174
Sandal Castle, 33–4, 50
Sandwich, 59, 65, 74, 78, 103, 147, 164, 188, 207, 211, 214–16
Sayer, William, 172–3, 193, 199
Scotland, 214, 216, 221
Scott, Sir John, 117, 121–2, 178, 212
Seine, River, 69
Sellow, William, 214
serpentines, 75, 85, 118, 162–3, 165–6
Severn, River, 92
Sforza, Francis, Duke of Milan, 103
Shakespeare, 17, 21, 40, 190–1, 225, 236
shipbuilding, 59, 74–5
ships, 18, 20, 38, 41–5, 58–60, 63–4, 68–9, 72–8, 90, 106–8, 123, 130, 133, 142, 145, 147, 162–4, 176, 186–9, 211, 214–16, 229; *The Antony*, 45; *The Trinity*, 48, 68–9, 76
Shooters Hill, 103
Shorne, John, 222
Sittingbourne, 129–31, 137
Skelton, 61
Smithfield, 115
Sodbury, 92
Southampton, 68, 215, 217–18
Southwark, 70, 104, 107–8, 120, 125–7, 136, 143, 145–7, 150, 167–70, 174, 228, 233
Spain, 64, 75
Spicing, 130, 147, 170, 175–6, 177, 187, 212
Stafford, Henry, Duke of Buckingham, 28, 30
Stafford, Humphrey, Duke of Buckingham, 64
Stanley, Sir William, 38, 50
Stanley, Thomas Lord, 38

starlings, 107, 153, 166
Statute of Truces, 63–4
Stepney, 186
Stockton, Sir John, 108, 110–11, 121, 130, 136, 142, 148–9, 177, 183, 194, 205
Stoke, battle of, 200
Stow, John, 70, 89, 101, 104, 106, 149, 168, 182, 185, 233–5
Stratford, 186, 212
Styford, 61
Surrey, 78, 122, 124, 178, 214, 226
Sussex, 78, 124, 179, 214, 226
Sutton, John, Lord Dudley, 113–14, 149, 177, 198
Swilgate, River, 99
swivel guns, 75, 163
Swynford, Katherine, 60

Talbot, Thomas, Viscount Lisle, 62
Taunton, 91
Testwood, Robert, 224
Tewkesbury, battle of, 18, 92–8, 100, 102, 115, 117, 133–4, 138–43, 161, 171, 190–3, 195–6, 205, 197, 207, 211, 217–18, 229–32, 236; Abbey, 95, 99–100; Bloody Furlong, 99, 101, 152; burials, 94, 101
Texel, 41
Thames, River, 18, 69, 76, 78, 103–8, 123, 130, 132, 142–50, 162, 164–6, 168–9, 175–7, 181, 186–8, 193, 209, 211
Threadneedle Street, 112
Tower of London (see also specific entries), 18, 20, 24, 26, 29, 36, 38, 42–3, 54, 57, 70–4, 79, 87, 91, 102, 104–8, 113–14, 129, 132, 142, 145, 147–9, 158, 165–6, 171–4, 177, 180, 182, 184–5, 189, 190–1, 194–201, 204, 207–9, 212, 218–19, 221, 228–9, 232–4, 236
Tower Wharf, 105
Towton, battle of, 34–5, 48–9, 56, 66–7, 96–7, 113, 122, 179, 219
Treaty of Péronne, 43
Tudor, Jasper, Earl of Pembroke, 37, 92, 217

Urswick, Sir Thomas, 54–5, 110–12, 155, 177, 182–3, 194
Usk, River, 75
Vaughan, Sir Thomas, 190–1, 201
Veere, 44
Venice, 107
Vere, John de, Earl of Oxford, 45, 50–2, 55, 70, 84–6, 214, 217
Vergil, Polydore, 18, 99, 231

Wakefield Tower, 158, 174, 193–4
Wakefield, battle of, 33–4, 46–8, 50, 60, 67, 96, 114, 128
Walcheren, 44
Wales, 67, 70, 75, 88, 91–2
Walpole, Horace, 190
warbow (see also archery), 66, 117–18, 161, 166, 165
Wars of the Roses, 17–18, 20–1, 26, 31, 33, 42, 46, 60, 74, 78, 80, 82–3, 91, 94–5, 110–14, 116, 130, 135, 147–8, 179, 186, 190, 225, 233, 235; armies in, 96, 134, 177–8, 180, 215, 223; artillery in, 161–3, 166; economy during, 29, 39, 109; Kent in, 120–4, 128, 226–7
Wat Tyler, 121, 236
Waurin, Jehan de, 56, 205, 216–17
Waynflete, William, Bishop of Winchester, 42
Weilingen, 42
Wells, 91
Welles, John, Viscount, 200
Welles, Margaret, 200
Welles, Richard Lord, 37
Welles, Sir Robert, 37–8, 162
Wenlock, John Lord, 30, 95–6, 98–9, 138
Wesel, Gerhard Von, 84–5, 87
Westerdale, John, 49
Westminster, 35, 43, 47, 70, 100, 117, 125, 142, 144, 146, 190, 200, 204, 209, 215, 221–2, 224
Westwell, 220
Weymouth, 90–1, 96
White Tower, 105
Whityngham, Sir Robert, 138
William I, 105
Windsor, 62–3, 91–2, 192, 202–4, 206, 222–5
Woodville, Anthony, Earl Rivers, 38, 42, 52, 57, 68–9, 112–18, 134, 142–4, 146, 148–9, 154, 177–8, 184–6, 188, 190–1, 194, 199, 201, 213
Woodville, Sir Edward, 47
Woodville, Elizabeth, Queen of England, 36, 39, 115
Worcester, 101, 134
Wrottesley, Sir Walter, 73–4, 78, 163, 176, 179, 188, 214

York, 33, 35, 48–9, 107, 221
Yorkshire, 33–4, 45, 48–9, 60, 67, 73–4, 78, 101, 112, 120, 134–5, 216

Zeeland, 42